Howard Zinn Speaks

Howard Zinn Speaks

Collected Speeches 1963–2009

Edited by

Anthony Arnove

AAKAR

HOWARD ZINN SPEAKS
Edited by Anthony Arnove

First Published in India 2016

ISBN 978-93-5002-454-6

Published in agreement with Haymarket Books, Chicago for publication and sale only in the Indian Subcontinent (India, Pakistan, Bangladesh, Nepal, Maldives, Bhutan & Sri Lanka)

Published by
AAKAR BOOKS
28 E Pocket IV, Mayur Vihar Phase I, Delhi 110 091
Phones : 011 2279 5505, 2279 5641
aakarbooks@gmail.com; www.aakarbooks.com

Printed at
Mudrak, 30 A Patparganj, Delhi 110 091

Table of Contents

Introduction
by Anthony Arnove

My work with Howard Zinn over the last decade was punctuated with frequent enthusiastic calls and e-mails, his dispatches from the road and the home front. I remember Howard calling the morning after he appeared on stage at a Pearl Jam concert. Eddie Vedder had brought him out on stage in front of tens of thousands of Pearl Jam fans and handed him a microphone. "I gave the best speech of my life last night," he said. "It was three words long: 'End the war.'"

As a speaker, Howard understood the power of brevity, of never making anything simple complicated. He understood the power of the dramatic pause, letting his audiences have a moment to take in his thoughts, the power of humor to convey radical ideas in a compelling and dramatic way—and the power of the simple word "no." "They say war is the only solution," he'd say in one of his many talks delivered against the ongoing wars in Iraq and Afghanistan. "No . . ."

Our relationship began with a call, when I happened to pick up the phone one day at South End Press, where I was working as an editor at the time. He was calling to see if South End might have work for a friend of his who had just been released from prison after a number of years. That, of course, was exactly the kind of radical Howard was.

Other calls over the years were more mundane. He and Roz had listened to the Bob Dylan album I'd sent him. Or they'd watched a film

Brenda and I had recommended. The Red Sox had beaten the Yankees.

I had the great privilege of working with Howard on the book *Voices of a People's History of the United States*, which then led to dozens of live performances that we cast, produced, and narrated together, and then the movie *The People Speak*. If Howard loved a specific performance, he didn't even use words to describe it. There'd just be a visceral "Mhmmm" and his remarkable smile would grow into a full grin. After our first few Voices performances, I figured out that I had to tell the sound technicians to turn off Howard's microphone during the readings, because otherwise our tapes of the performances would pick up his sounds of pleasure during particularly good readings.

Filming our documentary *The People Speak* in Boston one afternoon, Howard observed that the camaraderie between our cast members, the sense of collective purpose and joy, was a feeling he hadn't experienced with such intensity since his active participation in the civil rights movement. Since Howard's passing, I have thought often of that moment, which crystallizes for me what made him so compelling an example of someone committed to, and enjoying to its fullest, a life of political activism.

Howard jumped into the civil rights struggle as an active participant, not just as a commentator or observer. He decided that the point of studying history was not to write papers and attend seminars but to make history, to help inform grassroots movements to change the world. He was fired from Spelman College as a result, and risked losing his next job at Boston University for his role in opposing the Vietnam War and in supporting workers on the campus. When there was a moment of respite after the end of the Vietnam War, Howard did not turn back to academic studies, or turn inward as so many other 1960s activists had done, but began writing plays, understanding the importance of cultural expression to political understanding and change. He also began writing *A People's History of the United States*, which came out in 1980, right as the tide was turning against the radical social movements he had helped to organize.

A People's History would provide a countercurrent that developed and grew as teachers, activists, and the next generation of social movements developed new political efforts and new movements. Howard was there to fight alongside them.

Throughout, he reminded us of the history of social change in this country, and kept coming back to the essential lessons that it seems we so often forget or need to learn anew: that change comes from below; that progress comes only from people resisting and organizing—workers going on strike, consumers boycotting, soldiers refusing to fight, saying no to injustice and war. He reminded us that we cannot rely on elected officials or leaders, that we have to rely instead on our individual and collective actions: social movements, civil disobedience, and political protests; that change never happens in a straight line but always has ups and downs, twists and turns; and that there are no guarantees in history.

But Howard added a distinctive element to these arguments by embodying the understanding that the shared experience of working alongside others for political change is the most rewarding, fulfilling, and meaningful life one can live. The sense of solidarity he had with people in struggle, the sense of joy he had in life, was infectious.

The stereotypical image our corporate media presents of the left, especially the radical left, is that it is humorless, boring, and out of touch. Howard shattered this convenient caricature. His voice, as this collection of speeches clearly illustrates, combined personal conviction and powerful historical narratives with comedic punch-lines that delivered keen social observations and compelling political criticism. These qualities are in full view in his play *Marx in Soho*, which manages to simultaneously reclaim Marx from his critics and his Stalinist distorters while bringing down the house with humor that evokes Sid Caesar and Zero Mostel.

Howard knew how lucky he was—with Roz, with his family, with his experiences of being part of movements for social justice and the friendships he formed in them. He conveyed this with a sense of joy that was inspiring. He communicated to everyone around them that they mattered, that they were an active part of history making.

In an article on Eugene Debs that Howard wrote in the 1990s, he said, "We are always in need of radicals who are also lovable," and said what we need to learn from Debs is a "determination to hold up before a troubled public those ideas that are both bold and inviting—the more bold, the more inviting." When David Strathairn read those lines at a celebration of Howard's life and work in California soon after his passing, it was clear to all of us that those words described Howard as much as they did Debs. Howard's ideas were bold, inviting, inspiring. As is his example—and that is something that, like the remarkable life force Howard had, is still so very much with us.

There are, from time to time, people who can crystallize the aims or goals of a movement in an especially compelling way, who can rally greater numbers of people to take a particular action and make a lifelong commitment to activism. But such people cannot substitute for a movement. Eugene Debs, who understood this problem well, once put it this way: "I am no Moses to lead you out of the wilderness . . . because if I could lead you out, someone else could lead you in again." That was the spirit of Howard: think for yourself, act for yourself, challenge and question authority. But do it with others. As he writes in *Marx in Soho*, "If you are going to break the law, do it with two thousand people . . . and Mozart."

I think if Howard were here today, he would be excited by the boldness and inventiveness of the Occupy movement. I know he would appreciate the humor and creativity of its slogans, particularly those drawing attention to the important issues of class that are usually so hidden here. But I think Howard would also want to make a connection between the dispossession of the 99 percent and the obscene spending on our nation's endless wars. He would have appreciated the placards calling for money for schools, health care, and jobs, not for war, and the placards saying we should Occupy Wall Street not Palestine.

I think Howard would also have something to say about the question of Occupy's demands. I am reminded of one of the slogans of the French struggle of 1968: "Be realistic, demand the impossible." By "demand the impossible" I do not think the French meant demands that were literally utopian. I think they meant we should raise demands that are achievable, but not within the logic of the current system. So, for example, we are told that universal health care is unrealistic, that we can't afford it. But we can. And there are other demands we need to make. We want to house the homeless. We want education and jobs for everyone. We want an end to our nation's wars.

I believe Howard would also be thinking of ways to involve more people in the Occupy movement, new ways of bringing the energy of Occupy into cultural expression and new arenas of social activism, such as the exciting work to occupy homes that have been foreclosed and to engage in neighborhood-based actions such as Occupy the Hood. As important as the spaces at Zuccotti Park and other encampments have been, these spaces are ultimately too small to contain all the people we want to be part of this movement. We need to think about new spaces we can occupy and new tactics for expressing our goals and principles.

As we look at Howard's lifetime of work, and his remarkable example, he has something else to teach us that is very important. As urgent as the present moment is, we need to build and strategize for the long term and have the patience to weather the attacks and challenges that are coming. The kind of change we want, systemic change, will not happen overnight or even this year. People are now raising questions about the entire system, about capitalism, that cannot be addressed by electing a new president—as more and more people now realize—or Congress.

This moment in which popular protest worldwide is toppling dictatorships, and forcing even establishment discussions to address vital social issues, is one Howard had worked years to bring about and did so much to contribute to making possible. It was something he knew would come. He had the unwavering belief that people would eventually rise up and seek a more just society. It was something he would have been so overjoyed to see and to be part of.

It is my hope that this collection of Howard Zinn's speeches will connect with a new generation of people, inspiring them and reminding them that history matters, that we do not have to begin anew, and that we can draw inspiration and lessons from those who have come before us.

Note on the text

I have made very minimal editorial changes to the text, respecting the conversational nature of Howard's talks. If someone appears in the text by last name only, the index provides the full name. In the few instances when I have cut any text beyond a word that Howard himself corrected in a speech, I have noted the cut with ellipses. In a few cases where he clearly left out a word implied by the context, I have added it without the distraction of brackets.

1

Southern Influence in National Politics

Student Nonviolent Coordinating Committee conference, Atlanta, Georgia, April 12, 1963

Howard Zinn was an adviser to the Student Nonviolent Coordinating Committee and wrote the book SNCC: The New Abolitionists *to document their important work. In this speech, delivered at the Third Annual Spring Conference of SNCC, he questions the title of his talk given by the conference's organizers and challenges the audience to ask tough questions about the challenges facing the civil rights and student movements.*

Maybe at some point in this talk, if that's what it will be, I will get back somewhere and maybe at some point in it there will be some relationship between what I say and the title "Southern Influence in National Politics." If so, it will be an accident. But what I really want to talk about is just politics, or maybe just national politics, or maybe a number of other things connected with it. I'll tell you why I don't like to talk about Southern influence in national politics: because it perpetuates a kind of mythology which I think is very prevalent in American thinking, and probably in foreign thinking about the United States, and that is that we have here a fine, decent, democratic, beautifully structured, lovely country which the South is spoiling. We have some great statesmen in this country, we have a good country, a fine president, a magnificent Supreme Court, a wonderful set of laws, a great constitution, a magnificent heritage, and all of this is being spoiled by a few miserable, evil Southerners. And I don't think this is true. And you know this isn't true.

And the fact is ... I was thinking to myself, "I can't tell these people anything that they don't feel in their bones." But, you know how it is, your job is to talk, you have to talk, so you talk. The thing that's wrong with that myth is this: racism is not a Southern characteristic, it's a national characteristic. Racism is not a Southern problem, it's a national problem. And this has been a very easy way for us to dispose of the whole situation. We've done it all the time. This nation historically, we often forget, has been for most of its existence a slave nation. Well, I'm counting its existence from the seventeenth century as a social entity. And we have been slave more than we have been free. And if you count our existence from the Declaration of Independence, the years that we've been a slave nation and the years that we've been a free nation are pretty close to equal. It's not a matter of North or South. We find this out when we go north, and we find this out when Negroes move north. Negroes leave the South and they go north, and they get on an express train which doesn't stop until it gets to Harlem. We like to think that in Missoula, Montana, there is no race problem, that all you have to do is move a hundred Negroes into Missoula, Montana. England found this out. We had great romantic notions about England, and how the English were free from prejudice. And then West Indians moved into certain sections of England, and things began happening.

This is beyond the South. Our problem is not basically that Eastland is vicious, but that Kennedy is timid. And this is something I think we haven't recognized sufficiently. Now, to put it another way—and here I'm not trying to take the onus off the South—the South has been treating the Negro like a dog, but this has been so because the nation has allowed this. If you look at the position of the Negro in American history, the Negro has always been a minor issue, and I mean that. He's always been somewhere on the outskirts of American concern, he's never been a major issue in the thinking of Americans, and certainly not in the thinking of the American national political structure.

There was one point in history, that period around the Civil War, when the Negro became a hitchhiker on a national train which was moving toward economic development and expansion. Because he was a hitchhiker, when he refused to get off they passed the Thirteenth and Fourteenth and Fifteenth Amendments and this, this was a great thing. But that was one momentary flash in American history. The rest of the time the Negro comes second, third, fourth, or nineteenth on the list of national concerns. And this is true even today, when we think that race and the Negro and all of this is very important to the Kennedy administration. Just take a look at the priority number that civil rights is given and all of the things that the Kennedy administration does and all the things that it speaks about.

I want to say a few things about the Kennedy administration, only because it happens to be in power now and only because it is our natural example for the whole problem of—is this a Southern crime or is this a national crime? We have too long treated what we have done with the Negro in this country as a kind of an aberration on the part of what is otherwise a normal, healthy American society. And this is completely false. It's as if you knew somebody who was a very nice, sweet person most of the time, and just one day a week he went out and found somebody and killed him and ate him. And then, if you had to write a letter of recommendation for this person, you would say, "Well, this person's very dependable, reliable, conscientious. He has one little fault, which we're trying to correct." Now, the Kennedy administration has played this myth of Southern conspiracy, Southern evil, to the hilt, and it's easy for them to play it because there's a basis of truth to it. The worst racism is in the South, the worst acts of violence are in the South, the worst senators come from the South. In fact, I could go further and say they come from Georgia, but there are people here from Mississippi who would have to argue about that. . . .

More than half of the standing committees of the Senate are chaired by Southerners, and the administration says, as every administration has said, Well, you see, this is the problem we face, this is built into the situation.

Not quite so. Because outside of this framework, above and beyond it and over it, the administration has had an opportunity to do things it had wanted to which could have nullified this power setup, changed it, and in some way created a possibility for decent civil rights legislation in Congress. When Kennedy was elected, if you can remember, there was some expectation, some hope, in the field of civil rights, and I was expectant like everyone else. He had not yet taken office, he had been elected, he was to be inaugurated, but Congress had convened and Kennedy men were already in power in Congress. Mansfield was majority leader, and the Kennedy machine, that great machine, which had succeeded in winning the election for Kennedy by a magnificent manipulative process, was now operating in the Senate. There was real hope.

So the Senate opened, and the very first thing that happened was that there was a battle on Rule 22, a very important rule for civil rights, because Rule 22 decides when you can shut off a Southern filibuster. And it says you can only shut it off when you have two-thirds of the Senate voting to shut off debate. And liberals have been trying to get rid of Rule 22 for a long time, so they can stop a Southern filibuster, so they can get civil rights legislation through Congress, particularly through the Senate, which has been a big stumbling block and which has been a scene of so many filibusters. So the first battle comes with the opening of the Senate right after Kennedy is elected, and a vote is taken on amendment of Rule 22 to make it easier to stop filibusters, and the vote is 50-48. Two votes made the difference. If two votes had switched there, we would have had a tied vote and Nixon, it was clear, with all the things we say, would have voted to change the rule. Kennedy—and everybody who had observed the political scene at that time, in a sense, agrees pretty well on this—Kennedy could have switched those two votes and didn't. Now we don't know what went on behind the scenes. One man who wrote a book on Kennedy, called *Kennedy in Power*, says that a deal was made between Kennedy and the South to go slow on civil rights and return to other things. We don't have documentary evidence on this. All we know is that Kennedy did not fight to change the rules at this very crucial point at the opening of the Senate.

And since then, again and again, as the Senate has opened and as opportunities have occurred to change this rule, to create a possibility for civil rights legislation to pass, Kennedy has muffed, has stayed home. There was a time when Kennedy was in Congress, when Kennedy was in the Senate—he'd just written his best-selling book *Profiles in Courage*—and somebody said about Kennedy, "As a Senator, he shows lots of profile but very little courage." And this began to look true for him as a president also.

We face a real problem here because we are the victims of visual power. That is, if somebody looks vigorous, we think he is vigorous. If he looks young and so on and so forth, and he strides the right way, or moves the right way, talks the right way, we get an impression of vigor, of strength, of courage. Yes, of vigor. But, it hasn't worked that way with the Kennedy administration.

At the opening of the 88th Congress, in early '63, there was another opportunity to change the rule. Again, Kennedy stayed out of the fight. Senator Joseph Clark of Pennsylvania, one of the rare men in the Senate, stood up in the Senate on February 19, 1963, and opened his speech in an unusual way for the Senate. I say unusual because senators are very polite to one another. And he stood up and he said, "Mr. President"—he was talking to the president of the Senate, Lyndon Johnson—"Mr. President, I desire to address the Senate on the subject of the Senate establishment, and how it operates." And then he proceeded to do something which just isn't done in the higher political circles. He proceeded to name those members of what he called a Senate establishment, the top important powerful senators who decide what goes on in the Senate, who decide what bills go through and what bills don't go through, and most of these turn out to be Southerners. And somewhere there at the top of the list is Richard Russell of Georgia. And another person near the top of the list is a personal friend of Kennedy's. This is the establishment, these are the people who control the Senate steering committee, and the Senate steering committee is the committee that decides what happens and what doesn't happen. . . .

We have the Senate steering committee, and the steering committee is dominated by Southerners and Mike Mansfield, who is a senator, who is Kennedy's man, who is majority leader, and who has the power to do something about the steering committee, and is much too courteous to his friends in the South. When Clark got up on the Senate and said this about the Senate establishment, Mansfield was very much disturbed. He's a nervous man, he gets disturbed at things like this, because he doesn't like people to say things out loud in public that they are supposed to keep private. And he said . . . in effect, "There are certain people that are in our party and we must be nice to them no matter what region of the country they come from." Well, Clark didn't make any headway. Clark pointed out, back in '61, when Congress first convened in the new Kennedy administration, Clark knew that people would argue that Kennedy was impotent when it came to Congress, that Southerners controlled things, there wasn't much Kennedy could do. Clark pointed to an interesting historical fact. He pointed to this because he was able to take the initiative really, to go back into the records of the Senate caucuses. This is really a secret thing, and the secretary of the Senate, as a matter of fact, wouldn't let any member of Clark's staff go into the historical records to see what previous caucuses in the Senate had decided. He said only a senator himself may go, thinking that Clark, like the other senators, couldn't get out of his office and go over and pore through the archives. But Clark did. And he came up with something interesting, and that was that in 1913, when Woodrow Wilson's first Senate convened, the caucus, the Senate caucus, became a scene of quiet revolution. And about twenty-three committee chairmen were replaced by Wilson at that time in order to put into the chairmanship people who would put through Wilson's program. That wasn't a civil rights program. It was mostly a program of economic reform. But Wilson wanted those bills passed, and he made sure that he would put into the committee chairmanships the kind of people who would get those bills passed.

Clark was saying, in effect, "Jack, you could have done something like this. It was done in 1913, a long time ago." Well, Kennedy has not done this sort of thing. Kennedy has played, as you know, a very interesting game. He's done just enough to prevent his image from collapsing in the minds of the twenty million American Negroes, just enough. He barely skirts the edge, no more. He invites Martin Luther King Jr. to the White House. He also invites John Patterson of Alabama to the White House. Things even out. He appoints Negroes to fairly high office, but he also appoints as director of the Export-Import Bank of the United States—which interestingly enough has the job of deciding where money goes to which colored peoples of the world, and most of them are—a guy named Merriweather, who was campaign manager for John Patterson of Alabama, who was also campaign manager for Admiral Crommelin, both of whom are—to say extremely racist doesn't mean anything anymore, no, they're beyond extreme racist. But this is a man who gets director of the Export-Import Bank. He appoints and makes a big deal of appointing Thurgood Marshall to the circuit court, but on the other side he appoints four staunch segregationists to federal judgeships in Mississippi, Louisiana, Arkansas. And since then he's also appointed a real nice one in Georgia: Elliot. You people from Albany all know your friend Robert Elliot, who when somebody makes a constitutional point in court, Elliot says, first to himself, You know I've only been on the bench a short time, and he says, "Let me go home and think about this." And goes home, and six months later he comes back and, of course, he always rules against. . . .

The Kennedy administration, and people who are not antagonistic to it—as I seem to be—people who are, you know, newspapermen who work for nice conservative newspapers, say, "Well, this administration likes to manipulate. It likes power. It doesn't really care about things. You almost give it any job to do, it will do it well. It doesn't care what it has to do. It's efficient." And it's a strange thing, in the American political system we have come to value efficiency more than we have come to value decency. "He is able, an able man," is the greatest thing you can say about anyone. People no longer talk about who's a good man and who's a bad man, but who's an able man. The Kennedy administration is able. What it's able for is something else, but it's able.

I won't say any more about the Kennedy administration, because I'm afraid you may get the impression that I'm critical of it. The truth is, and

I really want to straighten this out, I have nothing against the Kennedy administration that I don't have against every administration that we've ever had in the history of this country. And I mean it. When people say, you know, they count them up, and they say, "Kennedy has done more for civil rights than any other president," you know, okay, all right. But don't bother me with that. People who keep scorecards don't really know what's happening in the world. And the point is not how much has been done. The point is how much has to be done, and the point is, how much can be done which isn't being done? How much power does Kennedy have which he is not utilizing? Here's a man who is in control of the most fantastic aggregate of power that any nation has every held in the history of the world, and he can't do anything with it to protect one or two people in a little town in Mississippi. This is incredible. You see? . . .

No, it's not Kennedy. It goes beyond Kennedy, and it goes I think to our national history and to our national political structure, to our system and to our values. It's much more deep rooted than that. And I suppose the problem is that basically we've always, even when we've been fairly liberal at times, it's been a white liberalism. Racism has been dominant in our history and in our actions throughout. And what I'm really arguing, I think, is that we've got to look at our national political structure, and we've got to recognize that there's something about the national political structure itself—no matter who is in power, whether the Democrats or Republicans are in power—which gets in the way of solving the basic human problems that have to be solved in our time.

So this is important because here we have a whole bunch of people who are going out registering people to vote, doing a great job, and what do you do when you walk up to someone and say, "I think you ought to register"? What do you tell these people? Do you tell them, "I want you to register to vote because that really is all that's missing, all that's needed"? "You see, we have a beautiful working democratic mechanism here. The only problem is that you are left out of it. If you would just enter this beautiful democratic mechanism, and join in it, you will then be able to do the things you want to do." Well, I don't think this is an honest statement. I don't think this is true. I think it would be truer to say, "If you register, and if you vote, you will then have as much power as the rest of us, which is very little. Very little.". . .

I'm not singling out the American democratic system as against other systems. I'm not saying our system is worse than other systems. I'm just saying it's not that much better. And I mean this for this reason: any mammoth social organization in the twentieth century places huge obstacles between people's needs and power. And this is as true of the United States as it is of any other huge political mechanism in the world. And we sort of fool ourselves. We read the Constitution, we recite everything about the separation of powers, and pluralism, and two houses of Congress, and voting, and so on—and everything on paper looks good. But when you get down to it, there is something fundamentally wrong in that we cannot translate what people need into what is done at the top of this political mechanism.

There's a test for whether a political structure works, any political structure. A political structure exists in order to make sure—this is what we have supposedly set it up for—that nobody takes advantage of anybody else, because if we didn't have a political structure, people would ride roughshod over other people. And so we set up a political structure to defend us against this. We set it up supposedly so it will prevent people from exploiting others, prevent some people from getting rich and keeping others from getting very poor, to prevent some people from holding all power and denying power to others, to prevent people from discriminating against other people for irrational reasons. And we also set up a political structure to keep the peace, because this is important to people. They don't want to die.

On every one of these counts, most political structures in the world have failed. And on every one of these accounts, the American political structure today, in 1963, is failing. It's certainly failing in the area of equality. This I don't have to talk about. It's failing also in another important area, in the area of making sure that the wealth of this country, which is incredible, does not get siphoned off into relatively few hands and is not kept away from millions and millions of people.

In the last year or so, poverty has been discovered in America. I mean that. It's really been discovered. People have suddenly begun to write about the poor. They've been here all this time, they've been all around us—like the Negro has been around us, you know, but he can be right there but you don't see him. Ellison wrote about the "invisible man." Well, the invisible man not only applies to the Negro, but it applies to the poor in America. And we find that there are about 8.5 million families, about forty million people, who earn under $2,000 a year. But the picture that we present to the world, and very often to ourselves, is of an affluent society that is just doing great. Everybody is spending money, going here, going there, living it up.

Forty million people, under $2,000 a year. . . . Look at the concentration of wealth, on the other hand. One percent of the population, 700,000 families, own 25 percent of all of the money, stocks, bonds, real estate, all the tangible assets, in the country. And furthermore, this hasn't changed much over the years. There's been practically no change in the distribution of wealth in the United States in the last thirty or forty years. . . .

You read about a man who jumps off a bridge, you read about a man who shoots his wife, you read about a mother who drowns her children. And behind every one of these, if you look in the small print, you find economic deprivation. Well, this is a problem that hasn't been solved by this political mechanism. The poor are not represented in the political structure of this country any more than Negroes are represented in the political structure of this country.

And if we talk about peace, you can judge for yourself whether we have solved that problem. Everybody in this country is living with something that they push aside, push way down deep, which they don't like to face, don't like to think about. But we're living on the brink of something, and they know it. They know we're living in a dangerous situation, and they know that somehow our political mechanism has failed to solve this dangerous situation.

Now, what I'm saying, I think, all this sounds very pessimistic. We have no power. Really. Yes, we go to the polls every four years, and we elect somebody who has been selected for us at a national convention over which we had practically no control. It's interesting how we build our pictures of democracy: we elect everybody. You see, the candidates are chosen mostly in very neat political fashion by Democratic or Republican committees here and there, or by conventions here and there, most of which are manipulated by small groups of people. And every two or four years, we have an opportunity to go to the polls and make a mark or pull down the lever and say, "Which of these is going to get it?" And this is the extent of political democracy. Here's a great mechanism of politics and . . . every few years somebody says to us, "All right now, we'll let you touch this. That's it. And you'll change some little thing in here when you do it."

This *is* pessimistic. We don't have the power. We think we have the power. We're shut out. Lots of people are shut out. We want to register people to vote, and yet we know that when they do vote, they're going to be in the same position as everybody else. And yet we want them to register. And what's the answer to this? Well, this organization has provided a key to the answer, I think. The answer is to create centers of power which are outside of the official political mechanism, and which exert their own pressure, their own energy on the social structure and the political structure of the nation. This is what the student movement has done, this is what SNCC has been doing all along. One of the ways in which it can do this is to vote. There are things that can be done by voting, but I think it's important to recognize that this is a limited sphere of activity. Things can be done by voting against or for somebody, but this is only one of many pressures that can be exerted.

Now, you say, "What power do we have? What kind of power can we create? We don't have the money, and we don't have the high office." This is a fact. Just look around here. People around here just don't have the money, and they certainly don't have the high office. Where is the power? If you look at the world and the nature of society, you find that people utilize whatever power they do have. Somehow they find a power which is peculiar to them or which they can use. Looking at it superficially, a child doesn't have much power. A child is weak and small and helpless.

And yet a child learns how to use its own kind of power to bring pressure on the social situation to get something that it needs. Women very often are powerless, until they learn—as the women [in *Lysistrata*] did, when they stopped war in their own special way—that they have a special kind of power which they can use. Well, people in an organization like this have a special kind of power, and we've all used it. And we all have to continue using it. And I don't know how to define it, but it's the power that people have when they get together and they let other people know how they feel in one way or another. It's a power of pressure. Maybe it's a power of embarrassment. It's a power of annoyance, of embarrassment, of pressure.

Two nights ago, four of us went into Leb's restaurant in Atlanta to just sit in, just quietly. Really, not what you could call a sit-in, two white and two Negro. And it created an embarrassment for the proprietor. He didn't want to arrest us, and didn't want to have us there. And yesterday, when one of the fellows called him to sort of check up, he said, "You know, I'm sorry for the way I behaved yesterday, refusing to serve you. You were sitting there for hours. You obviously were hungry, and I even took away the water that the busboy had sneaked over onto your table so that you wouldn't be thirsty." He said, "I'm sorry I was unreasonable." I don't know if he really thought he was unreasonable. But anyway, he wants to talk. He wants to confer.

Slight power of pressure, embarrassment ... and this is a man with money, with prestige, and we're just poor people who are hungry. But SNCC has created such centers of power—and it can again. And I'm trying to say—and I think I'll end because I think as soon as I mention that word "hunger" . . . I shouldn't have done it—that the national political structure of our country is not the beautiful oiled mechanism that just needs the vote to solve our problems. Always—and this I think is the real meaning of democracy—people must create their own centers of power, must never get drawn in, sucked in, enticed, into the official mechanism. They must talk to the mechanism, they must put pressure on it, but they must never be captured by it. This is what SNCC has succeeded in doing, and this, I think, is what it and other organizations must continue to do.

I said I would get back to … to Southern influence in national politics, and I will by saying that I think there's a different kind of influence that can be exerted in national politics than has been exerted up to this point. The South has Senators Eastland and Russell, but the South also has the student movement. The South has something. The South has always been behind. Now the South is ahead. And I mean that the South has something to offer the rest of the country. We have something here that they just don't have elsewhere. This is what those idealists have talked about. . . . And maybe this is an unusual opportunity for us to show the rest of the nation what can be done. Maybe this is the only kind of setting in which this kind of power could be created. . . . This is the kind of Southern influence on national politics which would be meaningful.

I just want to end by saying this: remember the purpose of fooling around with politics and political mechanisms, and all this nonsense, the purpose of it all, eventually, is to do away with it. The purpose of getting into and trying to do something with a political mechanism is to do away with political mechanisms. The purpose of creating any kind of structure is to enable you to get away from it. All we want to do is have a world in which we can do naturally what we want to do with one another. All we want to do is have a world in which we can just relate to people the way we want to relate to people, in which obstructions aren't placed in our way. That's all we're trying to do. Maybe, temporarily, in order to accomplish this, we're going to have to exert pressure on the political structure. But in the end, I think—well, as I heard somebody say one time, I think, we shall overcome.

2

Speech against the Vietnam War on Boston Common

Boston, Massachusetts, May 5, 1971

Zinn was an early and outspoken opponent of the Vietnam War. This speech—one of many he gave in his lifetime on the Boston Common, often accompanied by his wife, Roslyn—can be heard in part in the documentary You Can't Be Neutral on a Moving Train, *which shares a title with Zinn's autobiography.*

Six young people who were in jail with me yesterday in Washington, DC, were arrested for walking down a street together singing "America the Beautiful." If Thomas Jefferson were in Washington yesterday walking down the street, he would have been arrested. He was too young, and he had long hair. And if Jefferson had been carrying the Declaration of Independence with him in Washington yesterday, he would have been indicted for conspiring to overthrow the government along with his co-conspirators George Washington, John Adams, Tom Paine, and a lot of others. So obviously the wrong people are in charge of the machinery of justice, and the wrong people are behind bars and the wrong people are calling the shots in Washington. The whole world seems to be topsy-turvy. And what we want to do is try to set it right.

A lot of people are troubled by civil disobedience. As soon as you talk about committing civil disobedience they get a little upset. But that's exactly the purpose of civil disobedience, to upset people, to trouble them, to disturb them. We who commit civil disobedience are disturbed too, and we need to disturb those who are in charge of the war, because the president, by his lies, is trying to create an air of calm and tranquillity in people's minds when there is no calm and tranquillity in Southeast Asia, and we mustn't let people forget that.

And those people who get troubled and excited about civil disobedience have got to have some sense of proportion. The people who commit civil disobedience are engaging in the most petty of disorders in order to protest against mass murder. These people are violating the most petty of laws, trespass laws and traffic laws, in order to protest against the government's violation of the most holy of laws, "Thou shalt not kill." And these people who commit civil disobedience don't do harm to any person. They protest the violence of government.

We need to do something to disturb that calm, smiling, murderous president in the White House. Now they say we disturb even our friends when we commit civil disobedience, and that's true. But the history of civil disobedience in this country and in other parts of the world shows that people may at first sight be put off by civil disobedience, but at second sight, at second thought, they learn that the protesters against war are right, and after a while they join us in their own way, and that's why we must carry on.

The Congressmen, you see this in the newspapers, while seven thousand people are arrested in Washington, you see Congressmen coming out in the headlines saying, "Oh, that's bad. You're upsetting those of us in Congress who have worked so hard. You're rocking the boat and so on and so forth." Well, we need to upset Congress. We need to disturb Congress, because for six years the president has carried on an unconstitutional war, and for six years the bodies of Americans have been coming home in plastic bags, and for six years the villages and countryside of Vietnam have been destroyed, and these members of Congress have been sitting there silently, passively, voting the money for this war. And if these Congressmen don't like the upsets to courtesy and decorum represented by civil disobedience, then let them courteously, separately, put an end to the murder in Vietnam by stopping the funds for the war, or by filibustering or impeaching the president and the vice president and impeaching every high official in government. Let them not criticize those who in anguish cry out with the only means we have left, with our energies, with our spirits, with our bodies, against the abomination of this war.

It's been a long time since we impeached a president. And it's time, time to impeach a president, and the vice president, and everybody else sitting in high office who carries on this war. The Constitution says—article 2, section 4—that the president and the vice president and other civil officers of the government may be impeached for, and I quote, "high crimes and misdemeanors." Is not making war on the peasants of Southeast Asia a high crime?

We grow up in a controlled society, and the very language we use is corrupted from the time we learn to speak and read. And those who have the power, they decide the meaning of the words that we use. And so we're taught that if one person kills another person, that is murder, but if a government kills a hundred thousand persons, that is patriotism.

We're taught that if one person invades another person's home, that is breaking and entering, but if a government invades a whole country, and searches and destroys the villages and homes of that country, that is fulfilling its world responsibility.

When nuns and priests, horrified by the burning of children, disrupt actions that brought about the war, actions that do no violence to human life, they're arrested for conspiracy to kidnap. And when the government reaches into a million homes and snatches the young men out of them under penalty of imprisonment, and gives them uniforms and guns and sends them off to die, that is not kidnapping. That's selective service. So let's restore the meaning of words. And let's tell the world that the government has committed high crimes. And that we don't want to continue being accomplices to these crimes. And we have to do that, and we have to say that in every way our conscience compels and every way our imaginations suggest.

And so the veterans will throw away their medals, and GIs will refuse to fight, and young men will refuse to be drafted and women will defy the state, and we will refuse to pay our taxes, and we'll disobey. And they'll say we're disturbing the peace, but there is no peace. What really bothers them is that we are disturbing the war.

For two weeks, for two weeks we have not let the country forget about this war. The veterans in their ways, the mass meetings in their way, the disrupters in their way . . . and we must continue disturbing the war and the makers of the war. We must not give them a moment's rest until the soldiers and war planes are out of Southeast Asia. And so, tomorrow morning, early in the morning, let's all go to Government Center. All of us. Let us, let us be nonviolent. We are going to be protesting against violence. We may break some petty laws. We may interfere slightly with business as usual. But these are not terrible crimes. There are terrible crimes being committed, but sitting down and locking arms, that's no terrible crime. War is the great crime of our age.

We may be arrested, but it's not a shame to be arrested for a good cause. The shame is to do the job of those who carry on the war. You policemen, you policemen around here who are going to be called on to make arrests tomorrow, remember it's your sons also that are taking off for war to be killed. And it's your sons, your sons as well as ours that they want to die for the profit of General Motors and Lockheed. It's your sons too, your sons too that they want to die for the political profit of the Mayor Daleys and the Spiro Agnews. . . .

So you policemen will have to put away your clubs and put away your guns, put away your tear gas. Become nonviolent. And learn to disobey the order for violence. You agents of the FBI who are circulating in the crowd, hey, don't you see that you're violating the spirit of democracy by what you're doing? Don't you see that you're behaving like the secret police of a totalitarian state? Why are you obeying J. Edgar Hoover? Why are you obeying the lies of an executioner, acting like a dictator from Paraguay rather than a public servant in a supposedly democratic state? Remember, members of the FBI, you are secret police, and you ought to learn what the German secret police did not learn in time. Learn to disobey.

So you police and you FBI, if you want to arrest people who are violating the law, then you shouldn't be here. You should be in Washington. . . . You should go there immediately and you should arrest the president, and his advisers, on the charge of disturbing the peace of the world.

3

Thinking about Vietnam: Political Theory and Human Life

Location unknown. January 27, 1973

This is the only speech in this book that is based on Zinn's typescript rather than a transcript of his actual remarks. It's unusual in that he didn't write out most of his speeches and delivered them extemporaneously. I found it among some papers in his archives shown to me by his daughter, Myla Kabat-Zinn, and was struck by its incisiveness. Howard's handwritten changes to the typescript are sometimes difficult to interpret, and some of his asides in parentheses were clearly meant as prompts for him to extemporize on certain topics. I have cut a few of these parenthetical asides where I thought they might be distracting to the reader.

It is January 27, 1973. The United States has been bombing Vietnam for eight years now. This evening, a cease-fire goes into effect . . . but no one knows when it might start again—or where. Who can believe any more the words of political leaders? They have laid their hands on the Bible, which says "Thou shalt not kill"—while ordering the killing of thousands. They have sworn to abide by the Constitution—and ignored its requirements. They have gone to church, while the planes they have dispatched were dropping bombs on churches eight thousand miles away. Remember the scene in *The Godfather* where the leader of "the organization" attends a baptism and listens to the words of the holy father, at the exact moment when his assistants are carrying on an orgy of murder throughout the city?

At Christmastime 1972, it was summed up. . . . While bells in American cities tolled "peace on earth, good will to men," B-52 bombers, eight-engined monsters that were built to carry hydrogen bombs, dropped thousands of tons of bombs on the most heavily populated streets of Hanoi and Haiphong. At least two thousand men, women, and children were killed. Other thousands were crippled, mutilated. The largest hospital in Hanoi, called the Bach Mai—White Blossom—was hit by thirty bombs, and afterward there was nothing left but piles of rubble, and beneath that, the bodies of twenty-five doctors and nurses, dead, others struggling and crying out in the debris. . . .

At first the Pentagon denied the hospital had been hit. "We only target military objectives," said its spokesman. On national television, a few days later, he said the hospital had been "partially damaged" and that the bombing was "accidental."

We need to think about that. Was the bombing of the Bach Mai hospital an accident? Was it deliberate? Or was it something indefinable in words like those? Was it something more complex, which, if we could analyze it, might give us clues to a world of apologetic barbarism?

We need to think about the whole war in Indochina. Because it is a matter of life and death. Fifty thousand Americans died in that war. And over a million Vietnamese. Imagine seven million Americans dead—that's the proportion. Six million Vietnamese had to flee their villages. Imagine a disaster that forced forty million Americans to settle in refugee camps far from home.

All over Vietnam now, there are men, women, and children without arms, without legs, without eyes. And a million American men have returned from there, many of them wondering: what for?

Yet to fix our minds on Vietnam alone would be to hypnotize ourselves. Even if no more bombs ever fall again on Indochina, we all remain in enormous danger. Because the fleets of bombers, the stockpiles of bombs, the napalm and white phosphorus and nausea gas, and the desire to use them, still exist. The government officials who ordered them into action are still in power. The wheels of deception still turn. And no one knows where the next Indochina will be.

We need to think about that war while its heat can still bend and reshape the iron frames of our thought. To think about violence and about deception—about ends and means—about the prince and the intellectual—about the use and abuse of history. About governments and their claims to immaculate conception—about money and empire—about human nature and war—about loyalty to government. And also about how we can change things, about the customary channels: representative government and voting—about confrontation and civil disobedience, reform and revolution, compromise and toughness, what can we learn from Thoreau, Lenin, or Alinsky. About power, in its different forms—and, mostly, about how to save and make beautiful the lives of people in a time of cruelty. Where is Emma Goldman, now that we need her?

All those questions are there, on that wounded subcontinent of Southeast Asia. It remains to be seen if any answers are there, too.

We might begin by thinking about thinking. To see what are the limitations of human thought. A carpenter, or a scientist, or a musician studies the limitations of the instrument to be used, but also tries to see how far its possibilities can be stretched.

How come Richard Nixon initiated, in 1970 and 1971, invasions of Cambodia and Laos, to "destroy the communists' capability to carry on offensives in the 'South,'" with the result that by 1972 the communists had increased their strength in these countries, controlling 80 percent of the countryside, and were able in the spring of 1972 to launch a great offensive in South Vietnam that carried to the environs of Saigon?

How come those who have so much knew so little? Or rather, how come their huge technical apparatus gives them much knowledge about small things, and little knowledge about big things? They may know . . . all the things that North Vietnamese leaders say over the radio to their own people, and maybe even to one another. But they don't know how people really think, how people really feel. And in a world where the thoughts and feelings of the large masses of people can shake the greatest empires, stop the largest military machines, this is crucial.

We make so much of something called "intelligence." But people are more limited by their position than by their intelligence. And as much by high position as by low.

It is strange but true. Precisely because they have so much—because they are members of the establishment, because they sit on top of a mountain, because they are rich, and educated, and privileged—their knowledge is severely limited. In two ways. First, as to facts. As to what is true. There is a whole world of fact that men in government offices, in war rooms of the White House, in the cubbyholes of Congressional offices, in the board of directors' rooms at General Dynamics, do not know. They do not know the daily experience of people who are cold, who are hungry, who sleep in the mud, who are tortured in jail, whose homes are destroyed by shells. Not knowing the conditions of such lives, they do not know the thoughts or feelings that such conditions create.

And so they don't know the most important facts of a century in which the masses of people—long ignored by the white Western powers—make history: the thoughts, the feelings of Chinese peasants, of Vietnamese villagers, of black villagers whether in Africa or in Alabama, of slum-dwellers in Havana or Harlem. That's why they are continually surprised by these people who rise up when they are supposed to be contented, who sometimes even win when they are supposed to lose.

Even uneducated, ignorant people learn from their mistakes. But it is a sign of how severely limited is the thinking of people in the big white house on the hill that they keep making the same mistakes over and over again. They miscalculated the people in China, sticking with Chiang Kai-shek until it looked so absurd in the face of reality, until it looked so silly to the rest of the world, that Nixon finally traveled to Communist China, swallowing old words. And they miscalculated the Vietnamese. If those who have the most history books available to them do not learn from history, it must be a problem not of their intellectual resources but of their angle of vision, their position.

At a conference of scholars in 1968, Henry Kissinger, not yet a White House adviser, spoke of "a lack of historical knowledge" among Americans in conducting foreign policy. "For example, it is amazing that no one seems to have systematically studied, before we went there, what the French experience was in Vietnam."

But if they keep repeating in Vietnam the same mistakes the French made there, surely it isn't because the facts of the French experience aren't available to them for study. They may, because of their position, not look for those facts; or, if they do look for them, interpret them differently, because their high position keeps them ignorant not only of certain facts (of what is true) but of certain values (of what is right). Or, to put it more accurately, they may know what is "right" for them, that is, for men in high position, but not what is right for people in another position, much lower than theirs.

This is one of the most important discoveries we can make as we think about thinking and its limitations. That people in different positions not only have different experiences not easily knowable to others, but they have different aims; what is right, or good, or beneficial for some may not be for others. We understand this easily for people in different nations, because we grow up with strong notions of "national interest," of "us" and "them," of "friendly nations" and "enemy nations." But to talk of "we Americans," and "our nation," and "national security," covers up the fact that in this one nation there are people in high and low positions, and the security of one may be the insecurity of another group, both inside the boundaries of "America."

In that same conference in 1968, Henry Kissinger said (you can find this in a book *No More Vietnams?* edited by Richard Pfeffer), "I never understood, even before I knew anything about Vietnam, why we thought we could achieve with sixteen thousand men what the French could not do with two hundred thousand men."

Let's look at that carefully. It could mean: the French couldn't win over the Vietnamese with 200,000 men; maybe this was because the Vietnamese had a cause they believed in, their own independence, and independence is a cause which brings better morale, better fighting ability, than the cause of imperialism, of keeping control of a colony, which is all the Frenchmen had to motivate them. And so the Americans are not going to do any better, because they, like the French, do not have a right cause to believe in. Bluntly speaking, any foreign power trying to control Vietnam is wrong, and that very fact will make it incapable of winning.

But such an interpretation ignores Kissinger's position in life. He has been a high-level adviser to men like Kennedy, Rockefeller, Nixon. He is close to the establishment. His employers have an interest in maintaining and expanding American power in Asia. They are anti-communist and pro-capitalist. Why are they interested in Southeast Asia? As a memorandum from the Joint Chiefs of Staff put it in April 10, 1950, just as the United States was beginning its large-scale aid to the French war in Indochina:

> The mainland states of Southeast Asia also are at present of critical strategic importance to the United States because:
>
> a. They are the major sources of certain strategic materials required for the completion of United States stock pile projects;
>
> b. The area is a crossroad of communications;
>
> c. Southeast Asia is a vital segment in the line of containment of communism stretching from Japan southward and around to the Indian Peninsula.

Those three concerns may be important to generals and businessmen and political figures high up in the American establishment. But not to the Vietnamese peasants, and not necessarily to the average American family, whose sons might be going to Vietnam to fight and die for those interests.

Look again at Kissinger's words: "I never understood . . . why we thought we could achieve with sixteen thousand men . . ." Now a second interpretation seems more reasonable: that we could not possibly defeat the Vietnam revolutionaries with 16,000 men, but with 300,000 or 500,000 men, with heavy bombing.

To the establishment, winning this "crossroad of communications" eight thousand miles away might be worth sacrificing all those American lives; to the American whose life is being sacrificed, or to the wife, or children, or parents, whose position is different, that might not be right.

So it may be a matter of life and death for some of us to understand that men in high office are severely limited in their thinking about a problem like Vietnam by their position. There are things they don't know, that we or others might know. There are things they don't care about that are very crucial to us.

People in lower positions in life are also limited in their thinking. For one thing, they have a hard time just collecting facts, because the sources of information and the means of communication are controlled by those on high. The government keeps secret from the public what it feels like keeping secret. It was a government official, James Hagerty, former press secretary to President Eisenhower, who in March 1972 told the House Committee on Government Operations about the classification system marking documents "Secret" and "Top Secret": "All too often, classification also seemed to depend either on the whim or the play-it-safe attitude of government personnel who were merely following the old Washington adage: 'If in doubt, classify it.'" Thus by 1970 there were five million pages of "Top Secret" documents in government files.

The government hides things. Giant newspaper chains, television stations, decide what is important for people to know about. So the public knows what the mass media want the public to know. During Nixon's first tenure in the White House, although twenty thousand American soldiers died in Vietnam and four million tons of bombs—more than in World War II—were dropped in Indochina, the newspapers and TV played this down.

Those who are subordinate in the society, whose education and time and resources are limited—poor people, black people—are often prevented, within the narrow world in which they live and work, from knowing that there are others, in equally narrow worlds, who have the same kinds of problems. Thus they feel isolated and impotent. But even if they overcome that feeling, even if they rebel, they are subject to a special limitation on the thinking of the rebellious: rage against the going order may distort their view, may drive them into actions that will not change their condition, may lead them to overestimate their strength, while the intimidated ones of their own group underestimate their strength. I heard a black South African revolutionary, who was conscious of this problem, tell an American audience: "I must not exaggerate the situation in South Africa to make it more dramatic for you, because that will fool me as well as you. And our movement depends not only on our not being fooled by others, but not by ourselves."

If a person's position, high or low, distorts and limits his thinking, then can the person in the middle, the scholar, the intellectual, who is not of the establishment and not of the oppressed classes, escape these limits? Karl Mannheim, a German social critic of the 1920s, saw the ruling classes as limited by "ideology" and the rebels limited by "utopia," and suggested intellectuals might have a more accurate perspective. In olden times, he said, intellectuals were direct servants of the court—Brahmins, Confucian scholars, medieval scholastics. But now there were intellectuals of all classes, and so had more room to think freely.

It would be pleasing to think that I and my colleagues in the universities—historians, political scientists, economists, philosophers, and so on—were, unlike the establishment and the ordinary citizens, in a special position to know more, to think more clearly. Thinking is our profession.

Here, too, however, it turns out that the very situation which looks favorable for knowing more leads us to know less. The world of books, of scholarly journals, of the classroom and the library, is a world of limited vision. The sounds and smells of the battlefield, the passions of the struggle in the streets, are out of hearing, out of sight. Exactly the distance from trouble, which lets us think we can see more coolly, more wisely, cripples our understanding of the real world. From books and documents we can know about the war in Vietnam. But to know the war we would need to feel it more immediately than we do.

Am I saying that human beings cannot transcend their environments, cannot use their imagination? No. Isn't this exactly the quality which distinguishes us from other forms of life? Of course. But in order to leap over the walls of our situation, we need to recognize them as being there, rather than priding ourselves on our "detachment" from what we want to know.

We are taught, as students, to avoid "emotionalism," to be "objective." And so we might learn the history of Laos, and the figures on how many bombs the United States dropped on Laos in 1968 to destroy the Plain of Jars. But how could we know what that destruction really meant to the people in the villages there, unless we could be there are the bombs fell, and if not that, listen to the words of someone who was there? . . .

Perhaps the greatest limit on the thinking of professional scholars is the emphasis in universities on the idea that you are being "scientific" if you stick to "facts" and avoid "value judgments." I suppose that is true if a scientist is someone who works on a problem, not caring what use will be made of his work. But a scientist given the order to "figure out how to kill a million people with nerve gas" could say, "I refuse. I think I'll figure out instead how to make nerve gas harmless in case you use it." He's being just as scientific, having made a judgment about right and wrong, a "value judgment," before he does his technical work, as his colleague who goes to work on nerve gas without a murmur. But he's being more human, it seems to me.

Can "political scientists" leave it to others to make the value judgments while we just dig up facts and tie those facts together with theories, oblivious of the effect of those facts and theories on the world? Doesn't that view limit our thinking in such a way as to put us in danger of control by those whose values may be antihuman and murderous?

Yet one of America's leading political scientists, a president of the American Political Science Association, Heinz Eulau, wrote in *The Behavioral Persuasion in Politics* that while something called "man" is the goal of the political scientist, we "disagree on the nature of man." "Is he a man who must be controlled because he is brutish and nasty? Or is he a man who must be liberated from the shackles of oppression to live a dignified life? These are philosophical questions better left to the philosophers."

Of course we "disagree" on the nature of man. Does this mean that we cannot decide whether a man "must be controlled" or "must be liberated"?

And if we cannot take a stand on this most fundamental question, how can we decide what we should work on? Shall we perfect the instruments of control or figure out how to liberate people from oppression? We might even decide that some people (kings, presidents, generals?) need to be controlled to stop them from being brutish and nasty . . . while others (ordinary folk) are brutish and nasty because they are controlled, and so must be liberated.

When a leading political scientist says, "These are philosophical questions better left to the philosophers," is he surrendering the most important judgments of all, but not to the philosophers (who will throw the question back to anthropologists or social psychologists, or someone else not likely to do much with them)? He is surrendering these judgments to the politicians, to the men in power, because when citizens—especially the most "educated" and "informed" citizens—refuse to pass judgment on the most crucial questions, then the politicians can make those judgments for them.

Eulau says: "It is the function of science to understand and interpret the world, not to change it." Science has no choice. Its work will change the world; and if it doesn't ask "In what direction will my work change the world, for good or bad?" then it has failed to ask the most important question of all. Then it is a zombie-science, doing whatever work is given it by those who are already in charge of changing the world. And how can it "understand and interpret" the world, if it doesn't understand the most fundamental fact about it: that there are those who want change, and those who don't, that there are changes that mean death, and others that mean life, and that if the scientist doesn't decide where he stands on change, others will decide for him?

So the professional thinker, if he is bamboozled by a narrow and inhuman conception of "science," is most limited in his ability to know: to know even the most elementary question for himself—what shall I work on? what shall I investigate?

Why do intelligent, educated men—doctors of philosophy, political scientists, historians, and so on—mostly stay within those boundaries of thought that keep them away from the most urgent questions of life and death, but in comfort and security? They live—I should say we live—in a modern society which pays them a fairly good salary and gives them pleasant work, but where the threat of unemployment is always there for someone who has not been chosen for tenure. That threat is lessened, that promise is heightened, by staying within the rules of the game: Don't teach or write about subjects that might rub your dean or president or department chairman the wrong way, that might get the alumni riled up. Stick to the old catalog of courses. Play it safe.

I am not talking about deliberate surrender on the part of scholars. It is, rather, an unconscious, almost automatic behavior in the academic world, not to make yourself conscious in a troublesome way. This explains why, through eight years of war in Indochina, so little attention was given by professional scholars in the regular curricula of the universities to Vietnam. The teach-ins of 1965 through 1968 were necessary to try to educate a whole generation of students about Vietnam in a way that ten thousand courses in social science had neglected to do. A linguist (Noam Chomsky), a baby doctor (Benjamin Spock), and a chaplain (William Coffin) became experts and educators on Vietnam, while the Asian scholars were working on the Ch'ing dynasty. A graduate student who spoke fluent Vietnamese, had worked in Vietnam for four years, was gracefully led to work on the Ch'ing dynasty in China rather than on Vietnam. A historian had difficulty getting tenure in Asian studies because he was paying too much attention, he was told directly, to Vietnam, and not enough to his specialty—medieval China. True, there were a few specialists on Southeast Asia (George Kahin of Cornell) and in international relations (Hans Morgenthau) who turned their attention to Vietnam. But the younger students had to form a group outside the regular professional associations, the Committee of Concerned Asian Scholars, in order to concentrate on the war in Indochina. The regular professional organization, the Association for Asian Studies, could hold its annual meeting in 1969, at the height of the Vietnam War, and not schedule a single one of its hundred or so panels on that war.

So we need to know these boundaries placed around us, those pressures, subtle or direct, on us, if we are going to go beyond them—we professional scholars—to deal with the most urgent matter of human concern. Of course, knowing them is not enough. We need to do something about that power that threatens unemployment or insecurity or merely disapproval to those who step out of line. Again, knowing and acting are intertwined: only when we act, press against our limits, do we begin to understand, to truly know them.

Once we defy these limits, we find we have resources which society has given us as professional thinkers—information, time, skills—to use in ways that the leaders of the society might find annoying. Then why do they give us these resources? Because they need us. Because the structure of wealth and power in a modern country is held together by the work, and the loyalty, of the entire population. It is a society held together not only by force but by consent. The more modern a society it is—the more technical its economy and the more people vote for representatives—the more it keeps force inconspicuous—bringing out the police and army only when it has to, for those, here and abroad, who rebel—and rests much more on the consent of the population.

But—assuming you were one of those leading powers of the society—how can you get a population to give its consent to your control, to turn over its taxes to whatever you consider important, to turn over its sons to the army? In a modern, sophisticated country, you use persuasion. And because you are modern and have some wealth, you can afford to give some of this wealth to a whole profession of persuaders: publishers, movie producers, broadcasters, university presidents, and a whole army of professionals who work for them. They will create the consent, not by a bullying kind of persuasion but by a quiet laying out of facts and ideas, which have all the look of neutrality and objectivity, but which keep people relatively happy with the existing policies.

Scholars and university professors have this soothing effect too on the population. True, there are radicals and dissenters here and there, but they are a minority. But the political leaders of the nation are gambling that most of the professional communicators will create enough general consent in the society so that the few troublemakers will not be effective. In fact, the existence of dissent can be pointed to as proof of how free and democratic the nation in, and even help to pacify the population.

But it is a gamble. Which means there is a chance for the dissenter to win, even if it is a small chance. In the case of the Vietnam War, the gamble of the political leaders was a winning one, for eight years. But it was a shaky game, with the opposition becoming so threatening that a compromise peace, and a temporary military evacuation, had to take place in January 1973. Even an enormous technology of consent—TV, radio, newspapers, churches, schools—cannot work if the facts are so obviously ugly that one or two of them escaping through the web can shake people's faith in their leaders. This seems to have happened in the Vietnam War. But the war did continue for eight years, and even at its "end," the structure of military power that had destroyed Vietnam was still intact and could be used again. This means that the system of mystification, of creating support and preventing disobedience, must be very powerful, very effective. It must not only defend itself against embarrassing facts; it must have a defense in depth, in case some facts get through.

Let me suggest how I think the system's defense in depth works to mystify, to pacify, the population whose consent it needs. I can see a five-line defense (maybe others will see three, or eleven, but I offer this as approximation).

First: keep out other facts besides the official ones. In Saigon, every day, there was what newspapermen called the Five O'clock Follies, where the US gave them the official account of the war news that day. In order to discover what was omitted they had to go out into the field themselves. It was not considered proper to use the North Vietnamese or National Liberation Front accounts of what had happened. Thus, a story that appeared in the Hanoi publication *Vietnam Courier*, in the spring of 1968, about a massacre of civilians by American soldiers at Song My, was ignored. Much later, due to the daring of a noncompliant soldier, Ronald Ridenhour, and a noncompliant journalist, Seymour Hersh, the story of the My Lai Massacre got out to the world. But the US government did all it could to keep secret its own decision making (which didn't come out until the Pentagon Papers were released over the government's objections in 1971). And the major sources of news for the American public remained official briefings in Saigon, Defense Department press conferences in Washington, presidential addresses on nationwide television.

But suppose the facts—or some of them—do get out, and endanger the web of consent spun over the country? There is a second line of defense. You admit the embarrassing facts (a massacre of civilians, the elimination of democratic rights by the government you're supporting, the high morale of the enemy, the popularity of the rebels), but declare that these are single, unconnected facts, not typical of the whole picture. One massacre shouldn't condemn a whole war; one police-controlled election shouldn't condemn our ally; one admirable NLF program doesn't represent communism in Vietnam. The war as a whole is still a good one.

But if there are too many facts, too much evidence, to make this claim, then you can still admit this particular war is unfortunate, but insist that it is not part of a larger pattern of US government policy. It is a freak, an aberration, an accident, a mistake, the result of a particular personality in the White House.

For instance, you can do as Arthur Schlesinger did, at a conference at the University of Chicago in 1968 in which a number of scholars were discussing what went wrong in Vietnam (you can find the transcript of the conference in Richard Pfeffer's *No More Vietnams?*). Schlesinger said the Vietnam intervention, which was not in the national interest, could be understood in the light of our historical framework: The historical framework is comprised of two entirely honorable strands in American thinking about our role in the world. In time past these two strands were responsible for some of the most splendid moments of our international behavior, but they reached a final and tragic misapplication in Vietnam.

This kind of explanation says: this history of American foreign policy consists largely of "honorable" strands, which account for "splendid moments" in our behavior, but they were not applied well in Vietnam. In this way Schlesinger can throw the corpses of Vietnam overboard in order to keep afloat the ship of traditional American foreign policy.

Or the embarrassing facts can be attributed to ignorance, to mistakes. If only the president had listened to the CIA. If only he had listened to George Ball instead of McGeorge Bundy. If only he had . . . This explanation fastens on the individual president's errors, not on the nature of the whole policy, on which all postwar residents agreed.

Or the trouble can be attributed to the psyche, the personality, of the president, maybe his early upbringing. So we find a respectable political scientist, James Barber, of Yale, writing in his book *The Presidential Character*, that it is important for us to distinguish between four types of presidential personality: the "active-positive," like FDR, Kennedy, and Truman, who use power and enjoy it; the "active-negative," like Nixon, Johnson, and Woodrow Wilson, who want power but don't like it; the "passive-positive," like Taft and Harding, who enjoy people, not power; and the "passive-negative," like Coolidge and Eisenhower, who don't enjoy power and probably don't enjoy anything. All of this is a lot of fun, but it does not explain how, no matter what type you had in the White House in the twentieth century, American power over Latin America was maintained, or no matter who was in the White House after World War II, the same basic policy of controlling Vietnam held fast.

All of these explanations of mistake-aberration-psyche are useful in protecting the overall structure of foreign policy, in sending people off on wild chases for more informed experts, or better-balanced presidents, rather than looking deeper at the whole structure of foreign policy and of society. These explanations might sacrifice a particular president but will keep the system safe.

However, if this defense fails, if people, reading some history, see a pattern of policy too persistent to be explained by personal or historical deviation from the norm, there is a third line of defense. It goes like this: All right, there is a deep structure to these events. In fact, it is so deep there is not much anyone can do about it. It is a matter of human nature, or historical inevitability, or destiny. It is not our actions that brought the war on, and it is not our actions that can change things. Therefore our job is simply to study what is our fate.

For instance, at that same conference at which Schlesinger spoke, there was Samuel Huntington, a political scientist at Harvard who helped the US government with its planning of counterinsurgency programs. (Huntington, at one point in the Vietnam War, referred to the movement of masses of refugees from the countryside, driven to Saigon by American bombing, as "urbanization.") Huntington explained that the rising opposition of Americans to the war in Vietnam was attributable to television. He pointed out how many more deaths there were in the Korean War, without great protests. Watching the deaths on TV was what did it. (It did not seem to occur to Huntington that perhaps Americans simply found the Vietnam War much harder to understand and justify than the Korean War.) He then gave a more impressive explanation of the antiwar feeling in the United States: "The shift in opinion on foreign policy in the mid-1960's appears to be simply the latest manifestation of a regular alternation of American attitudes toward foreign affairs between introversion and extroversion."

Huntington now produced the "Klingberg cycle." Some ingenious political scientist had found in American history eight alternating cycles, in which the American people swung about every twenty-five years from extroversion—an energetic foreign policy—to introversion, sticking closer to home. This made it easy to understand the opposition to the Vietnam War. Our last extroversion period started in 1940, with World War II. Our twenty-five years of extroversion were up in 1965. Therefore we were now ready to go back to an emphasis on domestic policy. As Huntington says:

> The swing to introversion in the Klingberg cycle is clearly a fact, and it is precisely this fact that causes the national trauma over the Vietnamese War. At an earlier point in the cycle such a war would not have caused so much commotion. But not even Lyndon Johnson could successfully buck Frank Klingberg.

This explanation, coming from a chairman of the political science department at Harvard University, should give every ordinary citizen not blessed with a higher education in political science a sense of supreme confidence in his or her own ability to figure things out. We can pass over flaws in Klingberg's pretentious chart: he lists 1919–40 as introversion, a period in which we intervened a number of times in Latin America; he lists the Civil War period as extroversion, although that might be the most internal of all our national crises; and he lists the period 1871–91 as introversion, although we then fought a series of bloody battles against the Indians comparable in ferocity to the Civil War.

More important, must one not be incredibly closed off from the facts of the Vietnam War not to be able to understand that the opposition to the war might come from the nature of the war itself, as revealed to the American public, yes, by television, and also by newspapers, magazine articles, teach-ins, and protest actions? Was it not conceivable that the opposition came from the fact that the American public found unconvincing the claims of the government that it was fighting an "invasion from the North," when Secretary of State Rusk was saying on television, before the Foreign Relations Committee in early 1966, that 80 percent of the rebels were from South Vietnam? Was it not conceivable that the public could not understand what 500,000 American troops were doing in a tiny country, halfway around the world, to stop communism among fifteen million people, when there were already a billion people in the world under communist regimes, when there already was a tiny communist country just ninety miles from Florida? Why would the communist conspirators of the world cleverly start a row of dominoes ten thousand miles away when they already had a domino in the Caribbean Sea? Was it possible that the public could not understand how the bombing of villages, the napalming of children, could be justified in the name of decency? Was it possible that the public could not understand how we could support a dictatorship in Saigon in the name of freedom?

Huntington's "Klingberg cycle" was a perfect device, if anyone could accept it, for persuading people that the political protest of citizens doesn't matter; our policies, our national moods, are all foreordained by some mystical cycle. The closest Huntington comes to explaining this cycle is that "the people of one generation may well think domestic policy important because their fathers thought foreign policy so." Why this should happen, he never explains.

Suppose this particular form of mystification fails. Suppose people will not accept historical inevitability, or cyclical fate, and insist that there is something they can do. Then a fourth line of defense appears: If you must do something, do what we suggest you do, what people have always done. Work through the regular channels. Write a letter to your newspaper or Congressman. Vote in the next election. Above all, don't disobey the law. In this way, the need to act is kept within harmless limits. No demonstrations, no civil disobedience, no disrespect for authority, no implication that the political system, as it now stands, is not good enough to change a basic policy.

And if people do go beyond these limits, and do burn draft board records, lie down in front of troop trains, sabotage bomb plants, expose secret government papers to the public, to the point where the public becomes aroused, either by the war itself or by the disruption of normal life, there is still a fifth line of defense. The government can yield a little, can surrender part of its policy but not all of it, can change elements of its program but not give up the basic principles. It can pull out ground troops but keep bombing with their force. It can stop bombing Vietnam but keep bombing the South. It can stop bombing Vietnam and continue to bomb Laos and Cambodia. It can yield some control but not give up the basic principle that it should control Southeast Asia. It can allow the communists this piece of territory which they have been fighting for since World War II, but not give up the principle that anywhere else communism rises in rebellion against a regime we support, we will attack it and try to destroy it. The government can yield to the popular demand for peace in this case but still hold on to presidential power, which might be used for war in another case.

They are gambling that we professional scholars and ordinary citizens will give up at one or another line of this defense of the system. And so they give the scholars time and opportunity to teach and write. They give the citizens a certain minimum of free speech and expression: the right to hold protest meetings, to air an occasional antiwar program on television, buried in a mass of cool and neutral news, in the barrage of official press conferences and speeches. They are gambling that both scholars and citizens will stay within the limits, will go past one or two defense lines, but not all of them, that the consent of the public at large to the war will remain.

In the Vietnam War, they did not quite win their gamble and did not quite lose it. Even though they were able to continue the war for eight years and bring incredible devastation to Indochina, they had to pull back to a last line of defense. In January 1973, the American troops are getting out of Vietnam, and the bombing has stopped there, but the air bases in Thailand and Guam, the aircraft carriers in the sea, are capable of sending out their deadly cargoes in a matter of hours; the president's power over war and peace remains great; the structure of wealth and power in this country remains geared to waste at home, death abroad.

Establishment officials gambled that the public would accept the Vietnam War as it had all other wars. This time they were surprised. Priests and nuns surprised them—the Berrigans and others. Students surprised them, in colleges and universities, even in high schools and elementary schools, across the nation. Daniel Ellsberg and Anthony Russo, "whiz kids" who had worked for the government in Vietnam, surprised them by releasing the Pentagon documents to the American public. After a while, even middle-aged, middle-class Americans surprised them, no longer believing the stories handed out by government. Above all, the GIs surprised them, by the thousands, expressing their antagonism to war, throwing their medals away in anger and defiance. During the last brutal bombing the war, the Christmas B-52 saturation bombing of Hanoi and Haiphong, came the first refusal by pilots to fly bombing missions in Vietnam, from Captain Michael Heck, a B-52 pilot, and Captain Dwight Evans Jr., who flew an F4 Phantom fighter-bomber.

The nature of the government's defense in depth suggests what scholars—and other citizens—might do to break through the web of mystification around the Vietnam War, and around the workings of the establishment. A good place to begin is with history.

4

Academic Freedom: Collaboration and Resistance

Twenty-Third T. B. Davie Memorial Lecture, University of Cape Town, South Africa, July 23, 1982

Zinn was truly international in his thinking and spirit. He welcomed chances to speak abroad, to break down national boundaries and build new ties of solidarity. He also came to represent to millions of people around the world "the other United States" of striking workers, civil rights workers, antiwar voices not represented in the mainstream media in the United States or abroad.

All of you assembled here understand, I am sure, that an invitation to lecture in South Africa cannot be received casually. You know—and there is no point in my summoning up a spurious courtesy to ignore this—that the name South Africa immediately arouses powerful emotions among all people concerned with human liberty.

I remember, twenty-five years ago, when I was finishing my PhD at Columbia University and I was offered my first full-time teaching job, a post as chairman of the history department at a small college for Black women in Atlanta, Georgia. My father said: "Don't go." I was going into the Deep South of the United States, the mysterious, threatening South of William Faulkner's novels and Richard Wright's memoir of childhood. To my father, a working man who had never finished primary school, survival required caution, and that phrase "the South" brought immediate foreboding.

However, in August of 1956, my wife and I packed all our possessions into a 1947 Chevrolet, leaving barely enough room for two small children—and drove south. Living for seven years inside a Black community in the racially segregated South of the late 1950s and early 1960s, we did indeed find that which troubled my father: an atmosphere of fear and hate built on a premise of racial inferiority. But we found other things too, omitted from those crude general epithets used to describe and dismiss whole societies: we found Black people with high intelligence and indescribable courage, determined to struggle for an equal share of the fruits of the earth, the light of the sun, the living space, that freedom which the great philosophers, poets, and prophets of world history had declared to be the right of all human beings. And we found white people, not many, but enough to suggest the possibility of more, brave men and women ready to support the struggle.

As I contemplated your invitation, that memory reinforced what I had already come to believe very strongly—something put into words by a character in Lillian Hellman's anti-Fascist play *Watch on the Rhine*: "Remember, everywhere in the world there are people who love children, and who will fight to make a world in which they can live." I have lived in many parts of the United States. I have been to Canada and Mexico and Cuba, to Western Europe and Yugoslavia, to Japan and Laos and Vietnam, and wherever I have been, whatever the nature of the government, that statement of faith in *Watch on the Rhine* was corroborated. I have never before been to South Africa. I am sure that South Africa embodies the starkest truths that have been uttered about it. But I am equally sure that inside those truths are infinite complexities and surprises. I wanted very much to come here to discover some of these for myself.

Indeed, the terms of your invitation gave me an immediate good feeling: that this lecture itself would be an occasion for protest against a government edict which is such a violation of democracy, such an infringement of liberty, that men and women of good will everywhere must condemn it.

I feel honored to be a part of such an occasion. I admire you for your refusal to remain silent.

It must be said that attacks on human rights, while more flagrant and more frequent in some places than others, are to be found all over the world. One reads with horror the story of Steve Biko, and knows at the same time that in police stations everywhere, not only in right-wing dictatorships but also in countries that dare to call themselves socialist, and yes, in countries that are considered liberal democracies like the United States, people are taken into custody, beaten, and killed. The reasons given by the South African Security Police for the deaths of forty-five Africans in detention between 1963 and 1977 could come from the same handbook used by police authorities almost everywhere: "suicide by hanging . . . slipped in shower . . . fell down stairs . . . fell against chair . . . leaped from 10th floor window during interrogation . . . [and, as with Steve Biko] died in a scuffle."

There are place-names in every country that immediately evoke dread. In your country: Queensboro, 1921; Sharpeville, 1960; Soweto, 1976. In my country, in the 1960s and 1970s: Kent State, Ohio; Jackson State, Mississippi; Attica, New York—white students shot and killed by National Guardsmen for protesting the Vietnam War, Black students shot and killed by police for protesting segregation, Black and white prisoners shot to death by state troopers for taking over their prison in protest against intolerable conditions. All these victims were in the classic military position in which Natives, historically, have fought Europeans: sticks, stones, and bare hands against modern firearms.

So I have not come here to talk to you about the sins of South Africa. I cannot forget that my country was a slave society for two-thirds of its history—from 1619 to 1865—that is, 246 years. It is only 117 years since the Thirteenth Amendment to the Constitution was passed, abolishing slavery, only twenty-eight years since school segregation was declared unconstitutional in 1954, only seventeen years since Southern Blacks could vote without fear because of the Voting Rights Act of 1965. And it is zero years since Blacks received equal rights to work and wages, which is my way of saying that while overall unemployment in the United States today is 10 percent of the labor force, for young Black people the unemployment rate is 40–50 percent. With that past, with that present, no American can lecture South Africans about "your race problem."

Because injustice is universal, indeed among people of all colors, and because the longing for justice is also universal, we may be able to learn from one another, to keep in touch, to give support. I hope that my visit here is an exchange.

I do know that there is a standard warning issued to foreign travelers everywhere, written in invisible ink on our passports: you must not criticize your own government while abroad; to do so is unpatriotic. I must say, however, that I have never considered my criticism of the United States government as unpatriotic. If patriotism has any valid meaning, surely it means love and respect for the people of your country, indeed for human beings everywhere, and this may require honest criticism of your government, which is something quite different from your country.

Similarly, I have never thought that, as a matter of etiquette, people visiting another country should remain silent about injustices there. Should freedom of speech have geographical boundaries? How odd that governments find it proper to send armies across borders to kill, but think it improper that people should cross borders to speak.

So I will speak freely here today, as honestly as I can, as candidly as I dare. I confess that I do not know much about South Africa. I have read a few histories. I have read the novels and stories of Nadine Gordimer. I have seen the plays of Athol Fugard. I have also read some documents; one of them moved me deeply: the Freedom Charter that was adopted by three thousand delegates at the Congress of the People of Kliptown on June 26, 1955. That was four years after a one-day strike called by the African National Congress and the Indian National Congress to protest discriminatory laws. During that strike eighteen people were killed by police, and June 26 became a memorial day.

That Freedom Charter I found a remarkable document, a powerful statement for both political and economic democracy, as if the American

Declaration of Independence had been brought up to date and made concrete. I am quoting from it:

> The national wealth of our country . . . shall be resorted to the people. . . . No one shall be imprisoned, deported or restricted without a fair trial. . . . Imprisonment shall be only for serious crimes against the people and shall aim at re-education and not vengeance. . . . The law shall guarantee to all their right to speak, to organize, to meet together . . . to educate their children. . . . All shall be free to travel without restriction. . . . Men and women of all races shall receive equal pay for equal work . . . rents and prices shall be lowered, food shall be plentiful, and no one shall go hungry. . . . Free medical care and hospitalization . . . with special care for mothers and young children. . . . Slums shall be abolished. . . . The aged, the orphans, the disabled and the sick shall be cared for by the state. Leisure and recreation shall be the right for all. . . .

It shocked me to learn that this charter was later used by the government as proof of communism in treason trials. It seems to be unwise for the government to label as communist a statement so profoundly democratic, so concerned with freedom of expression, with sexual and racial equality, with the goal of plentiful food, land, medical care for everyone. The democracy asked in the Freedom Charter surely does not describe the Soviet Union. It is a description of a society which does not exist anywhere on earth, but is eminently desirable by any rational and humane person.

Another document I have read: the speech of Nelson Mandela to court in 1963 before he was sentenced to life in prison, for sabotage and conspiracy to overthrow the government. He admitted to planning sabotage, as a desperate measure, wanting to avoid rebellion, terrorism, and bloodshed, preferring to use violence against property rather than against people, in order to call the attention of the world to the situation of Black people in South Africa. He admitted to being influenced by Marxian thought but also by Gandhi, Nehru, and others. He advocated some form of socialism but also admired Western parliamentary democracy. He said:

> I have fought against white domination and I have fought against black domination. I have cherished the ideal of a democratic and free society

> in which all persons live together in harmony and with equal opportunities. It is an ideal which I hope to live for and achieve. But if needs be, it is an ideal for which I am prepared to die."

I cannot see how any decent person can help but admire that aspiration, that spirit. Surely, a person of such sensibility, such idealism, such courage, should not be in prison but in the leadership of a society reconstructing itself as a democracy.

So a bit of reading is all I can claim about South Africa. But I do know something about what that remarkable Black American Dr. W. E. B. Du Bois called "the problem of the twentieth century, the problem of the color line." Living and teaching in a Black community in the Deep South of the United States in a period of transition and turmoil was an education. Also, having taught history and politics for more than twenty-five years, first in a small Southern college, then in a large Northern university, I have had to do some thinking about the question of academic freedom.

I am encouraged by the third paragraph in your admirable dedication, which says, "We believe further that academic freedom is essential to the pursuit of truth and is best assured in a free society which recognizes fundamental human rights." To me, academic freedom has always meant the right to insist that freedom be more than academic—that the university, because of its special claim to be a place for the pursuit of truth, be a place where we can challenge not only the ideas but the institutions, the practices of society, measuring them against millennia-old ideals of equality and justice.

My own background led me to such a definition. I was brought up in a working-class family, worked in a shipyard for three years from the age of eighteen, then enlisted in the US Air Force and saw combat duty as a bombardier in the Second World War, all this before I became a student of history and political science at New York University, then Columbia University, later Harvard University.

From the start, I was skeptical of the academy's claim to objectivity. The world I had known was one of hard class war, of holocaust and atrocity (I had participated in at least one totally senseless bombing of a village of civilians), of injustice and unremitting conflict. It was a world, as Albert Camus wrote, divided between pestilences and victims, and it was our responsibility as human beings not to be on the side of the pestilences. In a world so divided, no institution can claim neutrality, not even an institution as clever as a university, so righteous in its claims to objectivity, and so wrong in that righteousness.

Even before I set foot in my first university classroom, I suspected this, and yet in the years that followed, as a student, then as a member of various faculties, I found that my recurring naiveté—assiduously fostered by the academy—had to be again and again overturned by reality. The reality is that I live in a country where 1 percent of the population owns 33 percent of the wealth, where one hundred giant corporation control half of the economy, where cabinet members, presidential advisers, and top military men move back and forth from government to high corporate posts like shuttles on a loom, weaving a giant web of influence from which no institution can remain free.

When I was in Spelman College in Atlanta, one could easily conclude that here was an autonomous institution, free from outside control, a private university with private funds, a lovely campus fragrant with magnolias and honeysuckle, where a minority of white faculty could love and work among Black students and Black colleagues, where the racial segregation laws that operated in the city outside the campus walls could be forgotten, and where learning could go on, untrammeled and free. Indeed, as if to emphasize the independence of this enclave from the harsh racial division of the world outside, a stone wall and barbed-wire fence enclosed the campus.

My family and I lived on campus, and it was our eight-year-old son who one day pointed out that the strands of barbed wire on top of the fence were angled in such a way as to make it harder for students to get out of the campus than for intruders to get in. He was an expert on barbed wire, and it was left to me to put together the evidence and draw the political conclusions.

The college now had its first Black president but was ultimately ruled by its board of trustees, almost all white, and had been financed from its beginnings by the Rockefeller family; two Rockefellers were still on the board. Far from being independent of the outside world, the college, I began to understand, was fulfilling the historical pact between Northern and Southern capital which marked their reconciliation about thirty years after the Civil War. Another party to that pact was Booker T. Washington, the Black leader, who offered the white South Black labor in return for industrial training and some education, offering Blacks a measure of economic integration if they would quietly accept social and political segregation.

In this agreement, Northern philanthropist-industrialists, finding economic allies among rich white Southerners, would subsidize Black education. Southern politicians would let the Black colleges do as they liked inside their protected enclaves, so long as they turned out the Black teachers, social workers, ministers, even a few doctors and lawyers, to serve as a segregated community of Black men and women who crossed the border twice—morning and evening—to do menial work in the white part of town. And so long as the Black students stayed inside the fence and did not interfere with the patterns of segregation in the city outside, the pact was sealed. There was academic freedom inside the walls, and economic enslavement outside, to the satisfaction of Northern millionaires and Southern white politicians. There was the cooperation of a few Black administrators, and the compliance, for a long time, of young Black students, promised careers and a measure of American success, along with that long-withheld pride of accomplishment.

My wife and children and I, by chance, came on the scene when the students at Spelman and other Black colleges in the South were getting ready to withdraw that compliance. It was 1956.

Two years earlier, the Supreme Court of the United States had ruled that the Fourteenth Amendment to the Constitution, which declares that no state can deny to any person "equal protection of the laws," means you cannot have segregation in state-supported schools. That amendment had been passed in 1868, so it had taken eighty-six years for the Supreme Court to come to this conclusion. There were many reasons for the court decision, but one of them is rarely mentioned in American history textbooks: Africa. It was the time of cold war. The United States was vying with the Soviet Union for standing among the new colored nations of the world and, continually embarrassed by those who pointed to racial segregation, needed to say something dramatic on this issue. The Supreme Court decision allowed the United States to speak out grandiloquently. The government could then sit back while the praise rolled in from all sides, and do nothing to enforce the decision.

Other people, however, Black Americans, would not let the words rest on the printed page. It was, indeed, their long persistence that had led to the court decision. In late 1955, Black people brought their first mass action in the Deep South: the boycott of buses in Montgomery, Alabama, to protest segregation. Maids, laundry workers, and handymen were walking three, four, five miles every morning, and again every evening, for a year, until that day when the news came: they had won, and now could sit wherever they chose on the buses in Montgomery. One of them, an elderly Black woman, walking back home in the midst of the boycott as the sun set, was asked, "Aren't you tired?" Her reply became famous: "Yes, my feets is tired. But my soul is rested."

In Atlanta, in 1957 and 1958, my students began venturing off campus. They had always gone into town to buy food and clothes, but this time they were shopping for freedom. They kept asking for books at the Atlanta public library, which was reserved for whites. The librarians became embarrassed in refusing the requests of Black students for books like John Locke's *An Essay concerning Human Understanding* and John Stuart Mill's *On Liberty*. They worried about the public unveiling all this in an impending lawsuit against them. So the Carnegie library of Atlanta one day quietly opened its membership to Blacks.

This was prologue. In the spring of 1960, all over the South, Black students walked off their campuses to sit in at downtown lunch counters and restaurants, and would not move until served. "We don't serve niggers" was the standard statement of refusal. And the classical reply became: "That's not what I want. I want a sandwich." Black laughter became a weapon in the struggles that followed, along with hymns of freedom and acts of sheer courage.

And so my students at Spelman did the same. By the hundreds, they broke the ancient pact, went into town, sat in, refused to move, were arrested, and went to jail. Some of us on the faculty joined them in their sit-ins, their demonstrations. When our students came back from jail they were different: they would never be the same again. Neither would Spelman College. Neither would the South. Once their academic freedom has been just that—academic. Now it would have at least a measure of reality, because they had crossed the barrier of the academy and joined the struggle in the world outside.

When I moved north and began teaching at Boston University in 1964, I learned that the pact to limit academic freedom, to keep it behind barbed wire whether actually or symbolically, was not confined to Southern colleges. I knew that from the beginning of the United States, there was a partnership between business and government on behalf of a wealthy elite, and that the power of this elite depended on a compliant population, trained in the primary and secondary schools to become the underpaid work force of an immensely rich country. What I began to see was the role of the universities: to train the middle managers—the professionals, businessmen, administrators—who would become a useful buffer between upper and lower classes.

In short, the pact I had learned about in the South was only part of a larger, longer-standing agreement in American higher education, in which the students collaborate to maintain the social structure as it is. In return they are given jobs in the middle and upper levels of that structure, as engineers, doctors, lawyers, professors, businessmen, scientists, selling their skills to those who run the society, for a price which gives comfort and security.

Sometimes this service given by the university is direct, immediate. When police went on strike in Boston in 1919, they were replaced by students from Harvard University. In wartime, college students who have been trained in the Reserve Officers Training Corps are sent off to the front, and patriotism pervades the campus. In the great Widener Library at Harvard there is a mural of a Harvard student off to fight in the First World War, with the inscription "Happy is he who in one embrace clasps death and victory."

When the bugles of war sound, the so-called independent and humane centers of learning in every country open wide the school doors to march their students down from the hilltops of higher learning into the valleys of death.

When the United States sent more than a half-million troops into Vietnam and carried out massive aerial bombardments of towns, villages, and countryside, dropping more bombs than had been dropped in all theaters of World War II, the front-line troops came out of the primary and secondary schools, where children are raised in an atmosphere of salutes to the flag, pledges of allegiance, and reverence for military heroes. The colleges and universities played their part. Michigan State University trained police officers for the Saigon government, which the United States had installed in power in 1954. Campus units of ROTC expanded to train junior officers to serve in Vietnam. The Massachusetts Institute of Technology and other prestigious universities housed research units that were involved in the development of weapons for the war. From the faculties of Harvard and other leading institutions came the presidential advisers, the consultants and planners for the war. Vietnam became the modern version of a historic African experience—wars of so-called civilized nations against so-called primitive people—in this case, the civilizations of napalm against the primitive idea of self-determination.

The fact that I have been describing in American education—submission to the state in return for the promise of success—was broken in the 1960s by students on campuses all over the United States. In the great universities, in the small community colleges, students decided, en masse, that the war against the people of Vietnam was an abomination, that the government of the United States was not be to obeyed in the carrying out of crimes. And so they demonstrated, occupied buildings, marched, picketed, held giant rallies and teach-ins, burned their draft cards, refused to be inducted into the military, and found themselves soon part of a national movement of protest against the war.

They were joined by priests and nuns, by middle-class Americans, by artists and writers, by millions of people all over the country, and ultimately by soldiers in the field, who wore black armbands of protest, refused to go out on patrol, and put out newspapers on army bases denouncing the war. A situation was created where the government finally decided it did not have the support at home to carry on a war against the determined revolutionists and nationalists of Vietnam.

At Boston University, there were all-night teach-ins pointing out the facts of the war. Faculty and students lay down on stairways and corridors to bar the way of men from the Dow Chemical Company, manufacturers of napalm, who were recruiting students for their business. There were blockades of buildings where recruiting officers for the US Marines has been invited by the university administration to sign up students.

It was a magnificent movement, remarkably nonviolent, refusing to do harm to any person, but determined to stop the war, to break the law if need be, to go to jail. And tens of thousands went to jail: on one day alone in Washington, DC, fourteen thousand antiwar protestors were arrested. It was an era when many of us got a small taste of what prison is like. I did not think I could talk about politics and history in the classroom, deal with war and peace, discuss the question of obligation to one's brothers and sisters throughout the world, unless I demonstrated by my actions that these were not academic questions to be decided by scholarly disputation but real ones to be decided in social struggle.

Can we in the universities fulfill our obligation to society, to the principles of justice and equality, unless we renounce those pacts with the devil? Can we accept a measure of wealth, privilege, and status in return for quiescence and obedience—in short, for the surrender of freedom? Can we accept unquestioning subservience to the state when the state nowhere in the world represents its people, in their variety, in their fullness? It is the essence of modern democratic theory that governments, to be considered legitimate, must rest on the consent of all the people, and on the principle that all human beings, of whatever sex or color, are equal in their right to life, liberty, and the pursuit of happiness, that governments which are destructive of these rights are not legitimate.

I am paraphrasing, as you probably know, the American Declaration of Independence, but the ideas are universal. The United States today, recklessly squandering the nation's wealth—over a thousand billion dollars allocated for the next five years—to build superfluous weapons of mutual annihilation, while children, old people, sick people are in need, while the arts fade for lack of funds, while ten million are out of work and the cities are in decay—is violating the spirit of its own Declaration of Independence. The Soviet Union today, by its deprivation of basic liberties, by its ironic imitation of capitalist America in militarism and waste, is betraying the philosophy of Karl Marx, who, in his critique of Hegel's writings on the state, emphasized freedom as the goal of communism and supported the principle of popular sovereignty. Because that principle is being violated everywhere in the world today, we require a vast effort of cooperation among peoples everywhere, in defense of all our lives and liberties.

With all that I have said about governments, however, I must point out that there is a form of control operating in the university which is more insidious than governmental control. I am speaking of self-censorship, self-control, where the interests of the state, of the great corporations, are internalized by the academy itself: its administration, its students, its faculty. That is the most effective form of control, because it takes on the appearance of freedom, even self-determination.

Everyone collaborates in this control, simply by pushing, day to day, their traditional roles. No external restraints are needed to ensure this, only the invisible coercion exercised by a system rich enough to offer job security, promotions, social standing, and comfortable incomes, and powerful enough to withhold these rewards from the unorthodox. External control is then replaced by a whispering in the inner ear, with the single message: play it safe. In this way, behind a facade of academic freedom, the university, with the cooperation of the faculty, will turn out able and docile students who will dutifully, efficiently play their trades to keep the wheels of the economic system turning, and who will obey the state when it summons them to service, especially to war.

Thus, without extraordinary measures, in the natural course of its operation, the academy weeds out undesirable faculty, students, courses, by a panoply of political devices masquerading as lofty academic standards. Through a process of almost natural selection, a structure of quiet coercion is created, within which a prudent professor then works. The rule of safety then dictates the substance of scholarship and teaching. Probably all here can illustrate this from their own experience. I will point to a few examples from my own fields: history and political science.

Note, first, that these are two separate departments, to avoid contamination. Why spoil political theory with a dose of historical reality? Why test Locke's notion, of an original contract pleasantly agreed to by all the members of society, with the actual history of the American Constitution, which speaks for "we the people" in the very first words of its preamble, but which, in fact, was drawn up by fifty-five wealthy slaveowners, merchants, bondholders, in such a way as to assure protection of the interests of their class.

Also, political science is not to be joined to economics—that would be equivalent to interracial marriage. A study of textbooks on international relations used in American universities has shown that virtually no attention was paid in these texts to the influence of corporations on US foreign policy, despite voluminous evidence attesting to such influence. The average student of international affairs will not learn that International Telephone and Telegraph helped to plan the overthrow of the Allende government in Chile, or that United Fruit participated in and profited from the CIA's program of armed overthrow of the Arbenz government in Guatemala, or the three reasons given most frequently by the National Security Council for US involvement in Vietnam, in its secret memoranda of the 1950s, were "tin, rubber, and oil."

You will find in the American study of politics an enormous attention to voting and an obsession with all the details of legislation and parliamentary government. This is presumed to simply describe reality. However, in all complex situations there is a choice of what to describe. There is no such thing as mere description, because each choice has different consequences. To describe is, therefore, to prescribe. It is true that Americans have been voting every few years for Congressmen and presidents. But it is also true that the most important social changes in the history of the United States—independence from England, Black emancipation, the organization of labor, gains in sexual equality, the outlawing of racial segregation, the withdrawal of the United States from Vietnam—have come about not through the ballot box but through the direct action of social struggle, through the organization of popular movements using a variety of extralegal and illegal tactics. The standard teaching of political science does not describe this reality.

Nor does the teaching of history, which in the main emphasizes the laws passed by Congress, the decisions made by presidents, the rulings of the Supreme Court, and relegates the work of social movements to minor notice. The identification of political action with voting, attributing social change to the beneficence of authorities, has a distinct effect: it teaches young people that if they want to bring about change, the ballot box is the way. But what if students were taught about another reality: the history of strikes, boycotts, demonstrations, refusals of military service, the development of mass movements? It is not a matter of chance that the choice of what to describe in the process of social change is the choice safest for the existing social system, which then uses punishments and rewards to make it also safest for teachers and for students. The choices have made an air of neutrality, but can one be neutral in a world which is already moving in a certain direction?

What if one overcomes all these restraints, from outside and inside, and proceeds to teach, to write unstintingly, on behalf of radical solutions, to present sophisticated radical analyses, to become bold theoreticians of social change? What if one seizes the territory of theory and remains there, with enough provisions—that is, books, documents, bibliographies—for a thousand years, never venturing outside except for scholarly meetings?

I am sure we all know the jet-set Marxists, the mandarins of revolutionary theory, who, whenever there is a call to walk on a picket line, are en route to an international conference on the withering away of the state. I am suggesting, I suppose, that the theorist of radical change who does not act in the real world of social combat is teaching, by example, the most sophisticated technique of safety.

I have been talking to you as if to students of history or politics. But you may be engineers, scientists, artists, physicians. For you, the internalized control, the once-conditioned, now automatic reflex action for prudence is based on an even simpler maxim: stick to your lane, stay in your field, leave politics—problems of war and peace, racial oppression, class exploitation, sexual equality—to someone else. A neat formula for the continuation of things as they are: just as people are artificially divided into races and nationalities to keep them apart, and preferably in conflict with one another, divide them also into specialties. Let word spread through the culture that one who ventures out of one's assigned field is not a true "professional."

I think of J. Robert Oppenheimer, who supervised the development of the atomic bomb in the United States and then, as part of a scientific panel advising on the question of what to do with it, affirmed the political decision to drop it on the city of Hiroshima, He said later than he didn't really know what was going on politically and thought it best to let the political leaders decide.

In contrast with Oppenheimer, there was Albert Einstein, also brilliantly gifted in his field, who insisted throughout his life in speaking his mind on questions of war and peace, armament and disarmament. Refuse to fight, he said bluntly, to the young people of all countries. Refuse to make the weapons of war, he said to the populations of countries preparing for war. And when these ideas became widespread enough, Einstein said, wars must end.

Today, in the United States, the doctors, most conscientious of specialists, said always to be ready to send a person with an earache on to someone else who specializes in left ears rather than right ears, have begun to speak up loudly on the question of nuclear war. Organized into one of the fastest-growing groups of citizens in the United States, the Physicians for Social Responsibility, they have initiated a national campaign to alert the nation to the dangers of nuclear war and the necessity for disarmament. Other specialists have been stimulated to organize similarly: artists, businessmen, social scientists, teachers, writers. Because of this, it was possible last month to assemble in New York the largest antiwar demonstration in the history of the United States—three-quarters of a million people calling for a halt to the arms race. Einstein, I think, would be pleased.

I have wanted, as you can see, to go beyond the more crude inferences of the state, to suggest that the most important limits on our freedom are our own. If enough of us broke through our own restraints, no outside force could suffice to deny our freedom. Modern systems of control still depend on force, in emergencies, but for day-to-day discipline they depend on the compliance of vast numbers of people. When that compliance is withdrawn, en masse, even force is inadequate to hold back the impulse for justice.

Please understand that I am addressing myself while I am addressing you, admonishing myself, reminding myself, trying to keep my own spirit of resistance intact even while I speak to you of yours. And what I am asking of you, what I am asking of myself, is not simply to help someone else to achieve justice. I believe that the time is past for philanthropy, for missionary work, for good samaritans and kindly advisers. We are all in it together. History has come to that point. We have run out of time and space and boundary lines. We are all crowded together on a planet which must find universal brotherhood and sisterhood, across lines of class, of race, of religion, of nationality—or we will all go down, whether it be nuclear holocaust or endless civil war.

5

Second Thoughts on the First Amendment

University of Colorado at Boulder, October 25, 1989

Zinn frequently visited Colorado, where he gave talks to colleges and regularly spoke at benefits supporting the work of David Barsamian's invaluable Alternative Radio *program and radio station KGNU. This talk was followed by a benefit for the Left Hand Books and Records collective's tenth anniversary.*

One of the things that I got out of reading history was to begin to be disabused of this notion that that's what democracy is all about. The more history I read, the more it seemed very clear to me that whatever progress has been made in this country on various issues, whatever things have been done for people, whatever human rights have been gained, have not been gained through the calm deliberations of Congress or the wisdom of presidents or the ingenious decisions of the Supreme Court. Whatever progress has been made in this country has come because of the actions of ordinary people, of citizens, of social movements. Not from the Constitution. You think of whatever progress has been made in this country for economic justice. Obviously, not enough progress has been made for economic justice, looking around at this country. You have to look around. You have to walk through a whole city. If you walk through half a city you'll be mistaken. You have to walk through a whole city and you see the class structure in the United States, the hidden story of American prosperity. So obviously we haven't made a lot of progress, but we've made some progress. We got it down to an eight-hour day. We call it, professors, those people I used to associate with, an eight-hour day is a long day. People worked twelve and fourteen and sixteen hours and six days a week and seven days a week, and then at a certain point we did get it down to an eight-hour day for at least a lot of people. How was that done? It wasn't done through the Supreme Court. It wasn't done through Congress or through the president. An interesting thing about this much-touted Constitution, it doesn't say anything about economic rights, at least not for people. It has something about freedom of contract, which is not an economic right for people but for corporations, but the Constitution has nothing about the right of people to breathe fresh air or to live in a decent house or to have medical care or to make enough money or to work not too many hours. There isn't anything about that in the Constitution. Whatever was gained in that way for working people was gained through an enormously rich, complex history of labor struggles in this country. This has been mostly ignored in the history books that have been written.

When I was going through the history training process, being trained as a historian—you know, they snap a whip and hold up a book and you jump at it—I learned very little about labor history. Then I began to read on my own about labor history. I was interested because I had spent three years working in a shipyard and I thought, hey, that's what interests me. I saw what hadn't been told about labor history, what magnificent events had taken place, what struggles people had gone through, what sacrifices, what risks, what courage had been shown, what had been demonstrated about the possibilities of what human beings can do once they get together, what people had gone through and what drama there was. I wondered where Hollywood was. Talk about drama! Hollywood was struggling to get a bit of drama into some stupid movies and here were some of the great dramatic events in American history. It wasn't there in our culture, our books, our literature, on the screen. That's how whatever modicum of economic justice we have was gained.

What about the rights of women? Where is that in the Constitution? People have been struggling to get something into the Constitution about that, but there isn't. Whatever has been gained for women, and something *has* been gained for women in this country over the years, especially in this century and especially maybe in the last ten or fifteen years, but whatever has been gained has been gained through the struggles of women themselves. Emma Goldman made this very clear when they were campaigning at the beginning of the twentieth century for women's suffrage. She said, "Look, I have nothing against women's suffrage." She didn't want to alienate too many people. She had already alienated almost everybody. She had seven friends left. She didn't want to alienate them. She said, "It's okay. It's good for women to vote. Men vote, sure, why shouldn't women vote? But look, don't kid yourself. The vote isn't going to get you much. Look what it's gotten men." She said whatever women get they're going to have to get through direct action against the circumstances of their oppression, against the situations that oppress them in the home, in the workplace, in the community. They're going to have to act directly. Forget about Constitutional amendments and law and this and that. They may follow, but they will follow, not lead.

This is the point I'm making about how things have happened, how things have changed: what progress has been made is perhaps no more vividly illustrated than in the case of Black people in this country. Yes, there is something in the Constitution. There was something in the Constitution. What there was in the Constitution was bad. It affirmed slavery. That's why William Lloyd Garrison and the New England Slavery Society went out to their annual picnic and Garrison held up a copy of the Constitution and held a match to it and burned the Constitution. They're getting excited about the flag? How would they like that? The Constitution. You remember guys used to burn their draft cards and politicians went apoplectic? What about burning the entire Constitution? He burned it because he said it's a covenant with hell.

Then finally, when they did amend the Constitution, and they didn't amend it just because Congress thought one day, "Hey, it would be good to have equal rights." The Thirteenth, Fourteenth, and Fifteenth Amendments came after an enormous struggle. I'm not just talking about the Civil War. I'm talking about the struggle that preceded and took place during the Civil War, the antislavery movement. It was that movement that created the atmosphere in which slavery could be done away with. It was that movement that created the pressure that pushed Abraham Lincoln to write that rather piddling document called the Emancipation Proclamation. It was piddling. It had great moral force, but if you read the language of the Emancipation Proclamation, it was so meager. He said, "I now declare the slaves free in all the areas where we can't enforce it. In all the parts of the country where we can enforce it, the parts that are fighting with us, you don't have to worry about your slaves. They're still around." But whatever happened then, the Thirteenth Amendment, the Fourteenth Amendment, resulted from the pressure of the antislavery movement, the atmosphere created by that enormous movement, which started out very small. And then when the Thirteenth, Fourteenth and Fifteenth Amendments were passed, finally we had in the Constitution the obliteration of those terrible words that made it a proslavery document, finally we had in the Constitution words about the equal protection of the laws and life, liberty, and so on. Property, yes, you can't leave that out. But when we had those noble words about equal protection of the laws, finally, and you can't deny people the right to vote on the basis of race, color, or previous condition of servitude, there it was, powerful, finally. The states can't do this to anybody. And everybody knows it was ignored.

So you have it in the Constitution. It didn't mean a thing. For one hundred years it was ignored. The Fourteenth Amendment didn't take on any meaning until Black people rose up in the 1950s and 1960s in the South in mass movements in the hardest, toughest, most dangerous places for anybody to rise up anywhere. They created an excitement, an embarrassment to the national government that finally began to bring some changes. They made whatever words there were in the Constitution and the Fourteenth Amendment have some meaning for the first time. That's what did it.

Then of course on the matter of foreign policy and the Constitution, the Constitution has a few things to say about foreign policy. That hardly means anything, as has become clearer and clearer. Who pays attention to the Constitution? Does the president pay attention to the Constitution? The Constitution says it's Congress that declares war. Does the president pay any attention to that? He makes war when he wants to make war. Korea, Vietnam, who cares about what the Constitution says about who shall declare war. So if you're going to do anything in foreign policy, like if you're going to help stop a war, you're certainly not going to do it through the channels, through the Supreme Court or Congress. There's the Vietnam War. They actually gave a Nobel Prize to Henry Kissinger for helping to stop the Vietnam War. It's enough to make you want to build ninety-seven statues to Jean-Paul Sartre, who refused the Nobel Prize because he said it was a political prize. Imagine giving one of the architects of the war a prize for helping to stop the war because he signed that treaty at the end. But the war was not stopped by any of the formal institutions of government. In fact, we learned somewhere, maybe in elementary or junior high school, that the Supreme Court is the guardian of the Constitution and when anybody does something that violates the Constitution the Supreme Court is there to say, "No, you can't do this." So these GIs from the Vietnam War came up before the Supreme Court and said, "We refuse to go to Vietnam because it's an unconstitutional war. You're the Supreme Court. Okay." The Supreme Court didn't rule against them. It just refused to hear the case. Wouldn't discuss it. The Supreme Court is great on little things. But you get to matters of life and death, it's nowhere. So a movement had to be created in this country to stop the war. That's what happened. It bypassed the formal institutions of government, bypassed that sheepish, timorous, obsequious Congress that kept voting money for the war again and again, bypassed all the institutions and created an enormous commotion and tumult in the country and scared the president and Congress. You have to read the Pentagon Papers about what attention they were paying to public opinion and demonstrations and draft refusals to see how it affected their decisions about the war and their decision to start retrenching and not escalating the war any more.

That's what democracy is. It's what people do on behalf of human needs outside of, sometimes against, the law, even against the Constitution. When the Constitution was proslavery, the people had to go not just against the law but against the Constitution itself in the 1850s when they were doing all that civil disobedience against the Fugitive Slave Act. People have to create disorder, which goes against what we learn about law and order and orderly society and you must obey the law. Obey the law. Obey the law. It's a wonderful way of containing things. I was reading something, I made the mistake again of reading. Somebody interviewed Gertrude Schulz-Klinck. Anybody here ever heard of Gertrude Schulz-Klinck? She was Chief of the Women's Bureau under Hitler. Did you know there was a Women's Bureau under Hitler? He was a great person for women's freedom. Schulz-Klinck made sure that women were doing what had to be done for the state. That was her job. She's still around, having fun. Somebody interviewed her about the Jewish policy of the Nazis and asked her how come people went along with it. She said, "We always obey the law. Isn't that what you do in America?" That's a nasty thing to say. We're just doing what you do. We obey the law. You obey the law. Even if you don't agree with the law personally, you still obey it. Otherwise, life would be chaos. We don't want chaos. We want order.

On the other side you have Garrison, and the abolitionists saying, "Let's not create too much commotion. Let's do things more quietly. Yes, I'm against slavery too, but you're really speaking too loud." Garrison replied, "Slavery will not be overthrown without excitement, a tremendous excitement." That has a lot to do with democracy.

Now I'm finally going to get to the subject of my talk.

This was all preliminary. Then I'll have a sort of post-thing, and about two minutes of my talk. I wanted to create a context. We always claim that when we go on and on about something, we're creating a context. I wanted to create a context for talking about the First Amendment, because what I'm going to say about the First Amendment fits into this general theme about what democracy really is and whether democracy comes to you through the existence of these formal institutions or whether it requires all sorts of action and organization and risk and sacrifice and energy which goes on outside of the formal apparatus and which is engaged in by ordinary people. So second thoughts on the First Amendment.

First thoughts on the First Amendment. I suppose we all have them. You read the First Amendment, hear about it, write essays for the *Reader's Digest* essay contest on Bill of Rights Day, and how wonderful it is to have a First Amendment: "Congress shall make no law respecting the establishment of religion or abridging the free exercise thereof, abridging the freedom of speech or the press or the right of persons peaceably to assemble, to petition the government for redress of grievances . . ." It's a terrific amendment. It makes you feel good to have something like that in the Constitution as the basic law of the land, the highest law of the land. Its language is absolute. There are no exceptions in it, no buts or howevers. It's there. It's flat. It's absolute speech. It's fantastic. But . . . this is a good but. There are bad buts. I will only use good buts. Freedom of expression does not depend on the First Amendment. Let me give you an example. It took me awhile to figure this out. It took me longer than it should have. I don't know exactly when I did, but I know one of the moments when I began to think about it very forcibly: when I was in the South teaching at Spelman College, which is a Black college for women in Atlanta, Georgia. I was teaching there for seven years, from 1956 to 1963. It was an amazing time to be there. I could see my students move from a situation that seemed absolutely courtesy, politeness, quiet, order and suddenly burst out in the way things happen when people have despaired that anything will ever happen in the situation and suddenly things happen. Then you realize that you don't know anything about the way human beings are. You think you know what human beings are thinking by watching their external behavior. You don't know what's going on inside people, what they're thinking and feeling, what they're holding back, that they're waiting for the right moment, how indignant they are, how wise they are. You look at people not doing anything and you put them down. People are not dopes. People have common sense. There's a reality there, and people feel it. They may not say anything about it. It may not be practical to say anything about it. But when the practical moment comes, things will happen.

So my students began to do these things. One day, a group of students—we lived on campus—came to my house and asked, "Can we borrow your car?" I was a great force in the civil rights movement: I had a car and really played a key role. I said, "Where are you going?" They said, "We're going downtown. In fact, we have a question to ask of you. You teach constitutional law." I drew myself up to my full height. Oliver Wendell Holmes. "We're going to distribute leaflets on Peachtree Street in downtown Atlanta against racial segregation." You have to understand, Atlanta was as tightly segregated at that time as Johannesburg, South Africa. You didn't see a Black mayor, Black policemen, no such thing. It was like Johannesburg. "We're going to go downtown, to the white downtown of Atlanta, and we're going to distribute leaflets, we Black students, against racial segregation. Do we have a constitutional right to do that?"

The answer is easy for anybody who studied constitutional law. There are a lot of ambiguities in Supreme Court decisions, a lot of things that are uncertain. But there's probably nothing in the Bill of Rights on which the Supreme Court had been more firm than the right to distribute leaflets on the public street. That is clear. So the answer is an easy one: Yes. You have an absolute right to distribute leaflets on Peachtree Street. Don't worry. That's what I might have said if I were a real idiot. I was half an idiot, but not a real idiot. So I had to say, "Yes, you do have a constitutional right, but if a policeman comes up to you and says what policemen say in such situations, you can imagine what policemen say, something like 'Leave.' Policemen have their principles. They don't like the sight of people distributing leaflets on certain subjects on public streets. Policemen will say, 'Leave.' So what do you do then? Obviously, the policeman is not quite aware of the Supreme Court decisions. So you say to the policeman, 'Sir, I think I should inform you that I have an absolute constitutional right to do this, *Marsh vs. Alabama*, 1946.' At that point the situation is very clear. You have on your side the Constitution of the United States and the words of the Supreme Court. The policeman, all he has is his club and his gun." That stands for so much, tells so much about the difference between words on paper and the realities of power in the world.

What happened, of course, in the civil rights movement is that understanding that in some way because it was so clear and because Black people in the South had so much experience with it, they didn't wait for the Supreme Court to come to a new decision on the right of Black people to sit at lunch counters. In fact, the law was against that. If you studied constitutional law, you know that the law, by the early 1960s, had been set down in 1883 for civil rights cases, and private entrepreneurs, restaurants and hotels, were not covered by the Fourteenth Amendment. They could discriminate and you had no constitutional right to ask for service at a lunch counter or a hotel or any public place. So what did they do? That was the situation when those kids sat in in Greensboro, NC, in February 1960. That was the situation for all the subsequent sit-ins all over the South in 1960. They were going against the Constitution. But they won. They succeeded, one after another, as with demonstrations and persistence and mass arrests and television pictures going around the world and embarrassment and boycotts and trouble, places gave in. Constitution or no Constitution, whatever. Because what the movement did was to create a power as a countervailing power to the policeman with a club and a gun. That's essentially what movements do: they create countervailing powers to counter that reality of power which is much more important than what is written down in the Constitution or the laws.

Let me say a little about the First Amendment. It says, "Congress shall make no law abridging the freedom of speech." In 1791 the First Amendment was passed. Seven years later Congress passes a law abridging the freedom of speech. The Sedition Act of 1798 says that if you criticize the government you're going to be put in jail. No problem. The law's passed against the Constitution. The Supreme Court will take care of it, right? It goes into the courts. They try to put people in jail for violating the Sedition Act by criticizing the administration. They cite the First Amendment and the Supreme Court justices say, "Sorry, the First Amendment doesn't apply." "Why not? It says Congress shall make no law abridging the freedom of speech. They're abridging our freedom of speech." You don't understand. People are really very thick. They think they can just read words and know what they mean. Why do people go to law school? To see what words really mean. How do you become a judge? You don't understand. You have to go behind those words, far behind those words, and you have to look. It sounds Talmudic, something you'd ask at Passover: What does freedom of speech mean? You have to go back to British Common Law. Let's see what freedom of speech means in English Common Law. Really, that was the argument of the judges. English Common Law? We just had a revolution against England. It tells you a lot about revolutions. You had a revolution against England and your law is still English Common Law. You read Blackstone: "Freedom of speech means no prior restraint." That takes a little time. I can hear you thinking about it. I'm thinking about it myself. "No prior restraint." In other words, it means we can't stop you in advance from saying what you want to say, but once you say it we can put you in prison. I'm serious. Blackstone is serious. The Supreme Court is serious. They're all serious. Down to the present day, that is still what the First Amendment means. I'm serious. That's doubly serious. People are always astonished to hear this. You might say, if you were just an ordinary person, "But let's see. You're not going to stop me, but if I say it I'll go to jail. If I know that, doesn't that stop me? Isn't that prior restraint?" You don't understand. There are big differences between common law and common sense.

So there we are with no prior restraint. That's why Congress can pass laws abridging the freedom of speech. And it does, did, in the Sedition Act of 1798, and again in World War I. They passed the Espionage Act in World War I. The Espionage Act—another lesson, don't think you can tell a law from its title. Espionage Act, you think, "Oh, good, we don't want espionage. Who wants espionage?" It turns out the Espionage Act does have some things on espionage. It also has other things, like "You can't say this. You can't write this. You can't print this. You can't publish this. You can't utter this." They love the word "utter." I guess if you say it but don't utter it it's okay. The act said you can't say or publish things that will discourage recruitment in the armed forces of the United States. They passed this in 1917. The United States had just gone to war, joined that noble crusade World War I, where ten million men died in the battlefields and at the end of it nobody knew why the war was fought. Not an atypical situation for wars. At the end of it people look around at the debris and say, "Hey, what happened here?" The Espionage Act is passed. You can't say things that would discourage recruitment or enlistment into the armed forces of the United States. In other words, you can't speak against the war. That's what it meant. Do not criticize the war. Then it was tested.

The Socialist Party was quite strong in those early years of the twentieth century, really strong. You had fifty-seven Socialist locals in Oklahoma. I'm serious. It was a big movement. The Socialist Party was a big, powerful movement. Charles Schenck was a Socialist and distributed leaflets against the draft and against the war. He was brought in under the Espionage Act, which provided for up to twenty years in prison, by the way, for saying things, and he was convicted and he came up before the Supreme Court. He said, "How about the First Amendment?" The Supreme Court was unanimous. Oliver Wendell Holmes wrote the decision. He has a great reputation, an intellectual, one of the really awesome figures in American jurisprudence, intellectual history, et cetera. He actually corresponded with Harold Laski. Anybody who corresponds with Harold Laski must be okay. Holmes writes the decision. He says what people have said. You hear this all the time. Your mother said it to you, your brother-in-law said it, who knows? Somebody you heard said this: Freedom of speech is fine, but you can't shout "Fire!" in a crowded theater. How many times have you heard that? How many times have you opened your mouth and looked? That stops you. Who wants to shout "Fire!" in a crowded theater? That's the end of it. That takes care of that. Holmes, this brilliant man, gives this stupid metaphor, this ridiculous analogy, that Schenck distributing a leaflet criticizing our entrance into the war is like somebody getting up in a crowded theater and falsely shouting "Fire!" A clear and present danger to all these people. Who was creating a danger: Wilson by sending us into the war, or Schenck by protesting against the war? Who started the fire that's burning in Europe and that's killing all these people? What's going on here? A unanimous Supreme Court: clear and present danger. So they send nine hundred people to prison. They prosecute two thousand and send nine hundred people to prison under this Espionage Act, including Eugene Debs, the leader of the Socialist Party. Holmes writes that decision, too. I'm more bitter against people who are revered as liberals, people with three names. It was too much.

By the way, a guy who made a film was prosecuted under the Espionage Act. He made a film about the American Revolution. What's wrong with that, you might say? Think a moment. I hate to be patronizing. Teachers say, "Think a moment." Think. A film about the American Revolution. We were fighting against the British. This is World War I. We're fighting with the British. This film is going to arouse sentiment. It's going to divide the Allies. It's going to arouse sentiment against the British, and the British are our allies. So he violated the Espionage Act. He was found guilty and sentenced to ten years in prison. The guy who made this film. Ten years in prison. The film was called *The Spirit of '76*. The case was called *U.S. vs. Spirit of '76*.

The First Amendment has always been shoved aside in times of war or near war; 1798 was near war, 1917 was war. In 1940 when the Smith Act was passed was near war. The Smith Act was used against the Socialist Workers Party and then against the Communist Party for things that they said and wrote. In those trials against the Communist and Socialist Workers Parties, the courtroom was full with stuff the prosecution had brought in. What had they brought in? Guns, bombs, dynamite fuses? No, they brought in the works of Marx, Lenin, Engels, Stalin. That's like a bomb. So people went to jail. National security. People fall prostrate before the words "national security." All you have to do is use the phrase "national security." Oh, well, I'm sorry, do whatever you want to if it's for national security. Any of you read the transcripts of the famous Nixon Watergate tapes? At one point Nixon says to Haldemann—he always had this plaintive tone—"What'll we do, what'll we do, gee, what'll we say, what are they going to ask us?" Haldemann said, "Say it's national security."

A few years ago in Cambridge, in my part of the country, a debate was scheduled at Harvard between Alan Dershowitz, who teaches at Harvard Law School, a Zionist and strong supporter of Israel, and a guy named Terzi, who's a representative of the PLO at the UN. It was going to be an interesting debate. PLO vs. Zionist at Harvard. The State Department went to court to prevent Terzi from traveling from New York to Boston. Why? They were worried about his safety on Amtrak? Why? Because the appearance of this PLO guy in Boston and the things he would say might undermine the foreign policy of the United States. And the court upheld that. Terzi could not come. National security is invoked to keep people out, to keep out playwrights and Nobel Prize winners and writers. A lot of those writers overseas are socialists or communists or anarchists. Keep them out. National security.

The First Amendment, for a long, long time, only applied to the national government. It didn't apply to the states. The states could make any law they wanted abridging the freedom of speech. Georgia and Louisiana in the 1830s passed laws against the distribution of antislavery literature. Anybody who distributed antislavery literature in Georgia or Louisiana in the 1830s could be sentenced to death. It was not a violation of the First Amendment. It was perfectly constitutional because—here again you have to be careful reading things—the First Amendment says Congress shall make no law abridging the freedom of speech. It doesn't say Georgia shall make no law abridging the freedom of speech, or Louisiana. The states could do whatever they want. We never reckoned with the cleverness of the founding fathers and all of those people who write these things. When the Fourteenth Amendment was passed that might have put a little different thing on it, because the Fourteenth Amendment was directed against states now. The Fourteenth Amendment says no state can deprive a person of life, liberty. Now we can act against the states. If we say no state can deprive a person of liberty without due process of law, maybe that should include freedom of the press, so now we do have protection for freedom of expression against the states. That came up in 1895 with some guy who wanted to speak on the Boston Common. They wouldn't let him speak on the Boston Common without getting a permit from the mayor. The mayor wouldn't give him a permit. He went to the court and they say no, the Fourteenth Amendment doesn't apply. It wasn't until the 1920s, 1930s that this First Amendment was applied to the states. So we say, now the states cannot pass laws abridging the freedom of speech, except that anybody who went out on the street to say something or distribute leaflets or make a speech was still at the mercy of the police and the state. Nothing new. There's such a thing as the police powers of the state, which the Supreme Court brings up again. The state has police powers, and they're always balancing the First Amendment rights against the police powers of the state. The First Amendment doesn't say that your right to free speech should be balanced against anything. But the Supreme Court has decided, and it's a very handy thing, that it should be balanced against the police powers of the state, just as on a national level it's balanced against national security interests. On a state level, the First Amendment is balanced against police powers—whatever the state has to do to maintain order, et cetera. So some student who gets up in 1949 in Syracuse, NY, and makes a speech criticizing the government, gets arrested for it, goes up to the Supreme Court, and they say sorry, police powers of the state and so on.

What you're gathering from all this, I hope, is that the First Amendment is not as strong as it seems. I'm trying to hint at that. The First Amendment is not a bulwark for us. Interpretations by the courts are only the beginning of the problem, because the real problems come outside of court. Very few people get to court. Very few free speech cases are settled in court. Most free speech cases are settled out of court, that is, on the street or at work or in a family or at school, that is, they're settled in the world of reality. An enormous deal is made of what happens in the courts, what happens in the Constitution, Supreme Court decisions. The Supreme Court has said that high school kids can be censored. They said that last year. High school authorities have a right to censor the things that high school kids write. What if the Supreme Court had said high school kids cannot be censored? How much of a difference would that make in the reality of a high school and the reality of the authoritarian atmosphere of a high school and the reality of the power of principals, of teachers, et cetera? The fact that you have a constitutional right doesn't mean you're going to get that right. Who has the power there on the spot? The policeman on the street? The principal in the school? The employer on the job? The Constitution does not cover private employment. In other words, the Constitution does not cover most of reality. It doesn't cover most of the situations in which you need free speech. Therefore, you have to get it yourself. You have to do what the IWW, the Industrial Workers of the World, did. It did not have a constitutional right to go to the mining towns and lumber towns of the Northwest in the early twentieth century. The First Amendment had not been applied to the states. The states could do whatever they wanted to the IWW. The IWW was not a legalistic outfit. No. Arrest our comrade, our brother? We'll send a hundred people into that town. Arrest a hundred people? We'll send a thousand people into that town. We're going to fill their jails, their streets; we're going to make life impossible for them until we can finally speak on that street corner. That's what the free speech fights were. Emma Goldman did the same thing. She had no constitutional right to speak in these places. She was arrested again and again, especially when she spoke about birth control or marriage. That's much more serious than war. She came back. She refused to be silenced. She came back and spoke, was arrested and came back and spoke. What did workers do, being fired for speaking their minds? They formed unions to fight for better wages and hours and job security. That you can't simply be arbitrarily fired for something you said to your foreman. The union will come to your defense. The union will go out on strike if they fire you. People got together, collectivized, organized in order to defend themselves.

There are several problems about free speech that I haven't talked about which are very important. Everything I say, actually, is very important. Suppose they didn't interfere with your right to speak. Suppose none of these restrictions, none of these Supreme Court interpretations, no policemen interfering with you, none of these interferences were there. There you are. Say what you want. What resources do you have to speak out? How many people can you reach? You can get up on a soapbox and no one arrests you, and you reach two hundred people. Procter and Gamble, which made the soapbox, has the money to go on the air and reach five million people. Freedom of speech is not just a quality. It's a quantity. It's not a matter of do you have free speech, like, "In America we have free speech, just like in America we have money." How much do you have? How much freedom of speech do you have? Do you have as much freedom of speech as Exxon? There's a nice little radio station here, KGNU. I'm sorry, it's a great radio station, I was there, which proves it. But they're not CBS, NBC, prime time. They're trying to reach some people in this area and doing a wonderful job, but they have to fight for a small audience.

Resources. Who has the resources? The press is monopolized. Turn from CBS to NBC to ABC, it's all the same. Resources. The biggest problem with freedom of speech is the economic problem—who has the money to speak out, to reach large numbers of people. There is an additional problem. Suppose you even overcame that and you had the resources. Now you could speak and reach a lot of people. What if you then were in that position and you had nothing to say? Freedom of speech is meaningless if the sources of information are controlled, if the government is putting pressure on the press to withhold information as it did in the Bay of Pigs, as in the CIA overthrow in Guatemala. The government reaches in, the CIA hires people in the media to do their job for them. It's not that the press is being taken advantage of by the government. Noam Chomsky said something about it in his book *Manufacturing Consent.* He said you really can't totally blame the government for taking advantage of the press when the press seems to be so eager to be taken advantage of. Information: where are you going to get it? The government is lying to you. I. F. Stone: The first rule for newspaper people: governments lie. The government is lying to you and concealing information, deceiving you. You have to have something to say. You have to have independent sources of information.

It puts a tremendous responsibility on all of us. If we want freedom of expression, it's up to us. We have a tremendous job to do. We have to take risks. We have to speak out. The Constitution won't do it for us, nor the courts. We have to create social movements that create atmospheres of protection for people who will take risks and speak up. We have to create alternative sources of information. We have to do what was done during the Vietnam War when you had teach-ins outside the regular class curriculum, which had given people no information about Asia or Vietnam, just like the whole education system has given people no education about Latin America. This continent which is the closest to us, with which we have the most to do, we have the least education about. So we obviously need alternative sources of information. We need to do what was done during the Vietnam War: community newspapers, underground newspapers, alternate press services, such as Dispatch News Service, this little radical news service in Southeast Asia which broke the story of the My Lai massacre before anyone else did. There's a lot of work to be done in speaking up. We need to create that excitement about the issues of the time, excitement about the war, excitement about the misallocation, the waste, of the country's wealth on the military. We have to create excitement about homelessness and poverty and the class system in this country. We need information. People have to know things. People have to spread the information. That is a job that all of us have to be engaged in day by day. That's what democracy consists of. That's the only thing I've been trying to say.

6

1492–1992: The Legacy of Columbus

Madison, Wisconsin, October 9, 1991

The opening chapter of Zinn's indispensable A People's History of the United States *turns much of our traditional teaching of history on its head. By exploding the conventional narrative of Christopher Columbus's "discovery" of America, and looking at the conquest of the Americas from the standpoint of the indigenous population, he has led millions of people to question our national mythologies. In this speech, Zinn continues his reflections on the meaning of Columbus in the context of the "new world order" proclaimed by President George H. W. Bush.*

You must know that this is a remarkable thing that's happening now and this next year. That is, for the first time on such a scale and in such a way the customary celebrations of Columbus are being challenged all over the country. What's happening here in Madison is just one of those many, many events. There was a quadricentennial celebration, which probably you didn't attend, but I did, and this was four hundred years after, 1892. There were celebrations in various parts of the country. In New York there was a very special celebration, a monster celebration, five days of parades and military marches, naval pageants. There were a million visitors who came to New York for this. At one of these events the major address was given by Chauncey Depew. For those of you who recently read Gustavus

Meyer's *A History of the Great American Fortunes*, you will find Chauncey Depew mentioned a number of times. He was what you might call the main lackey for Cornelius Vanderbilt, a very well paid lackey. His job was to go to the state legislature with satchels of money and free railroad passes to make sure that the legislature passed the right kind of legislation. That was before the welfare state.

Chauncey Depew addressed this quadricentennial. He said, "If there's anything I detest, it is that spirit of historical inquiry which doubts everything. That modern spirit which destroys all the illusions and all the heroes which have been the inspiration of patriotism through all the centuries." I felt kind of bad, knowing what I was going to say. The people organizing this thing should feel guilty for what they are doing to the memory of Chauncey Depew. But I guess we're doing what he detests, thinking about history in a way that doesn't add to that wonderful glow of patriotism which has supported war and aggression over the years.

There's no real argument about Columbus and what he did. You probably know that. That is, there isn't a great deal of doubt about the major events that are described after Columbus arrived here in this hemisphere. It's generally accepted by his admirers as well as detractors that he was desperate to find gold, that he enslaved Indians, the natives, the Arawaks and the Tainos, that he "found" here. Nobody knew where they were. Only they did, you see. Sure, it's known, this is accepted also on all sides, that he was a good navigator, maybe even a great sailor, and adventurous and bold and courageous, good eyes. He almost was the first one to spot land. One of the sailors spotted it before him and was supposed to get a reward. The first one to spot land was supposed to get a reward. But Columbus decided that the sailor had not really seen land; Columbus was the one. This may be petty of me to point this out. But it's just another fact about Columbus. But there's no disagreement about the magnitude of this oceanographic achievement and about the intrepidness of what Columbus did. And there's no argument about the fact that he enslaved the Indians. He mutilated them. They were hunted with wild dogs and horses and all the armored paraphernalia that Spain of that period was able to muster up, and they hanged and burned at the stake people who resisted their domination. Columbus was a God-fearing man, a religious man. This is one of the most important things about him. If you look at the elementary school books given to kids about Columbus, the thing they emphasize is how religious he was and how much he believed in the Bible. So he erected crosses all over Hispaniola, which is the island which is now Haiti and the Dominican Republic, to I suppose represent his religiosity. He also, roughly around the same time, erected gallows all over the island. The gallows and the crosses sort of went together, as has generally been true in history.

Those basic facts about Columbus, as I say, are commonly accepted by the people who argue about Columbus. There's no real argument about those facts. The argument is about what to emphasize, or about what to leave out, because while those facts are known, not all those facts are presented. If you look, for instance, at the *Columbia Encyclopedia*, which I do every night before I go to bed, because it's named after Columbus, you will find in the long article on Columbus no word about the atrocities committed by Columbus and his brothers and colleagues when they came here. If you look up the entry in the *Columbia Encyclopedia* under Las Casas, the Spanish priest who was a harsh critic of what was being done to the natives on Hispaniola, you will find that there's an entry on Las Casas, fairly substantial, but nothing about his protests against what was being done to the Arawaks on Hispaniola.

So the problem is omission and emphasis. It's possible to mention all of those things, to be thorough, to mention all the facts, but to mention them in such an order as to give Columbus's seamanship at least as important a place in history as his killings and his enslavement. In my *People's History*, I mention the fact that Samuel Eliot Morison, the admiring biographer of Columbus, just went wild for Columbus. He was a sailor himself, and he followed Columbus's path across the ocean. He says that Columbus committed genocide. The word he uses is "genocide." But the word is buried somewhere in the middle of this long and adulatory volume, as if it were just another fact. I suppose you could write a biography of Hitler and talk about his remarkable achievements in Germany. He solved the unemployment problem, erected the autobahns, there are some marvelous architectural achievements to his credit, he brought order. There's a whole list of wonderful things that Hitler did. I suppose we could concentrate on this and just mention in an offhand way, "Oh, yes, by the way . . ." At the end of his book, Morrison is summing up his view of Columbus and be says, "Well, he had his faults. There was a dark side to him. But there's no dark side to the greatest of his qualities: his seamanship."

So the problem is, as always with history, rarely is there a problem in history of people outright lying, although yes, there is outright lying in history, a matter of omission or emphasis. The omission and the emphasis are not accidental. They're not oversights. What is emphasized and what is omitted represent the values of the historian or the recorder or the person who is telling about these facts. It represents the present values, the thinking going on today in the mind of the people recounting all of this. Sometimes you will hear, probably more and more as we get into the quincentennial, that these people who are criticizing the quincentennial, the people who refuse to celebrate it, have a political agenda. Which is a horrible thing to have. The president doesn't have a political agenda.

I was in a debate a few weeks ago at Kent State University. It was a debate about Columbus. I was debating against a Princeton historian. His point was, who are we to point the finger at Columbus and what happened there? This was, after all, the fifteenth century. You may have heard that argument before. You will hear that argument made lots of times. What right do we in the twentieth century have to judge the fifteenth century? Or to put it another way, in the fifteenth century people killed one another, exploited one another, treated other people as if they were nonhuman, violently conquered one another. So we mustn't judge. How lucky we are to be living in this time. That's the argument, from a Princeton historian.

But it really doesn't matter, education doesn't convey wisdom. I'm sorry to say this in a university. But there are values, aren't there, that transcend centuries, that are applicable to the fifteenth, sixteenth, seventeenth, eighteenth, nineteenth and twentieth centuries? There are values of human life, of concern for human beings, which are not limited to one historical period. Greek playwrights in the fifth century BC cried out against war in the same way that people in the twentieth century cry out against war. People at that time made war and visited atrocities against people, as the Athenians did against the inhabitants of Melos, just the way people do in our time. So it's absurd, it seems to me, to talk about this as being an ahistorical criticism, as being anachronistic to look back at that time. People who say that are themselves people who are accusing the critics of the quincentennial of having a political agenda. These are people who have a political agenda of their own, because everybody does. It's just that some people have it explicitly and other people claim they don't have one. They just go home at night and nurture it and come back in the morning ready to use it.

By the way, one of the proofs of the fact that there are transcendental values is simply that there are people in all times who protest against what is going on. It isn't as if they were the conquerors of the fifteenth century and they're the protestors of the twentieth century. They were the protestors of the fifteenth and sixteenth centuries. There were the resisters, of course they were the Indians themselves, who resisted and protested, the victims themselves. But there were also Spaniards who protested against what was going on. Bartolomé de Las Casas, the chief of them, who spent forty years in this hemisphere and went back and forth to Spain, taking up the cause of the Indians and crying out against things that he had seen with his own eyes. Even those who argued against Las Casas—there was another priest named Sepulveda who argued for the right to enslave and kill Indians on the grounds they were barbaric and uncivilized and unchristian and deserved what they got. But in all ages there are people who are on the side of the powerful and people who take up the cause of the victims.

So I'm arguing that the real argument is not about Columbus. The real argument goes across the centuries. The real argument is about Western civilization. The reason that people are so defensive about Columbus and anxious to maintain a glowing image of Columbus and what he did has nothing to do with Columbus. After all, it's really too late to do something about Columbus. He's not asking us for a letter of recommendation. The real point is now, and the people who are defending what Columbus did, what they really care about is now. What they really care about is what the discussion of Columbus says about what is called "Western civilization," that is, about five hundred years that have elapsed since then. They obviously are worried that the casting of too harsh a light on what Columbus did might also cast a harsh light on all those events that followed Columbus in the history of what we call Western civilization. It seems to me that there are certain key issues that are raised by the Columbus argument which need to be thought about. It's because of those issues, which are issues of today and not just issues of that time, because of the immediacy of those issues, that we reexamine what happened at the time and ask, what did it mean, and what does that tell us about the five hundred years since and about today?

One of those transcendental issues is conquest by violence. Columbus was the earliest, in this hemisphere, European imperialist. I don't like to use a word like "imperialism," because it shows a bias. But that's what was involved. In the five hundred years that followed Columbus, sure, Western civilization is something that we can point to as having achieved remarkable things in science and technology, medicine and literature, the arts. Nobody is denying that. The people who are asking for a second look at Western civilization are not trying to denigrate Shakespeare, eliminate the great works of modern literature from the curriculum. But there are questions to be asked about that history of Western civilization, and one of those questions is about that long, long history of conquest by violence which Columbus ushered in in this hemisphere and to which then Spain and Portugal and the other European countries came, and the United States then joined that expansionist game that all the European powers were playing. The expansion of the United States followed very much the pattern set by Columbus, that is, the elimination of native peoples in order to find riches.

I remember reading about westward expansion and hearing my teachers talk in junior high school about westward expansion and seeing the map on the schoolroom wall that was labeled "Western Expansion." It was one of those maps, blue and red and yellow, each one representing a jigsaw puzzle. It made you feel good that that string of colonies along the Atlantic coast had expanded. It was like a biological phenomenon, because it didn't hurt. Nobody was hurt by it. Everything was either a cession or a purchase. There was the Louisiana Purchase. I do remember feeling a certain pride. I remember the teacher pointing out that this was a terrific bargain, doubling the size of the country and getting that whole area from the Mississippi River to the Rockies for three million dollars. And furthermore, it was empty land. You could tell that by looking at the map. There was nobody there. It was not until a long time after, not until I don't know when—I'm embarrassed to say how long it took me to discover the important things I know today. It took me a while to discover that there were people living there in that Louisiana Territory, people whose home it had been for thousands and thousands of years, and who had to be displaced in order for the United States to plant its flags there and carve out that territory into states and say, "This is part of the United States." Hundreds of battles, wars, had to be fought against the people living there in order to establish that as part of the United States. But it was just a purchase.

Then there was the Florida Purchase. What happened? Andrew Jackson went into Florida with his army, killed a number of people, and Spain agreed to sell Florida, where also there were Indians, natives, but it was between Spain and the United States. And now the United States had it, and it was the Florida Purchase. Then there was the Mexican Cession. What does "cession" mean? I remember the first time I saw the word "cession," I thought, something has been ceded to somebody. The Mexicans "ceded" that great area of the Southwest to the United States: Colorado, Utah, Arizona, Nevada, California. They just ceded it to us. Why? Just good neighbor policy. The Latin hospitality, general friendliness. They ceded it to us. Then I read about the Mexican War, the war which we instigated, which President Polk planned before it took place, waiting for an incident which he could seize upon, as so many wars start on the basis of "incidents," most of them manufactured, like the Gulf of Tonkin incident as the initiation of big hostilities in the Vietnam War, or the incident in the Philippines in 1899 starting the military attacks in the Philippines. Here was an "incident" in this disputed territory between the Nueces River and the Rio Grande, and President Polk was announcing to the nation, "American blood has been shed on American soil." It wasn't American soil, but that's war. It was a very short war, with not too many casualties on our side, and we end up with 40 percent of Mexico, and that's the Mexican Cession.

So we've moved from the Atlantic to the Pacific, and then we moved outward and down into Columbus's area, down into the Caribbean, into Central America. There's that one chapter in the textbooks labeled "The Age of Imperialism: 1898 to 1903." That takes care of that. It's acknowledged. There was Teddy Roosevelt, Henry Cabot Lodge, Admiral Mahan, Manifest Destiny, moving outward. We go into Cuba to save the Cubans from Spain. I wondered why I had a funny feeling when I heard that we were going into the Middle East to save Kuwait from the Iraqis. Whenever we have been going anywhere to save anybody from somebody else, I remember that when we went into Cuba to save Cubans from Spain, in fact we expelled Spain and established ourselves in Cuba. Then American corporations moved into Cuba, American railroads and banks, United Fruit, and twenty million acres of land were bought for ten cents an acre. There we were, and our military posts were set up in Cuba. We wrote the provisions in the Cuban constitution allowing the United States to go into Cuba anytime we decided that it was necessary. Thus was Cuba liberated. Then we took Puerto Rico. Just a little bombardment, and Puerto Rico was ours. Then we took the opportunity to take Hawaii, a little farther away out in the Pacific, but waiting for us. Then the Philippines, which was very far away. But McKinley didn't know this. He didn't know where the Philippines were. It was pointed out to him on the map. He thought it was off the coast of California. It turned out to be off the coast of Asia. But there they were. They belonged to Spain. We had just defeated Spain. McKinley gave the same reasons for going into the Philippines that Sepulveda gave for killing and enslaving the Indians on Hispaniola. McKinley said, "We've got to go into the Philippines to civilize and Christianize them."

There's this history, this long history of expansion, of conquest, of violence. Somewhere, what Columbus did is there at the start of that long history. I'm not arguing that Columbus is therefore personally responsible for everything that happened, but it's just that to celebrate Columbus is to lose sight of what he represents in the history of Western civilization. What he represents is not something called "discovery" or "exploration"—all of these mild activities and admirable activities—or even "encounter," which people are beginning to use to describe what happened. "Encounter" suggests a meeting between equals rather than what it was, that is, conquest.

So there are issues like that that are raised by the rethinking of the Columbus story. The issue of dehumanization. The Indians were seen as subhuman, as creatures. They're not Christian. They're so different that they don't speak our language. It's true they're friendly and nice and warm and generous, as Columbus describes them in his journal. Nobody has a more kindly description of the Arawak Indians than Columbus, how they would just give what they had and not ask for things in return. But that didn't save them when they couldn't bring enough gold or when they had to be used for labor or when they had to be sent back in chains to Spain as slaves, as booty, to prove to Columbus's financiers that there was some value to his expedition and therefore there had to be more expeditions. And this dehumanization of conquered peoples is something that has followed the course of Western civilization over these centuries, as the European powers conquered Africa and Asia and as the signs in the port of Shanghai for the Western enclaves—the country clubs of the British and French had signs saying, "No Chinese or dogs allowed." That phenomenon of imperialism that has so marked the history of these last centuries, the dehumanization of black people in this country, the fact of slavery.

Aside from dehumanization, there's simply the fact of invisibility, of certain people being not within the purview of human consideration. That happened then and that still happens today. And in the latest war, of course, the Iraqis were not seen as human beings. That's the only thing that could account for the fact that we can accept the killing of so many people in Iraq, the bombing of cities accepted as just a glorious victory and an easy war. They didn't count. They don't count. It was sad to see General Colin Powell, himself a part of that American population that was for so long dehumanized, saying in response to questions about how many Iraqis had been killed, that it wasn't of great interest to him. That's part of the heritage of Western imperialism, that very nasty side to what we call Western civilization.

Another issue that transcends the centuries from Columbus's time to ours is the profit motive, which very often you hear about in admiring terms. The profit motive, the fuel of the modern industrial system. But the profit motive for Columbus led to genocide, and the profit motive across the centuries in the development of the modern industrial world, while yes, it has led to the creation of these enormous technological societies, these marvelous advances in communication and transportation, manufacturing and so on—the profit motive can do that and has done that—but it also meant that in the course of the building of these great industrial empires the cost of that so-called progress to millions of human beings was simply not considered. It's interesting how in the United States, when you study American history—I distinctly remember how the period after the Civil War, roughly from the Civil War to World War I, was looked upon in the history books as the Age of Enterprise, the age of great industrial progress. They would give you the figures on the miles of railroad that were completed in that time and how much steel was produced in that time. The figures were staggering; incredible industrial progress was made during that period.

What was left out of those textbooks was the cost to human beings of that industrial progress, of the deaths of tens of hundreds of thousands of people in the course of that industrial progress. In one year in the early part of the twentieth century thirty-five thousand workers lost their lives in industrial accidents. You can multiply that over the years and imagine how many hundreds of thousands of people lost their lives and how many millions were injured or how many lost fingers or arms. Five thousand railroad amputees in a year as a result of accidents on the railroads. The same thing done as our corporations moved down into Latin America. The railroad built across the Isthmus of Panama by Vanderbilt: five thousand laborers died in the course of the building of that railroad. And how many Chinese and Irish workers died in the building of the Transcontinental Railroad, which I remember from history as being one of the glorious feats of American history? The golden spike being driven there in Utah as the Central Pacific and the Union Pacific joined. What a great moment that was. But nothing was told to me about what went into that.

The profit motive, yes, free enterprise, private enterprise. We're delighted now to be thinking that everybody in the world is going to adopt it. Everybody's going to have what we have. Everybody's going to be able to build up their industry the way that we built up our industry, I'm not arguing for what they call the Luddite approach. "Oh, you want to go back, you don't want TV." That's the most serious accusation that could be made against anybody. "You don't want any of these modern things. You're antiprogress." No. But there has to be some proportionate response which involves figuring out how to make progress without killing people. How to make progress without poisoning people. How to make progress without polluting the air and the water, without endangering the planet and ruining it for our children and grandchildren. There must be a way of doing that and still, yes, making progress.

Yes, the criticism of what happened then and what has happened since is a criticism of what nation-states have done and a refusal to accept the glorification of flags and anthems and passports and military machines and all the other paraphernalia of nation-states that have made Western civilization that which Gandhi spoke about when he was asked, "What do you think of Western civilization?" He said, "It's a good idea."

Fortunately, that march of conquest and greed through the five hundred years since Columbus has not gone without resistance. After all, those glories of Western civilization that we talk about are not glories that were given to everybody. In fact, they were only given to a minority. The great technological marvels of Western civilization have not benefited most of the people of the world. Most of the people in the world are living in a state which does not resemble civilization as people want to think about it. Those people who are not benefiting from all these glories resisted it all through the years, just as Indians originally resisted Columbus and the Native Americans on this continent resisted, for a very long time, for hundreds of years, the conquest of this continent. The Seminole Indians in Florida fought a long war against the American army against great odds. The army could never really defeat them. They couldn't win either, but they refused to give up.

Working people in this country have resisted the glorification of private enterprise and insisted by all the things that they did, the strikes, the labor struggles, that they would not simply accept the natural results of what was called private enterprise, the natural results being the accumulation of wealth at the top and an absolute unconcern for the lives and the working conditions of the people who were responsible for working and building all these things. Black people resisted their situation and fought for their own freedom, and then when their freedom was given to them, presumably in legal form, by the Thirteenth and Fourteenth and Fifteenth Amendments, and then set aside and forgotten about, they reasserted themselves in the civil rights movement of the 1950s and 1960 and insisted that the Fourteenth Amendment be given life that had been denied to it before. So people have resisted all these years. What's remarkable is that the Native Americans of this country were supposed to be eliminated. Their sources of food, their basis for living being destroyed systematically, killed, pushed out of one part of the country, driven out of the Southeast across the Mississippi on those terrible, terrible death marches. Talk about the death march on Bataan, how terrible, what an atrocity it was. There was that death march of the Cherokees and Choctaws, the five civilized tribes in the 1830s and 1840s, and all of that. The Indians were supposed to be gone, driven into a section of the country called "Indian Territory." Now, this little part of Oklahoma is your territory. Then oil was discovered on Indian Territory, and all bets are off. Oil seems to be important in Western civilization. Oil seems to be responsible for a lot of cruelty and murder in the history of Western civilization. Gold also seems to be responsible. The Indians are scattered, isolated, invisible.

Then, just twenty years ago, they suddenly are here again. Where did they come from? They're here. They're occupying Wounded Knee, the site of that last massacre. They're occupying Alcatraz Island. They're battling for their fishing rights and demanding land all over the country. They've become a presence, a force. That's a remarkable fact, that now in this year of the quincentennial all these countercelebrations are being led by Native Americans. They're taking the lead in all of this, and suddenly they're visible again.

All of this bothers the defenders of Western civilization, those people who have benefited, apparently, from Western civilization, or who think they will benefit from it in some way. They are bothered by the fact that more and more Americans want to look at what happened then from a different point of view. Because we've been looking at it from one point of view for all these hundreds of years, looking at slavery from a white point of view, at Columbus from the white point of view, at women and the issue of sexual equality from the male point of view, looking at history from very specific, limited points of view. What's happening now, what's been happening for several decades now, is people have begun to ask to look at history from the point of view of those people who have been invisible, overlooked, oppressed. That troubles the defenders of Western civilization. That's interesting, because they're worried "political correctness" is inhibiting freedom. But they don't want people to be free to look at the data of history and to look at today from different points of view. And yet that's exactly what needs to be done if we are going to have a different kind of world. We're all going to have to look at what happened in the past and to look around us at what is going on now and look at it from points of view very different from those we were taught in school and those we were brought up with.

If we begin to see these things from these different points of view and understand one another, then we might be able to create that unity of purpose among these large numbers of people who so far have been left out of that apogee of wealth represented by Western civilization. If people can unite in those different points of view, then we may see remarkable changes take place. We know that it's possible for change to take place suddenly, surprisingly, unpredictably. We've seen that in various parts of the world. It's possible here in the United States, too.

Thank you.

7

A People's History of the United States

Reed College, Portland, Oregon, November 20, 1995

A People's History of the United States has now sold more than two million copies. In reality, this is a conservative figure, as countless used copies have been passed on to friends and family, teachers have photocopied its pages for students, and the book has been sold in dozens of translations across the world. By 1995, the book was beginning to gain a wider readership on campuses such as Reed College, where Zinn was in popular demand as a speaker and regularly drew hundreds of people, sometimes well over a thousand, to hear his talks. He gave this speech as part of a symposium called "On the Joy of Struggle."

I came across a book recently called *The Art and Politics of College Teaching.* Any of you ever hear of it? No. I'm not surprised. It's a kind of Machiavellian guide to people who want to teach in college. It's organized in the form of concerns. Concern no. 9—I skipped the first eight for your benefit—"Can I involve myself in causes, crusades and political activism as a professor? Answer: The institution of higher education may not look kindly upon such activities. Be wary of introducing your political conclusions or social thought into classroom situations. Be on guard not to take sides, if it is possible to avoid it at all. Play dumb." That's interesting. Until you get your PhD the advice is "play smart." Then after you get your PhD, "play dumb."

"Be somewhat submissive to the senior faculty." The only thing about that I didn't understand was the word "somewhat." I thought that took courage. If I had had that book available to me when I started my teaching career, who knows what I might have become. A dean, maybe.

I've always been interested in teaching as a profession and the whole idea of professionalism, which ties in with Machiavelli, that is, the idea of just doing well whatever it is somebody tells you to do, without asking why or what. I have something here that was written by Leslie Gelb, a writer for the *New York Times*, during the Gulf War, toward the end of the Gulf War. He was just ecstatic over the professionalism of the American army in the Gulf War. He had worked for the Rand Corporation and for the US government and was in the habit of not asking questions other than professional questions. So it is only fitting now that he should work for the *New York Times*. I remember that I saw a review not long ago of the autobiography of Leni Riefenstahl, the . . . I started to call her the "Nazi filmmaker," but then I realized, she wouldn't like it. So let's put it this way: she was a filmmaker who worked for the Nazis. The reviewer in the *New York Times* talked about her involvement with Hitler. When I say "involvement" with Hitler, I don't mean it in the sense of *People* magazine. She met Hitler a few times, had lunch with Goebbels, if you can imagine having lunch with Goebbels. In the world of film her technique is admired enormously. The reviewer ends up by saying something like "She may have compromised her morality, but her artistic integrity, never."

Then I remember when Mumia Abu-Jamal was facing execution last August. I don't know how many of you have heard of the case of Mumia Abu-Jamal. I remember at the very time, just before his scheduled date of execution, there was a campaign going on around the country, indeed, around the world to stop his execution. There was a meeting, it so happened, at that very time in Philadelphia, which is the site of all of that, of Jamal and MOVE, and the Pennsylvania governor coming into office promising to carry through all of the executions that were planned in the state of Pennsylvania. Just at that time the Association of Black Journalists met in Philadelphia and debated the question of whether they should call for a new trial of Mumia Abu-Jamal, which is what the campaign was for. E. L. Doctorow, the novelist, wrote an op-ed piece in the *New York Times*, saying, as many people did, "We don't really know the facts of this case. It's hard to know. We have conflicting evidence. Who can say for sure whether Mumia Abu-Jamal killed this policeman or not? But judging from the way the trial was conducted, from the way the witnesses were brought forth, from the prejudice of the judge, who was proud of having sentenced more people to death than any other judge, he deserves a new trial." That's what people were asking for, and this is what the Association of Black Journalists was debating. They finally decided not to call for a new trial but to make some statement short of that. One of the grounds for not declaring themselves boldly in favor of a new trial was that they felt it was not their job as journalists to do that. "Our job," as one of them put it, "is to advance ourselves professionally and to do everything we can do to advance the profession, and somehow this doesn't fit it."

I just thought of another example in my own profession—sometimes I consider myself a member of the historical profession, for speech purposes. During the Vietnam War there was a business meeting of the American Historical Association. At this meeting—you know these annual scholarly meetings, some of you may be really lucky and get to go to some of them. Right in the midst of the Vietnam War. At all these scholarly meetings all these papers are presented, but there's always a business meeting. The whole thing is attended by thousands of people who come from all over the country for that one annual meeting, and then there's a business meeting, which is usually attended by thirty-two people, because can you imagine how exciting would be the business of the American Historical Association? But this time, at this meeting, the place was jammed because everybody had heard that there was going to be a resolution introduced at the business meeting calling for the American Historical Association to denounce American policy in Vietnam and to call for the withdrawal of American forces from Vietnam. So everybody came.

We introduced the resolution. In fact, I confess that I introduced the resolution. Wearing dark glasses. We had a lively debate, as lively a debate as you can have at the American Historical Association. The resolution was defeated. The main ground for its defeat was that it really wasn't relevant to the work of historians. Immediately after our resolution, the resolution of what was called the Radical History Caucus—I don't know why I've always been part of something called the Radical History Caucus—but after that was defeated, somebody else got up and proposed another resolution which said exactly what my resolution had said, except that it added the words "because the money that's going for the war could otherwise be used to advance the profession of history." That resolution passed overwhelmingly.

So I'm glad you're all going to be professionals. The problem is how to work in a field without becoming a professional in that sense of the term, that narrow, warped, antihuman sense of the term. When I became a historian, when I entered what I soon discovered was a profession, I already knew that I was not going to be neutral. I already understood for myself that in teaching history or writing history my point of view was going to be there. I was not going to be what they called a disinterested historian. I had interests. I was not going to be an objective historian, because I didn't really believe objectivity was possible, nor was it desirable, unless objectivity meant telling the truth as you saw it, not lying, not distorting, not omitting information, and not omitting arguments because they don't conform to some idea that you have. But if objectivity meant not taking a stand, if objectivity meant presenting data without caring about the social effect of the kind of data you present, I didn't want that kind of objectivity. History was interesting to me, but I wasn't going into history because it was interesting. To put it another way, what was interesting about history was that it represented different kinds of interests. I was very much aware of that. I was aware as soon as I began to study history that you couldn't really be objective. You couldn't really just "recapture the past as it was," a phrase that was used starting in the nineteenth century, when history became a profession in an important sense, and an idea which is still heard today.

I remember reading not long ago an article in the *Times Literary Supplement.* I like people to think that I'm a regular reader of the *Times Literary*

Supplement. Actually I just stumbled on this issue, and there was an article by Gertrude Himmelfarb. I also like to drop her name once in a while. She's a historian, very well established, and I think it's fair to say a conservative historian. She argued in that article for trying to reproduce the past and get as close to it as possible, argued against what she called "postmodernism" in history. For her postmodernism meant not accepting truth, thinking that there is no such thing as established truth. She gave an example of how important it was just to find out as much as you can about any era: One of her students came to her very excited about a historical discovery. That was that Andrew Jackson's first message to Congress was written by George Bancroft. You don't seem excited by that idea. But my point is . . . if somebody hasn't found out anything before and you can bring a new fact to life, this is a very important thing very often, like when you work on a doctoral dissertation. You work in a field that nobody has ever worked at, no matter how unimportant the field is.

History is an infinite number of events, an infinite number of facts. Inevitably you must select from that number of facts those things which you are going to present, if you are going to write, if you are going to teach. What is going to go into this book, into your lecture, your classroom? There's no way of avoiding the process of selection. Once you make that selection, that selection is based on your point of view whether you acknowledge it or not, whether you even know it or not. There's a way in which you can reproduce the point of view that has been dominant in your culture without understanding that you are reproducing the dominant point of view. So you make a selection according to your point of view. You make a selection according to what you think is important. And different people think different things are important. Himmelfarb thought that finding out about Andrew Jackson's first message to Congress and who wrote it was important.

I say this because there's this huge emphasis—you know, how much discussion there is now about history and arguments about history, about history standards, national standards. That whole debate has gone about the standards drawn up in California, which led to a Senate resolution.

The Senate is very interested in history and culture and art and things like that. So the Senate passed a resolution overwhelmingly denouncing these history standards and calling for a history in which the United States would not be denigrated. So there is all this controversy about history. Much of the controversy ends up with talking about how it is important to know facts. That's what tests are based on: standardized tests are based on facts.

I remember a few years ago the *New York Times* did a survey of high school students to see how much history they knew. They do this every few years. They do a survey of young people to prove how dumb they are and to prove how smart are the givers of the tests. So they gave this test to high school seniors and it corroborated what they thought: young people don't know any history. They asked questions like "Who was the president during the War of 1812? Who was the president during the Mexican War?" I can see you thinking already. We're in a great quiz culture. All you have to do is ask a question like "What came first, the Homestead Act or the Civil Service Act?" You recognize questions like that because those are questions that appear on tests which enable you to get into graduate school. You can go very far if you know enough of those answers. You'll be Phi Beta Kappa. You'll become an adviser to the president of the US. Remember the book *The Best and the Brightest*, which is precisely about that point, that the people surrounding the presidents who made the war in Vietnam were the brightest people. They were the people who got the highest scores. They were Phi Beta Kappa. They were the architects of the war in Vietnam.

The *New York Times* decided it was important—they could have selected all kinds of questions, but they decided it was important who was president during the Mexican War. By the way, it was James Polk. I want to get that out of the way. You can forget about it now. I don't want for the rest of my talk for you to be thinking about that. There's nothing a speaker hates so much as a distracted audience. The *Times* could have asked an important question about the Mexican War. They could have asked, "How did the Mexican War start?" Ahh. Then they might discover, for anybody looking into how the Mexican War started, 1846–48, America goes to war against Mexico, ends up with 40 percent of Mexico's land, a little war, cleanly fought. It starts with an incident, one of those incidents which start wars, incidents which have a certain amount of deceit attached to them, in which an attack is fabricated or exaggerated or distorted and suddenly there's a cause for war. So there was this disputed territory between Texas and Mexico, the area between the Rio Grande and the Nueces River. Mexico claimed it for theirs and the US claimed it for theirs. A clash between the two troops, and immediately that's it. That's the end. That's enough. President Polk announces to the nation, "American blood has been shed on American soil." A little bit of an exaggeration. He wasn't sure whether it was Mexican soil or American soil. The nation is at war.

Of course, the decision to find a way to make war with Mexico had been made before that incident, just as the decision to go to war in Southeast Asia was made before the Gulf of Tonkin incident. But somebody looking into that might then have proceeded to examine our other wars and to examine how these wars start. They might have looked into the war in the Philippines at the turn of the century and taken a look at a fabricated incident which then enabled the US to make war in the Philippines against the Filipinos, who seem to want to run their own country. But they really aren't a civilized people, so President McKinley said, "We must Christianize them and civilize them." He said he got that message from God. The Filipinos apparently did not get the same message. They fought back, and there ensued a very bitter, bloody war which I remember when I went to school occupied a very small part of the history book, whereas the Spanish-American War, a short war in which we got the Spanish out of Cuba. The Spanish-American War. Cuba. Teddy Roosevelt. The Rough Riders. But the Philippines War, a long, bloody war in many ways like the Vietnam War, a war full of massacres in which finally we subdued the Filipinos and took it over: a look into how wars start might have led to some interesting conclusions about that war. It then might have led to the Gulf of Tonkin. That might have led people to ask more recently, "How did we, under Reagan, decide to invade Grenada?" What was the incident there? It was the medical students in trouble. Wherever medical students are in trouble, the US Army goes. Or Panama. It's hard to remember these things. They come and go so fast. There was another incident there. Somebody insulted somebody, and we can't take that. And besides, we want to eliminate the drug trade. If we get rid of Noriega, that will end the drug trade. In fact, it has worked. So in the course of it we bombard a few neighborhoods in Panama City and kill we don't know how many people.

But yes, there are important questions to be asked in history. But in order to do that you have to start with a point of view so that you will ask those questions. The idea of having a point of view is not to have preconceived answers, to be willing to be open for the answer, but the important thing about having a point of view is to ask important questions, on the grounds that history is important. It's not a game of trivia. It's not a way simply to become a professional, to produce another generation of historians who will produce another generation of historians. We'll all reproduce ourselves as historians while the world passes us by. All sorts of things are going on.

Of course, when you approach history that way, with a point of view, it can be dangerous to your career. People always wonder why it is that textbooks repeat the same stories over and over again, why history is taught the same way, why the same set of facts are told over and over again, and why the same things are omitted over and over again. In the very repetition of those omissions, those points of view become persuasive in telling you, "This must be a truth." If seven, eight, ten generations of kids learn that Columbus was nothing but a marvelous adventurer and great navigator, a real professional, and if everybody has been taught the same thing for a hundred years, it must be true.

If we teach it in a different way, if something has been taught the same way, or if you write something that's been taught a certain way and you deviate from that and start to teach or write something in a new way, that may be dangerous to your career. You may not even consciously think of it that way. You're not consciously selling out. It's just that in a society of economic hierarchy, a society of economic insecurity, a society where everybody is in some way insecure, middle class, working class, everybody's in a situation where somebody has power over them, power over their jobs, over their tenure, their promotion, their salaries—in every such situation there's always the thought or even the unthought, that felt need for safety. And safety results in teaching a certain kind of way, writing a certain kind of way, presenting the same set of ideas over and over again. That's safe. I guess you can put it this way: I never wanted to practice safe history.

I remember when the House Un-American Activities interrogated Daniel Boorstin. Do you remember the House Un-American Activities Committee? There are probably some people here who were interrogated. I don't want to point them out to you. You may remember that it had hostile witnesses who refused to talk about their political activities and organizations or to name their friends. Then it had what were called friendly witnesses. One of those friendly witnesses was Daniel Boorstin, who as you know is a distinguished historian. The word "distinguished" is kind of neutral. He assured the committee that whatever radicalism he had ever had he had left far behind. I don't know if I have somewhere a piece of his testimony before the committee. He told the committee that he had proved his opposition to communism in two ways. First, by participating in religious activities at the University of Chicago. Then he said, "The second form of my opposition has been to attempt to discover and explain to students in my teaching and in my writing the unique virtues of American democracy." That seems objective. If he had said, "I thought I would explain to my students some of the virtues of American democracy and some of the hypocrisies of American democracy," he wouldn't have been a friendly witness at that point.

I suppose that I came to history with a point of view. I came to the teaching and writing of history with a point of view already because I didn't go directly from high school to college to graduate school to teaching. I had a number of years between high school and college. At the age of eighteen I went to work in a shipyard and worked there for three years. I didn't do it as a sociological experiment, go around with a tape recorder and talk to my fellow shipyard workers: "How does it feel to work in a shipyard?" I came from the kind of background and family where kids didn't go to college, where at the age of eighteen you went to work so you could bring some money home, even if it was very little money, for the family. So I worked in a shipyard for three years. I have a chapter in this memoir which was referred to, *You Can't Be Neutral on a Moving Train*, called "Growing Up Class Conscious." I suppose I grew up class conscious. I grew up aware that most people in society worked on the kind of job I worked on, not in a shipyard maybe, it didn't matter what they worked at, but they worked at a job that they weren't crazy about but that they had to work at. They might be blue-collar workers and they might be white-collar workers or they might be steel workers or they might be advertising copy writers, but they were still mostly working at jobs which alienated them from the process of work and from the product of their work.

So I was aware that this kind of work existed and that there seemed to be some people in society who didn't do that kind of work. I very early on became aware that there was no particular relationship between how hard you worked and what rewards you got as a result of this work. I never believed, and I don't know when this started, but very young, I was no longer susceptible to that which you hear a lot around you, and I remember some of my students at Boston University would express something that is a recurring theme in American society. That is, if you work hard enough, you will "make it." You will become prosperous and successful if you work hard. If you haven't become prosperous and successful, it must mean you haven't worked very hard. I saw my father work very hard, all his life, and have very little to show for it. I saw my mother work very hard and lot of people like them. Then I saw people in society who were successful and prosperous. I couldn't figure out what they did. Either they didn't seem to be working very hard, or they were working very hard at producing terrible things and were very well paid for it. So I was class conscious at an early age.

The word "class-conscious" doesn't appear a lot in American society. It's sort of an embarrassing word. Our society is not supposed to be that way. Brazil, yes. Ecuador, who knows. Saudi Arabia. There are societies with rich elites and poor masses, but not America. You hear politicians accusing one another of appealing to class prejudices. Politicians are very careful not to be accused of that. I remember during the 1988 election campaign. Remember Bush and Dukakis? It's hard to remember that. But it will be on the next *New York Times* quiz. At one point Bush accused Dukakis of "arousing class hostility." Which really surprised me. I live in Massachusetts. Dukakis was the governor of Massachusetts. And the idea that Dukakis would appeal to class hostility somehow didn't ring true to me. That he would provoke class conflict? No. That he would provoke anything? The avoidance of class is very interesting.

I read a review. You'll be getting the idea that I do nothing but read reviews. Why read books? This was a review of a movie. For that matter, why go to the movies? This was a review in the *Boston Globe,* my hometown newspaper, which is one of the better newspapers in the US, which as you know is saying a great deal. The *Boston Globe* had a review of a new movie, *Germinal.* Some of you may recognize it as a novel by Emile Zola, about miners and the life of miners, a very powerful novel about the struggles of miners and their existence. A movie was made of it. The reviewer didn't like it. At the end of the review, as at the end of all reviews in the newspaper, and I don't know if they have that here in Portland, they give the rating: G, PG-13, R. Next to that designation, especially if it's R, they usually say why they gave it the R designation. Usually if it's R they will say "nudity" or "partial nudity" or "frontal nudity" or "side nudity." Or "scenes of violence" or "profanity." After the review of *Germinal* it was designated R. Then it gave the explanation: "depiction of intense suffering and class conflict." I didn't believe it, but I'm a naive person. I see things in the newspapers, I hear things from the mouths of politicians, and then I say, "I don't believe it." Which is ridiculous, because that's all you should believe. What else is there to believe? If I heard a politician say, "You know, the history of the US is the history of class struggle," then I wouldn't believe it.

But in fact this is a class society. And you could start a history of the US with that sentence. It would be absolutely accurate. But can you imagine somebody writing a textbook on American history for our very vulnerable students and starting off talking about our history as a history of class struggle? Can you imagine any major publisher publishing a book like that, with that first sentence? Would it take very long for the publisher to go through that manuscript before rejecting it? And yet it's an absolutely true statement. From the very beginning, on the North American continent, from those first centuries of what is called the "colonial period," the period before the American Revolution, we were a class society. We didn't all come here as pilgrims.

I remember going to school my impression was that those people who came from England all dressed in the same simple way. It was a very egalitarian society, and they signed the Mayflower Compact, which proved it. But no. In fact, there were people who came here as Black slaves, and other people who came here as indentured servants, large numbers of women came as you might say servants and sex slaves to serve the men who were already here, the labor force that had to be satisfied in some way. Others came here with enormous grants of land given by the king or by Parliament. So from the beginning there were very rich and very poor. That pattern continued all through American history. The poor resisted and rebelled. There were slave rebellions and servant rebellions, and the poor of the colonies rioted. The flour riots, the bread riots. The people attacked the warehouses where the flour was stored, flour that was not being made available to them because they couldn't afford the prices that were being charged for the flour. They stormed and opened up the warehouses and took the flour so they could make bread and feed their families. Riots against impressment, because they were being impressed to fight the wars of the British in the late seventeenth and eighteenth centuries. This was all before the American Revolution. Tenant insurrections against landlords. Crowds marching to jails and freeing the prisoners who had been imprisoned because of failure to pay their debts.

Then the American Revolution comes along, and one of its functions is to suppress class conflict, as wars are very often fought with that purpose. When I say "purpose" it suggests a more deliberate conspiracy than

I mean. But let's put it this way: one of the consequences of wars, very often one of the accompaniments of wars, is the creation of a country united against a common enemy and therefore a country which the leaders hope will put aside the internal conflicts, the class conflicts, the feeling of the poor against the rich, put that aside to face the common enemy—in the case of the American Revolution, England. It didn't wholly succeed, because even during the American Revolution there were rebellions. Soldiers, class conflict in the army. There's no class division more sharp and more humiliating than class divisions in the military. Privates were not being paid and officers were being paid very lavishly. So they mutinied and marched on the Continental Congress in Philadelphia and threatened it. A number of them had to be taken out by George Washington and their fellow soldiers ordered to shoot them as a lesson to the rest.

When the revolution was over, the class conflict continued, and that, to a great degree, led to the creation of the Constitution; that is, the Constitution was an attempt to create a nation in which internal conflict would be controlled. Those of you who have read the *Federalist Papers* or at least Federalist Paper no. 10 know that this was the argument that James Madison presented in arguing for people to ratify the Constitution. When the Constitution was presented in the various states for ratification, the argument was that there's a natural tendency for conflict. They even used the word "class," the word "faction." The basis of this conflict between factions is the division of property. Some people have property and other people don't have property. So you want to create a large republic which will be able to control this conflict. He wasn't worried about a minority faction, as he put it. He was worried about a majority faction, which meant most of the poor people. The way to control that is by having a big country, all thirteen states together. In that way it would be very hard—and they were very blunt about this in the *Federalist Papers*—to have a rebellion that starts in one part of the country spread very quickly to the rest of the country. It will be contained in time, before it spreads. . . .

The supposedly contending groups who run American society, Democrats and Republicans and Whigs and Democrats and Federalists and anti-Federalists, they really are part of the same elite group, with some differences. Madison and Hamilton agreed on this, although Hamilton preferred a monarchy but was willing to go along with representative government because, as Madison explained, if you have representatives, then if there is anger that arises in any part of the population, that anger will be filtered through the representative body, and by the time it gets through the representative body it will have been calmed down and subdued somewhat. As Madison put it, the reason for having this kind of government and this kind of constitution is to guard against things like a "rage for paper money." The people who owed money at that time, the debtors, wanted the state government to issue paper money—inflation, in other words. They've scared us with the word "inflation," but very often people in debt have wanted inflation so they can pay off their debts more easily. Farmers wanted paper money and wanted inflation. A rage for paper money, Madison said, is something we want to guard against, or, as he put it, "an equal division of property or any other wicked object." So they knew what they were doing, those founding fathers. They deserve our admiration.

As you know, the founding fathers were not a multicultural group. There were no women, no Native Americans, no blacks, and virtually no poor people. Fifty-five, fifty-three, maybe fifty-three and a half rich white men who as Charles Beard put it rightly, despite all the criticism he took for saying this, reflected the interests of the propertied classes. A strong central government was set up to protect the interests of the slaveowners and the merchants and the bondholders. A country that would be able to move westward and protect the people who moved westward to expand into Indian lands, a government that would be able to send an army out into Indian lands and get rid of the Indians and clear the way for white people to take over that land. Next time you hear somebody say, "We mustn't have big government," this country was founded on the idea of big government. The slaveowners needed big government. The manufacturers needed big government. The bondholders needed big government. The expanders needed big government. They all wanted desperately to have big government. The rich and elite in this country have always wanted big government.

Only relatively recently in this century have they worried about what big government may do. Because big government, for most of our history, has been big government on behalf of the wealthy interests. We've had a welfare state in this country for a very long time, but most of the welfare was given to powerful and rich corporations. It wasn't called "welfare."

The railroads in the 1850s got something like twenty million acres of land free from the states. During the Civil War the railroads got something like 100 million acres of land free from the federal government. A hundred million acres free? You try to get an acre of land, one. Just tell the government you want just a little bit of land, one acre. "They did it for the Union Pacific, they can do it for me." This is welfare on an enormous scale: subsidies to the merchant marine, subsidies to the manufacturers by increasingly higher tariffs, which are of course subsidies for the manufacturers and higher prices for the consumer. In 1931 Charles Beard, that same rascal who wrote *An Economic Interpretation of the Constitution*, wrote an article called "The Myth of Rugged Individualism." Recall 1931, in the midst of the Depression, there's an argument about should the government do anything to help the poor or should we leave it to private charities? All the people were saying, "No, we mustn't help all these people who don't have jobs anymore and who can't feed their families. In this country we have a tradition. People have always made it on their own." What Beard was asking was, Did Rockefeller really make it on his own? Did Vanderbilt? Did Harriman? Did they really make it on their own? Did Carnegie and the steel industry make it on their own? He listed in this article all the subsidies and grants that had been given by the federal government to the great corporations.

The history of legislation in this country is a history of class legislation. Legislation is rarely talked about in class terms. It's talked about as if all the laws that are passed apply equally to everybody. Like they will say, "Taxes are raised. Taxes are lowered. Do you want a tax hike or do you want taxes lowered?" It's kind of a meaningless question unless you ask, "Whose taxes? Taxes where? Taxes at what level?" The idea is to embrace us all in one great family, as if the measures that are passed by Congress apply equally to all of us. But of course they don't. We've had class legislation in this country ever since the very first Congress, ever since Hamilton's economic program was passed by the very first Congress. The first legislation they passed was tariffs for the manufacturers, banking partnership between the government, the government helping out private banking interests, a payoff to the speculators and bondholders, and taxes on the poor and an army ready to go out and collect those taxes if they refused to pay it, as happened very shortly in 1794 in the Whiskey Rebellion in Pennsylvania. Class legislation in a very straight line, from the Hamilton economic program right up through the budget bill now being debated in Congress. Right up through the oil depletion allowances of our time. Right up to the enormous subsidies to the aircraft industry which would have gone into bankruptcy after World War II if the US government had not given enormous and lucrative contracts to the aircraft industry and kept them alive. You go to the federal government when you're short of funds and ask them to keep you alive with a little subsidy.

So history can illuminate a lot of the issues that are presented to us today. And seeing history in class terms I think is a much clearer and more honest way of taking a look at our society than by pretending, as it pretends in the first words of the Constitution, "We the people of the United States," as if everybody established the Constitution of the United States and as if the Constitution was established for everyone.

I had a point of view about class, and I noticed that in my courses the development of the US as a great economic power was presented in such a way as to inspire us all. I remember feeling rather triumphant when they gave the figures on how many steel ingots were produced and how many miles of railroad track were laid, and how the Union Pacific met the Central Pacific and we finally had a transcontinental railroad. It was all glorious and heroic achievement, and yes, I was part of it. The Union Pacific and me.

It was only after I got out graduate school, after I had finished my PhD degree, that I began to learn something about American history. Isn't that what happens? You really learn after you get out of school. Sorry.

Then you read what you want to read. So I read labor history. I read the history of labor struggles in this country. In my history courses, what did I get? Did they tell me about the great railroad strikes of 1877? Did they tell me about the Haymarket Affair of 1886 and the execution of the anarchists in Chicago, which might have made me really think about justice in this country, just as it made Emma Goldman think about justice? She was just a teenager in Rochester, New York. She heard about the execution of the anarchists in the Haymarket Affair in Chicago and it galvanized her. She was never the same again.

I remember there was in the history books something about the Pullman strike. There was always something about Eugene Debs. You have a little bit about Eugene Debs and that takes care of socialism. You have the Pullman strike and that takes care of the labor movement. But I didn't learn anything in any of these classes about the Lawrence textile strike of 1912, a magnificent, dramatic episode in American history. Or about the Colorado coal strike of 1913–14 and the Ludlow massacre. I had to read about that on my own. I had to listen to a song by Woody Guthrie called "The Ludlow Massacre," which led me to wonder what was that about and to look into that and then ask myself, "How come none of this was told to me? How come the name Mother Jones never appeared in any of my history books or my courses? How come Emma Goldman never appeared in any of my courses? None of this."

So I wanted to teach and write about that which I thought had been neglected. I began to think there was a reason for neglecting that. Again, not a reason that seven people gathered in a room to plan, but a reason that comes out of the normal workings of a society, of an economic and social and political system in which power and wealth are concentrated at the top. I wanted to write about history from that other point of view.

I wanted to write about war from another point of view. I left a shipyard in order to enlist in the air force. I became a bombardier in the US Air Force. I don't know if I should tell you what war I was in, but maybe I will, otherwise you might think it was the Spanish-American War. I was a bombardier in the Air Force in World War II. I enlisted with all the enthusiasm that so many people went into the World War II with, because as you know that was the good war. Or, if you look at Studs Terkel's oral history *"The Good War,"* you'll notice that it has quotation marks around it. "The good war." Many of the people he interviewed who were in that good war came out of that war not as certain as they had gone into it. Not because they had developed an affinity for fascism. That was what gave us the moral purpose, the enthusiasm, a war against fascism. The assumption was—a very dangerous assumption—that if the enemy is evil then your side must be good. The enemy was evil. The enemy was unmistakably evil. But where we made the mistake was in thinking that therefore our side was good. If the enemy commits atrocities, therefore certainly our side wouldn't do that. We didn't match the Holocaust. That's a unique event in World War II. But in our indiscriminate, deliberate bombing of civilian populations, of working-class populations in German and Japanese cities, culminating with Hiroshima and Nagasaki, we committed atrocities.

What happened in World War II was what happened in war generally, and that was whatever the initiating cause, and however clear the moral reason is for the war in which one side looks better than the other, by the time the war ends both sides have been engaged in evil. So I came to the conclusion that war was an unacceptable way of solving whatever problems there were in the world—that there would be problems of tyranny, of injustice, of nations crossing frontiers and that injustice and tyranny should not be tolerated and should be fought and resisted, but the one thing that must not be used to solve that problem is war. Because war is inevitably the indiscriminate killing of large numbers of people. And that fact overwhelms whatever moral cause is somewhere buried in the history of that war.

So I wasn't going to teach about war in the same way after my experience. I wanted to tell about war from the standpoint not of the generals and the military heroes, but from the standpoint of the ordinary guys who were in the war. And maybe even to tell the story of wars from the standpoint of the enemy, the other side. How does the Mexican War look to the Mexicans?

My first teaching job was at Spelman College in Atlanta, Georgia. My first real teaching job. I had a few unreal teaching jobs. But Spelman College, Atlanta, Georgia, a Black women's college. I went down there in 1956 and stayed there, my wife and I and our two little kids. We lived in the Black community around Spelman College. Those were probably the most educational years of my life. Those were the years of the movement. My students and I became involved in the movement. From Atlanta I went down to Albany, Georgia, and Selma, Alabama, and Hattiesburg, Mississippi, and Greenwood, Mississippi, and Jackson and other places. I learned a lot. One of the things I learned was the capacity of human beings who seemed powerless to create enormous power just by their own acts of getting together, sacrificing together, taking risks together, and how against what seemed insurmountable odds things can change by people determined to change them. What could be a tougher situation than for Black people in Mississippi or Alabama or southwest Georgia to decide to change a deeply embedded set of social relations that had existed in those societies for a long time? It didn't look like it could be done, but it was done. To see that happen, and to see people who were quiet and silent suddenly speak up, people who were just going about every day doing their job, apparently. It was what they used to say: "People here are happy with their lives. Look at them. They're just going about their daily work." One thing I learned is not to mistake silence for acceptance, not to think that because people aren't doing anything at any particular time that they're not capable of doing something an hour from how.

I could see people change. My students at Spelman College were the most controlled students. They were taught to be controlled. They were supposed to be controlled. They were the daughters of maids and laundresses and porters and sharecroppers. They were supposed to go to college so they could lift themselves up into the Black middle class and make something of themselves. The idea was to stick to their work, stick to their studies and become successful and not get into trouble. The college was surrounded by a stone wall and barbed wire to make sure that's where you stayed, that's what you do. This was the kind of unspoken pact between the city fathers of Atlanta and the Black colleges of Atlanta, Spelman and Morehouse and Atlanta University. The pact was, You can have your nice Negro colleges. You can even have a few white faculty. We'll even let some white people from town come to campus at Christmastime to listen to the glee club. But in return, don't interfere with what happens in the city of Atlanta, which at that time was as tightly segregated by race as Johannesburg, South Africa. And yes, there was that wall around the campus. At a certain point the students leaped over that wall and went into the city.

It had been in them from a long time, from the time who knows at what age, four or five or seven or whatever age it was that they first became conscious, that they were looked upon as different by society. Sometimes my students would write to me about that first time in their lives when they became conscious of the fact that they belonged to a different group that was looked on in a certain way. One thing that white society in America has never been able to encompass, no matter how liberal and tolerant and understanding it is, it has never been able to comprehend the depth of feeling, the depth of indignation and anger, in people who have that history that Black people have had in this country. So when they behave in ways that are incomprehensible to us, like some of them exulting at the acquittal of O. J. Simpson, we say, "What's wrong with them?" forgetting that people are never reacting only to the immediate event. People are always reacting to their own lives.

What I saw and experienced in the movement at Spelman and then what I experienced later in the antiwar movement when I left Spelman—actually "left" is a kind of euphemism. How shall I put it? Fired. I was fired. We don't like to use that word. I was definitely downsized. I used to be 6'6". I went north and was offered a job at Boston University, just in time for the beginning of the big American escalation of the war in Vietnam. I became involved in the antiwar movement. I saw some of the same phenomena in the antiwar movement, that is, the apparent powerlessness of little groups of people protesting against a war fought by the most powerful military machine in the world, the most powerful nation. How could these little knots of a hundred people gathering on the Boston

Common in 1965, a little group here, a little group there, a petition here, a teach-in there, how could they do anything to stop a war waged by this enormous power? And yet you saw the movement grow and grow and grow, and the hundred people who met on the Boston Common against the war in 1965 become in 1969 at another meeting on the Boston Common 100,000 people. And something that then was reproduced around the country as perhaps two million people in October 1969 meet in various places around the country to protest the war. The population has turned around. The administrations, as powerful as they are, with all their money and military power, must reckon with the most important power of all, the power of people to refuse to do something that they are asked to do. The power of young people to refuse to fight. The power of soldiers who refuse to go out on patrol, the B-52 pilots who after a while refused to fly a bomber over Haiphong or Hanoi. The closing of ROTC chapters because they can't get enough people to join them. A resistance of apparently powerless people that becomes wide enough, widespread enough, to cause the people up there to put their heads together and to take the activities of these powerless people into consideration and to say, as they did at a certain point, "We can't go on like this. We must begin to move in the other direction." And finally, of course, with a major factor being the fact of being unable to win militarily in Vietnam, against again an apparently puny and powerless revolutionary national movement.

It is instructive to see this in the civil rights movement, in the antiwar movement. It coincided with what I had come to believe in studying history, that is, it is possible at various points in history, no matter how inconceivable it is, to change the policies of the people who run the country. It is possible for people, if they're determined enough and organized enough and indignant enough and energetic enough and are willing to take enough risks, it is possible for them to do extraordinary things. So I believe that's true today. I'm speaking at a time when there's a lot of discouragement. Most of my friends are depressed. I have begun to think it's a condition of being my friend, to be depressed. Why are they depressed? They must believe the media. The very people who say, "I don't believe the media," believe the media. The very people who say, "I don't believe the politicians, they all lie," believe the politicians. The politicians and the media tell us that they're in charge, that the Republicans have won a victory, that they're going to turn the clock back, and we believe them. They will try to do that, and they may succeed in doing it for a little while, and they may win some victories, but the fact is that they are working against a very, very powerful impulse in the American public which has been developed over quite a period of time. It's a very generous, good impulse. It's the idea that democracy should be real. That the wealth of this country should be much more equitably distributed than it is. That people who want to work should be able to work and if free enterprise won't give them work then a government program must give them work. But people should be guaranteed health care and a place to live and all the things that they need to live a decent life. This is a very, very rich country. It can do this.

You would think from reading, Sorry, we can't afford this. We can't afford child care. We can't afford to give school lunches to kids. We can't afford to give $500 a month to a mother taking care of two kids. We don't have the money for the arts. We have to cut money for music. We just don't have it. This country, with this enormous gross national product, truly *gross* national product. Wealth, which is concentrated in a small portion of the population, which is wasted on our military budget, which goes to all sorts of purposes other than human purposes.

There's a basis there in those facts and the existence, I believe, in most American people, not all American people, but large numbers of American people, of the sense of what is just and what is right. I believe that's the basis for people beginning to move, beginning to act, people to get together with other people, not to allow those people who are trying to convince us that they have it all their way. Why? Because they were elected by some small part of the population who voted unenthusiastically for them because they had nobody else to vote for? People begin to act, to move, to get organized in the smallest of ways, the smallest of groups. That's how social movements develop. If everybody understands that the smallest action may not have any effect, but it might join to millions of other small actions and at a certain point in history might bring about the kind of changes we want, might actually change policy, might actually boldly change policy and do something about the horrors of racism and the unequal treatment of sexes and the unequal treatment of gay people and the unequal treatment of children, do something about all those things. Because we certainly, approaching a new century, don't want to go into this new century repeating the history of the old century. And I think it's possible not to repeat that and to do something new and startling. And not only that, but whatever is accomplished—and you never know what you will accomplish, and anybody would be rash to predict, "Oh, yes, it's certain, great things will happen," except that I know that if you don't do anything, I know great things won't happen. If you act, great things might happen. But whether they do or not, in the process, in the course of it, by your action, by not simply living the life of a professional but having another life, it will be more interesting and more fun and more rewarding, and whatever is accomplished, you will feel that you have participated in something worthwhile all the time. That's worth doing.

Thank you.

8

A Call to Action: Abolish the Death Penalty

Harvard University, Cambridge, Massachusetts, March 11, 1996

Zinn helped launch the Campaign to End the Death Penalty at this event with Cornel West, Bill Keach, Robert Meeropol, and former death row inmate Lawrence Hayes. Throughout his life, Zinn corresponded with prisoners, spoke about the racism and injustice of US prisons, and worked for the abolition of capital punishment.

There must be a lot of feeling about this issue, and it's not just Mumia Abu-Jamal, it has to be more than that. Just as all the feeling that exploded around Rodney King was not just about Rodney King, it was something that went way back in history. When there's a long, *long* progression of injustices that goes on for a long time, the indignation builds up.

This issue of capital punishment has been addressed for hundreds of years. I mean that's what's so infuriating. We still have to deal with the state, the murderous state, putting people to death. In 1764, an Italian writer, Beccaria, wrote an essay, "On Crimes and Punishment," in which he laid out the argument against capital punishment. And this was the period of the Enlightenment. Soon after that British poet Percy Bysshe Shelley spoke out against capital punishment. And revolutionists, right after the American Revolution, cut down the list of capital punishment crimes, which was enormous under the king, in their revolutionary fervor.

You might say that the United States hasn't caught up with the Enlightenment. We're still working on that.

Karl Marx in the 1850s wrote for the *New York Tribune*. Marx wrote that capital punishment cannot be tolerated in any country calling itself civilized. It's a caution for any countries that consider themselves Marxist and continue with capital punishment.

But that's part of the emotion and the anger that I feel. I'm trying to restrain the anger, not to get violent . . . not to get murderous, but you know, just angry enough to do something, or to say something, or to get together with other people to organize to do something. It comes from the obvious injustice of it all. All those courtrooms and all those pillars, those signs reading "Equal Justice for All." You can't live in this society without knowing that there's not equal justice for all. If you're poor, you don't get equal justice. Maybe it should not be called "capital punishment" but "capitalist punishment." Because it is so connected with poverty, as imprisonment itself is connected with poverty.

I don't want us to lose sight tonight of the fact that capital punishment is just one part of that larger spectrum of evil which is punishment by prison. Which is a million and a half people in prison. Which means that somehow, out of all the things that have been done in society, out of all the presumably evil acts that have been done in society, high and low, by all sorts of people, they have singled out a particular part of the population for punishment and left other parts of the population untouched—and especially so if you're poor or if you're Black.

There was a brief period when the Supreme Court ruled out capital punishment because it was arbitrary and capricious and so on. You should know that that brief period followed an NAACP campaign. Courts don't do enlightened things on their own. Courts do enlightened things when something has happened in the society, when movements have been created.

The NAACP fought a campaign, case by case, to fight every capital punishment case and hold it up, and hold it up. And then the Court said, "Okay, it's arbitrary." So for a few years, there was no capital punishment.

Then they brought it back, on a 5-4 vote. It's always interesting how many lives hang on 5-4 votes.

Just thinking of the issue of racism and capital punishment, a capital punishment case came up in 1982, and the Supreme Court—in the case of a Black man who was convicted by an all-white jury and where every possible Black juror had been dismissed on peremptory challenges—the Supreme Court said they couldn't say that racial bias was involved in this. This was another 5-4 decision. How did the Court put it? I love the way judges talk. Well, discrepancy is "inevitable" in justice, they say, and also they didn't find a "constitutionally significant" risk of racial bias. It's not a matter of is there racial bias or is there no racial bias. The question is, is there a "constitutionally significant" risk of racial bias? If you're poor, if you're Black, and if you're political . . . well, Mumia Abu-Jamal had all of those things working against him, to be poor and to be Black and to be political.

We have a history in this country of putting people to death because they were political. In 1887, the anarchists of Chicago in the Haymarket Affair were put to death, not because there was evidence against them but because they were anarchists. Sacco and Vanzetti were put to death in 1927 right here in Boston—not because it is conclusively proved that they killed anybody but because they were foreigners, they were Italians, they were certainly poor, and they were anarchists. And, well, of course there's the Rosenberg case. People who come into court as people who have been politically radical receive far, far greater sentences than anybody else for the same kind of offense.

So there's all sorts of reasons to feel angry at the system. And perhaps, maybe most of all, there's the sheer hypocrisy of it. The sheer hypocrisy of the state, the government, declaring that somebody has committed a terrible crime. They've killed somebody. They may very well have committed a crime, but they may have not committed a crime. They may have killed somebody, or two people or seven people, or nine people, or they may be serial killers and they've killed fifteen people. This is the state which has killed infinite numbers of people in its history. And they are the ones making the decision that there are people who ought to be put to death.

The history of people who have been killed in labor struggles in the country by the police, by the National Guard, by the armies, is a very long and bitter and brutal history. In 1850, the first men—two tailors in New York on strike—were killed by the police. And after that, it went on and on and on. The Republic Steel Massacre in the 1930s. Back in the earlier twentieth century, the Ludlow Massacre, the National Guard and the killing and murders. It's gone on, and on, and on. And this to say nothing about war. And not just the killing of our own, but the killing of others. Which doesn't even come into the reckoning, of course.

I'm not asking for capital punishment for Nixon, or for Johnson, or for Ford. Yes, even Ford, who killed an untold number of Cambodians and about eighty-seven Americans as the result of a little incident that took place of the coast of Cambodia after the Vietnam War to show that the United States still had clout. But you think of the My Lai Massacre and you think of people walking away—the sheer hypocrisy of it all.

So that kind of indignation that one must feel at all of this is something that must be conveyed to other people. They recognize it as soon as you tell them. As soon as you ask people, "Isn't it true that poor people don't have a chance in the justice system?" they know it. That Black people don't have a chance? They know it. That radicals, anarchists, socialists, communists don't have a chance in the justice system? They know it. Remember, in the background of Mumia Abu-Jamal is MOVE. They assembled six hundred policemen and a helicopter, dropped bombs on houses, and they killed eleven people, including five children. Nobody ever gets brought into court for any of these things. I mean if we were bringing people into court as criminals for vicious deaths, the first people to be brought into court would be various presidents, secretaries of state, secretaries of defense, and joint chiefs of staff!

We know all the public opinion polls show that the public wants capital punishment. Well, the public wants what they're told again and again and again. And they believe what appears before them on television again and again and again, showing heroic cops, heroic forces of government, and vicious murders and so on and so forth. But if you look at the changes of public opinion over time, you see that the public changes its mind about capital punishment. The public can change its mind again if confronted with indignation, if confronted with information, and if it is just given the chance to think about it.

In the long haul, for capital punishment, for punishment itself, for the whole miserable jail system, the only long-term solution is a change in the society, a change in the distribution of wealth, a change in the economic system, a change in the social system, a change in the culture. It'll take . . . a few weeks, maybe longer. But the long term is something. You have to always work for the long term. Even while in the short term we struggle and fight and protest to save the life of the person who is about to be executed unjustly by a murderous state. In this immediate case, Mumia Abu-Jamal and everybody else who comes along with him and after him. So it's great to be here with all of you.

Thank you.

9

The Case of Sacco and Vanzetti

Northeastern University, Boston, Massachusetts, October 9, 1997

Zinn returned in many speeches and articles to the trial and execution of Nicola Sacco and Bartolomeo Vanzetti. As he wrote in The Progressive, *"What comes to us today from the case of the Italian immigrants Sacco and Vanzetti is not just tragedy, but inspiration. Their English was not perfect, but when they spoke it was a kind of poetry."*

How many of you know something about the case of Sacco and Vanzetti? How many really don't know about the case of Sacco and Vanzetti? Then there are some of you who neither know nor not know about the case of Sacco and Vanzetti. When I was growing up and becoming a political person, getting interested in politics and social issues, one of the things that sprang out at me as one of the most dramatic events in American history was the case of Sacco and Vanzetti. It plays a part in American history that so many other events have played, very special moments in history that affect an entire generation. There's a traditional list of these things which go as important historical events, like the Battle of Bunker Hill and things like that. But there's another kind of list, an alternate list, of events which did a lot to awaken people's political consciousness. The Haymarket Affair of 1886 was one of them. If you don't know much about it, look into it. Emma Goldman was a teenager in a working-class family, working in a factory in Rochester, when the Haymarket Affair took place. The arrest, conviction, and execution of a group of anarchists in Chicago in 1886, during a battle for the eight-hour day—when Emma Goldman heard about that, it changed her life.

So it is with the case of Sacco and Vanzetti, as it is for other people with the Rosenberg case. Who knows what effect the case of Mumia Abu-Jamal is having now and will have on generations of people to come? When we had twenty years ago the fiftieth anniversary of the execution of Sacco and Vanzetti, the governor of Massachusetts, Governor Dukakis, set up a commission. There's been a lot of discussion over the state of Massachusetts apologizing, doing something for executing these two men. Governments do that from time to time, they apologize. Khrushchev apologized. "Well, sorry, we killed a few people." Clinton has apologized for slavery. I don't want to make light of these apologies. Well, yes, I do. I have to hand it to Dukakis. He set up a commission to go back into the Sacco and Vanzetti case, and it came out with a report that declared the trial was unfair. There are also people who said Dukakis should pardon Sacco and Vanzetti. He thought it was a little late. They had been executed in 1927, and this was 1977. But his commission did come out with a report that said that Sacco and Vanzetti had not had a fair trial. This was an understatement.

When this happened, this aroused a reaction among people who defended the execution of Sacco and Vanzetti and defended the record of the authorities in Massachusetts. After all, the authorities were involved, the lower courts, the upper courts, Governor Fuller of Massachusetts. At the time, Peter Fuller, the son of Governor Fuller, was alive and living in Boston. He was more than alive. He actually ran a Cadillac dealership in Boston. He wrote a letter to the *Boston Globe*. He was known for several things, not just for being Boston's leading Cadillac dealer, but as a racer of thoroughbred horses. He was also a member of the board of trustees of Boston University. He was outraged at Dukakis's statement saying that Sacco and Vanzetti had not had a fair trial. He said this was "an attempt to besmirch a guy's record that we believe in and love, whose memory we cherish." Then he said, "We're sitting here in the last building my father built, the most beautiful car agency on the Eastern coast, and perhaps in the US." I didn't quite see what this had to do with the Sacco and Vanzetti case.

The issue is alive because the issue of justice is always alive, the issue of law, and not just of capital punishment but the entire judicial system. Just a brief summary of the events. It starts in the spring of 1920, not along after the end of World War I. There's a robbery and murder. This is very much a Massachusetts affair. There's a robbery in a shoe factory in South Braintree, Massachusetts, not far from here. The paymaster is killed and a guard is killed. Two people are killed. Shortly after that, it's not clear who did it; there are people who claim they were eyewitnesses. In any case, shortly after that, Sacco and Vanzetti, Nicola Sacco and Bartolomeo Vanzetti, were picked up on a streetcar going from Bridgewater to Brockton. They're carrying guns, revolvers. They are arrested for the robbery and the murder. That's the beginning of the case of Sacco and Vanzetti.

What follows then is years of trials and appeals. I should say something about the circumstances of that time, 1920. Why Sacco and Vanzetti? Was it because the evidence pointed to them? It's hard to say. The evidence in this case is so muddied and complicated that to this day people argue about whether Sacco and Vanzetti were guilty. There are people who say absolutely not. There are people who say they absolutely were. There are people who say Sacco was guilty and Vanzetti was not, a liberal compromise, I guess. But in any case, what happens in this period, Sacco and Vanzetti are anarchists. They're not just ordinary people found on a streetcar carrying guns. They'd been on lists. They were known to the police, to the Bureau of Investigation, the predecessor of the FBI. They have no criminal record, but they have a political record, big supporters of strikes. They would walk on picket lines. They would hand out leaflets. They're part of the anarchist movement on the East Coast. There was a special Italian anarchist movement on the East Coast. They're friends with Luigi Galleani, the editor of an anarchist publication, *Cronaca Sovversiva*.

What's happening now, after World War I, is that there is a wave of antiradical, antiforeign hysteria in the country. It starts during the war. During the war you have the buildup of hostility to radicals, to people opposed to the war. Congress passes the Espionage Act and the Sedition Act, and the Supreme Court affirms the constitutionality of these acts, which punish people for speaking out against the war. Two thousand people are prosecuted and about nine hundred sent to prison for violation of the Espionage Act or Sedition Act, basically for making speeches against the war. Eugene Debs, the socialist leader, was sentenced to ten years in prison for making a speech against the war. A woman is sentenced to several years in jail for making a remark which was overheard by somebody else that the socks that people were supposedly knitting for soldiers overseas weren't really getting to those soldiers. A movie is confiscated and banned and the maker of the movie is put on trial for violating the Espionage Act because the movie was about the Revolutionary War. In the Revolutionary War, the enemy was England. During World War I, England was our ally. So somebody who makes a movie in which England is the enemy when England is really our ally obviously doesn't know who are our friends and who are our enemies, and a person like that should be prosecuted. The name of this movie was *The Spirit of '76*, so the name of the case was *U.S. v. Spirit of '76*.

This is the kind of thing that went on. When the war was over, there was a bomb explosion. By the way, I don't want to paint the anarchists of this time as peace-loving, Martin Luther King type, nonviolent people. There were anarchists who believed in using violence against the class enemy, and there were anarchists who didn't. But the fact that there were anarchists who believed in this didn't mean that when an act of violence took place, therefore it must be that anarchists are responsible. That's what had happened in the Haymarket Affair, where nobody knew who was responsible for the bomb that exploded amidst the police in 1886, but since there were anarchists around in Chicago, and some of them had written statements advocating violence, it figured that they must have been responsible and therefore deserved to be executed.

A bomb exploded in front of the home of Attorney General Palmer, Woodrow Wilson's attorney general. This led to a great excitement and a search for radicals and bomb throwers and anarchists. It took the form mainly of breaking into the homes and meeting places of foreign-born people, on the supposition that that's where you were most likely to find bomb throwers and troublemakers. Thousands of these people were rounded up, held without bail, held without hearings, held incommunicado, and many deported. Two of the people deported were Emma Goldman, the feminist anarchist, and her friend Alexander Berkman. This is what was going on. The editor of *Cronaca Sovversiva*, Luigi Galleani, was deported. Another anarchist named Salsedo was picked up and kept by the Bureau of Investigation in an office on the fourteenth floor of a building in downtown Manhattan for six weeks, not allowed to see a lawyer or to talk to anybody. He was interrogated for six weeks. At the end of the six weeks, his body was found on the pavement below that fourteenth-floor office. The Bureau of Investigation said that he jumped. No one knows. Did he jump? Maybe. Was he pushed? Who knows? Did he jump because he was driven crazy by the Bureau of Investigation? Because he felt guilty, being an anarchist? Who knows?

I tell you about these events because they all had an impact on the thinking of the anarchist community and the foreign-born anarchists like Sacco and Vanzetti. It explains, and this is how they explained it, and it seems reasonable, why they were carrying guns. All of them, anybody in that community, was expecting to be raided or to be apprehended, seized by the police, interrogated, deported. They were carrying guns. Is that the explanation for them carrying guns? I don't know. I don't know if Sacco and Vanzetti were guilty. That's not the issue that interests me the most. Whether they were guilty or innocent, there were larger questions involved having to do with justice, the nature of justice and the way justice is meted out in our society, and the fact that that justice really doesn't have a lot to do with whether people are innocent or guilty of a particular crime. It has a lot more to do with who people are, what they represent, what they do in their lives, and what threats they pose not to this or that individual, but to the existing societal structure. It was assumed that the anarchists posed a threat to the existing social structure in the US.

When they were picked up, the record of the police interrogation does not suggest the police were most concerned about whether they'd committed the robbery and murder. Here are questions from the police interrogation: Police to Sacco: "Are you a citizen?" Sacco: "No." Police: "Are you a communist?" Sacco: "No." "Anarchist?" Sacco: "No." He's lying. Why somebody should lie to the police is beyond me. But he chose to lie to the police. The point is, what were they interested in? Whether he was a communist or an anarchist? What bearing does this have on whether he was guilty of this robbery and murder? The whole case was suffused by patriotism and appeals to the flag. That was the atmosphere in which it took place. At the very beginning of the trial, the judge, Judge Webster Thayer, said to the jury, "Gentlemen." There were no ladies on the jury. "I call upon you to render this service here that you have been summoned to perform with the same spirit of patriotism, courage and devotion to duty as was exhibited by our soldier boys across the seas." Strange kind of charge to the jury, putting them in the same position as soldiers doing their patriotic duty, especially in light of the fact that Sacco and Vanzetti had left this country, had gone to Mexico to avoid the draft. They were draft dodgers. They had not fulfilled their patriotic duty. Now the jury was going to fulfill its patriotic duty.

More of the police interrogation. Police to Sacco: "Do you believe in this government of ours?" Sacco: "Yes, some things I like different." That's a very diplomatic answer. He really likes things very different. Police: "Do you subscribe to literature from the anarchist party?" Sacco: "Sometimes I read them." "How do you get them? Through the mail?" "A man gave one to me in Boston." "Who was the man?" "I don't know." Again, were they looking for robbers, or people who subscribed to anarchist magazines?

The trial began immediately after Memorial Day. This was about a year and a half after that orgy of stupidity and death that was World War I. The military music was still in the air when the trial took place. In fact, twelve days into the trial, the press reported that the bodies of three soldiers were returning from France to Brockton and the whole town was turning out for a patriotic ceremony. All of this the jury could read in the newspapers. They could read newspapers as long as they didn't read reports on the trial. They were cut out. In the midst of the trial, the papers reported a gathering of five thousand veterans of the Yankee Division in Plymouth. In the trial itself, in the cross-examination of Sacco, he was prosecuted by Katzmann. Katzmann: "Did you love this country in the last week of May 1917?" I guess when you go through day by day, on some days you loved the country, on some days you didn't love the country. Sacco: "That's pretty hard for me to say in one word, Mr. Katzmann." Sacco's English was much better than Vanzetti's. Vanzetti had a much harder time with the English language. After he spent a number of years in prison, and after he reads, his eloquence in the English language is absolutely extraordinary. Katzmann: "There are two words you can use, Mr. Sacco. Yes or no. Which is it?" Sacco: "Yes." He did love this country in the last week of May 1917. Katzmann: "In order to show your love for this United States of America when she was about to call upon you to become a soldier, you ran away to Mexico."

This is the atmosphere of the trial. It's a very Anglo-Saxon jury and judge. The two defendants are Italian anarchists recently come to this country who were speaking English with Italian accents. The ethnic divisions in this trial are very clear. Webster Thayer, the judge, has specifically asked the chief justice to handle this trial. He wanted this trial. Strange things happened across the trial. There are many witnesses who place Sacco and Vanzetti in places other than the scene of the crime. A whole bunch of witnesses say that they saw Sacco in Boston. Sacco says he was in Boston at that time trying to get a passport in the office of the Italian consul. All these people are testifying that they saw Sacco in Boston. But all these people have Italian accents. A whole bunch of people testify that they saw Vanzetti at the time that the crime was supposed to have taken place in Plymouth selling fish. Sacco was a shoemaker, Vanzetti a fish peddler. But these people's words go right past the jury. Obviously, they're Italians. They're going to stick together.

There's a kid whose eyewitness testimony is very peculiar, very difficult to establish with absolute clarity. Eyewitness testimony is fraught with mistakes and misapprehensions. But still they use them. They call this kid who says, "We saw the robbers running away." They asked them, "Could you see their faces?" "No." "What could you tell about these robbers?" "I could tell that they were foreigners." "How could you tell?" "By the way they ran." You ever see a foreigner run? They are very funny runners. The judge made a famous statement, somewhere in the course of all of this going on at a Dartmouth football game. There must be something about a Dartmouth football game which lets the guard down. You think, I can say anything I want to at a football game. But no, you couldn't. He said to another Dartmouth alumnus, who was at the game, after he had turned down a motion for a new trial, "Did you see what I did with those anarchist bastards the other day?" The fellow he said this to swore out an affidavit to this effect. So you have to be very careful what you say to people at a football game. This was Webster Thayer.

There was very complicated ballistics evidence. I won't go into it, because I can't go into it. The ballistics argument has been going on for decades and nobody has come up with any absolutely clear-cut conclusion about what the ballistic evidence shows. My point is, one thing is sure, whether they were guilty or not, they could not possibly get a fair trial in the atmosphere of the courtroom in 1920–21. They could not possibly get a fair trial in the patriotic atmosphere of this courtroom and with this judge and jury. Sacco and Vanzetti were convicted, I would argue, more for who they were than for anything they could possibly have done. This is the importance of the case. It connects with so many other instances of how our justice system works. With some reflection and some study we know to be true, and that is, it is very important in our justice system, even more important than whether you did something or did not do something, it's very important who you are, how much money you have, what color you are, whether you are an American, and if you are a political radical. They had all these things against them, just as Mumia Abu-Jamal has them against him. He's black, he's radical, he's poor. Is he going to get a fair trial? Again, it's not known for sure guilt or innocence. One thing you do know for sure, so long as those factors are dominant, and those factors are dominant in a society which is filled with jingoism and hostility to foreigners and hostility to Blacks and hostility to radicals, and so long as the justice system is dominated by money, then the question of whether you actually did this or did not do this becomes secondary to these other factors.

Webster Thayer is asked six or seven times for a new trial. Different pieces of evidence are put before him. There's a prisoner who sends a message from prison that he was part of a gang that committed the robbery and murder. Who knows? Is it true? It might be enough to at least look into it. The judge doesn't want to look into it. He turns down these things again and again. The Supreme Judicial Court of Massachusetts goes along with Thayer in all of this. They never examined the facts of the case. It was a very common thing in courts of appeals that they don't examine the facts of a case. They only have to rule on matters of law. You don't have the right to a new trial. So you have these exasperating decisions that come down from courts in which somebody's life is at stake and they say, "Sorry, we really can't look over the evidence. That's not our job."

They tried to get the Supreme Court of the US to stay the execution. They tried to get Oliver Wendell Holmes, a justice of the Supreme Court, to stay the execution. All it takes is one justice. This was done for a while in the Rosenberg case, but Holmes would not stay the execution. Holmes is in any case one of the most overrated judges in Supreme Court history as far as liberalism and civil liberties. It was Holmes who wrote the unanimous decision that sent Eugene Debs to jail. It was Holmes who wrote the unanimous decision upholding the constitutionality of the Espionage Act.

The point is, they had their day in court. That's what people say. "What are you complaining about? They had their day in court." All the procedures were followed. They had a trial. They had appeals. It went from one court to another. The appeal went to the governor. The governor appointed a committee of three distinguished people. This is what executives do, take the onus off themselves. "Let's set up a committee of three important citizens and let them advise me and then I don't have to take the whole blame." How more distinguished a committee can you set up? The governor picked the president of Harvard University, the president of MIT, and a retired judge. You might say a cross-section of the community. They go over all the stuff and they come to the conclusion that Sacco and Vanzetti did not deserve a new trial.

Heywood Broun was a great journalist of that era, the 1920s and 1930s, and wrote a column for mainstream newspapers called "It Seems to Me." He was an unusual journalist, one, because he was a socialist, and two, because he was one of the organizers of the American Newspaper Guild, which started around that time. When people said, "We have three of the most distinguished people in Massachusetts go over the evidence and they said these guys are guilty," Broun wrote, "It is not every prisoner who has a President of Harvard University throw on the switch for him. . . . If this is a lynching, at least the fish peddler and his friend the factory hand may take unction to their souls that they will die at the hands of men in dinner jackets or academic gowns."

There were protests all over the country and all over the world, demonstrations in Buenos Aires, Paris, London. The lawyers kept trying to come up with new theories and new ideas and new bits of evidence. Sacco said, "Forget it. It doesn't matter. They want us to die. It doesn't matter what the evidence is." There are always people who think, "If you could only come up with the right kind of legal argument, the legal system will take cognizance of this." Sacco said, "No, you're wrong." He says, "Given who we are and given what the legal system is, it doesn't matter what argument you make in a legal brief, they are going to condemn us to death." "The only thing that would matter," Vanzetti said this, "is if hundreds of thousands, millions of people take to the streets and there is a clamor in the country. That's the only thing that might possibly stop them from killing us." There were protests, but they were not great enough and didn't match Vanzetti's standards for an enormous protest, and so on August 23, 1927, Charlestown Prison, where the electric chair was, crowds gathered outside, protestors, pickets. There were machine guns mounted on nearby buildings to control the protestors. People were beaten and arrested. Some distinguished literary figures participated in the demonstrations, Edna St. Vincent Millay and John Dos Passos. Albert

Einstein had protested against this, important figures in the arts had protested against this. And the labor movement, particularly the Italian labor movement, had supported Sacco and Vanzetti and organized protests, but they were executed.

I want to read to you something that Vanzetti had in his pocket when he was on that streetcar in Brockton the day he was arrested. What he had in his pocket was a leaflet advertising a meeting where he was going to speak. The leaflet said, "You have fought all the wars. You have worked for all the capitalists. You have wandered over all the countries. Have you harvested the fruits of your labors, the price of your victories? Does the past comfort you? Does the present smile on you? Does the future promise you anything? Have you found a piece of land where you can live like a human being and die like a human being? On these questions, on this argument and on this theme, the struggle for existence, Bartolomeo Vanzetti will speak."

Of course, he never got to give that speech. But I thought that says it. You don't want to let somebody make a speech like that. If that speech were made often enough, by enough people, to enough people, in a country where for so many people that message resonates, we might have some resounding movement for social change. So that was behind the case of Sacco and Vanzetti and the case of Mumia Abu-Jamal and behind so much of what goes on in our society and so much of what is called the justice system. It's important, especially in a law school, where it's so easy to become—I almost said besmirched—befogged with niceties of law. Behind the law, above the law, there are very powerful issues of class, race, gender, and social conflict. If we want justice, we are going to have to engage ourselves in some way in that conflict.

10

Emma Goldman, Anarchism, and War Resistance

Radcliffe College, Cambridge, Massachusetts, January 29, 2002

Zinn's interest in the life and politics of Emma Goldman led him to write not only a play about her, Emma, *but a screenplay that he hoped might one day be turned into a movie. Zinn saw in Goldman someone who defied convention and orthodoxy to live her life fully, passionately, and imaginatively.*

I'll start with Emma Goldman and then move into other things. Because I can never stay with history. I can never stay with the past. For me, I became a historian, and went into the past, really for the purpose of trying to understand and do something about what was going on in the present. So I never wanted to be a historian who goes into the archives and you never hear from him or her again. So my work on Emma Goldman was always connected with the things I was involved in, and active in, in the world. I had vaguely been aware of Emma Goldman. It was interesting—here I was a PhD in history, and what could be higher than that? Who could be better informed than a PhD in history? But here I was with a doctorate from Columbia, and Emma Goldman had never been mentioned in any of my classes, and none of her writings had ever appeared on my reading lists, and it's just that I vaguely remembered reading a chapter about her in a old book called *Critics and Crusaders*. There's a chapter on Emma Goldman. So I had this vague notion about Emma Goldman, but I didn't know anything about her.

Then I was at some conference in Pennsylvania and sometimes at conferences you run into interesting people. I ran into this guy, Richard Drinnon, a remarkable historian. I recommend a book of his that is not well known—but it's the not well-known books that you need to know about. He wrote a book called *Facing West*, a brilliant literary, political discussion of American expansionism into the far west, and the Philippines, and Vietnam. (You're going to find a lot of digressions in my talk, a lot of parenthetical remarks. Occasionally I'll come back to my topic.) But Drinnon told me he had written a biography of Emma Goldman: *Rebel in Paradise*. So I went to it, and read it, and it just astonished me. It made me angry about the fact that I had not been told anything about Emma Goldman in my long education. Here was this magnificent woman, this anarchist, this feminist, fierce, life-loving person. Of course, that led me to her autobiography, *Living My Life*, which, if you have not read, you should read. At a certain point, I decided to require it for a class—I had this class of four hundred students. At first I thought, "*Living My Life*—it's a big book. And will they really connect with this early twentieth-century woman, and here we are in the 60s?" They loved it. And they found in her what I found in her: free spirit, bold, speaking out against all authority, unafraid, and as the title of her book suggests, living her life, as she wanted to live it, not as the rules and regulations and authorities were telling her how to live it. So that got me interested in Emma Goldman, reading her, using her stuff in my classes.

I had always been interested in theater. My wife had acted, my daughter had acted, my son was in the theater and still is—I had always been interested in the theater and never done anything with it, always too involved in the South, and in the Vietnam War movement—and then came 1975 and I had a breathing spell.

So I wrote a play about Emma Goldman, and I had to make a decision. Her life was so long and full, and there's always in any work of art—I like to call what I do a work of art; everything I do is a work of art—a problem of what do you leave in and what do you leave out. And there's so much to her life, so I started with her as an immigrant girl, a teenager living in Rochester, New York, and working in the factory. Her political awareness taking a leap in 1886 at the time of the Haymarket Affair. How many of you know about the Haymarket Affair? I always have to take little polls, to avoid telling people what they already know. Of course I don't mind telling people what they already know—we all have to be reminded, right? Again and again. But the Haymarket Affair occurs in the midst of labor struggles all over the country for the eight-hour day. There's a strike against International Harvester Company in Chicago. The police come. It's the usual scene, police vs. strikers. But the police fire into the strikers and kill a number of them. At that time, Chicago was a great center for radical activity and anarchist groups. And the anarchists call a protest meeting in Haymarket Square. It's a peaceful meeting, but the police barge into the meeting, a bomb explodes in the midst of the police, a terrorist attack. Nobody knows who threw the bomb. But you know, when a terrorist attack occurs, it doesn't matter whether you know or don't know. You've got to go after somebody. The police have to find somebody. The FBI has to find somebody. The army has to find somebody. So they find eight leading anarchists in Chicago. Nobody can tie them to the throwing of the bomb, but they're anarchists. We have conspiracy laws. Conspiracy laws are very interesting. With a conspiracy law, you can tie anybody to anything. You don't have to do anything to become the defender in a political conspiracy trial. So they quickly find these eight anarchists guilty of conspiring to murder, and they are sentenced to death. Emma Goldman is aware of this. It goes up through the courts. The American judicial system is a wonderful system. Once gross errors have been made at a lower level, it's very often hard to overcome that because the higher courts will limit themselves in what they can review. They'll say, "Well, the jury and the judge considered the facts in this case, so all we have to deal with are the legal niceties, and we can't go over the facts." In any case, the Illinois Supreme Judicial Court approved the sentences.

The Haymarket Affair had become an international case. It was one of those cases that captured the imagination of caring people who see injustices. In our time, we've had so many such cases: the Rosenbergs, and Mumia Abu-Jamal, all these cases that become international causes. That was true of the Haymarket Affair. George Bernard Shaw sent a telegram to the Illinois Supreme Court, saying, "If the state of Illinois needs to lose eight of its citizens, it could better afford to lose the eight members of the Illinois Supreme Court." It didn't help. Four of them were hanged, and when the news came out and Emma Goldman heard about it, it excited her to the point of fury. She soon left Rochester, left her family, left a husband, almost an arranged marriage when she was so young. She went to New York and joined a little anarchist group. In New York she met Alexander Berkman, who became a comrade and then her lover. Then this little group of anarchists living in a collective in New York began putting out literature, handing it out, what these little left-wing groups do. Anybody who walks through Park Square or Harvard Square will encounter these people.

It's important to pick up their information, pick up those leaflets, because they will tell you things, these crazy, radical people, that you will never hear anywhere else. Anyway, she's part of this little group. And in 1892 there's a strike that takes place in Homestead, Pennsylvania, against the Carnegie Steel Works, and another very dramatic incident, the Pinkerton Detective Agency, which is a euphemism for strikebreakers, is hired by the Carnegie Corporation. Henry Clay Frick, whom you may know as an art patron, also a manager of steel works, employer of the Pinkerton strikebreakers. There's a gun battle and strikers are killed. And that fires up this little anarchist group in New York. They decide that they are going to do what has not been done in the United States but has been done a number of times in Europe, and that is to carry out a symbolic act, to show that the perpetrators of violence can also be the victims of violence. They decide to kill Henry Clay Frick.

So they argue about it. You can imagine this little group; they are not very experienced at this sort of stuff. They're discussing it all night. "How will we do this? Where will we get a gun?" Berkman volunteers to do it, and "We'll have to get him a new suit of clothes." If you're going to kill someone, you have to look respectable. And so he goes with his new clothes and his gun to Pittsburgh, and barges into Frick's office, and he's a very poor shot. He's an anarchist. What do you expect? He hadn't practiced this stuff. He knows how to hand out leaflets. So he only wounds Frick.

He's arrested, quickly tried, and sentenced to twenty-two years in prison. He's been Emma Goldman's lover, and while he's in prison, Emma Goldman becomes a nationally known figure, writer, lecturer, fierce woman. By the way, one of the great books about prison conditions and the whole issue of prisons is Alexander Berkman's *Prison Memoirs of an Anarchist.* It's not easy to get. It's a wonderful book. He spent fourteen years in prison, and by the time he came out, things had changed. He and Emma Goldman were no longer lovers. But very soon they founded an anarchist magazine together, *Mother Earth*, and were publishing things that nobody else would publish. They had by this time changed their minds about the necessity for occasional acts of symbolic violence. I say that to get them off the hook, make it sound nice. But ... they pretty much had a rethinking about this is the kind of thing you have to do. They were organizers, and Emma Goldman was an organizer of garment workers in New York while she was speaking all over, and yes, her personal relationship with Alexander Berkman ended. But they were still comrades, publishers of *Mother Earth*. I guess if you go into the library, you can find old issues of *Mother Earth*—fascinating stuff to read that will give you a history of that time that you probably won't get in traditional textbooks. Then Emma Goldman took up with—that's an interesting phrase, "took up with"—this man Ben Reitman. How many have heard of him? A few. Fascinating character. And Ben Reitman was a doctor, sort of. He was everything, sort of. But somehow he made his way through medical school by reading things on his own, listening to lectures, taking over for the lecturer, a famous physician, when the physician wasn't there. Ben Reitman just goes up to the podium and delivers a lecture on the same subject. And he was a swashbuckling character wearing a cowboy hat. He ran a street clinic for women who needed help, gynecological advice, needed abortions. And he was a risk taker and devilish person, a very handsome devil who absolutely captivated Emma Goldman, this independent woman who's not supposed to be captivated by anybody. And this is one of the interesting things about her life: she was a strong woman, she insisted on the independence of women, but when she fell in with (another nice phrase) Ben Reitman, she became absolutely swallowed up in this very, very passionate ten-year-long affair. And when he became her manager, he traveled with her all over the country, a man with enormous ego, tremendous appetite for everything, and when their letters were discovered not long ago, people who read them had to hold themselves in their seats. They were the most erotic letters. I don't know whether anybody writes such letters any more. There were biographies that came out that made use of those letters: one by Alice Wexler and another by Candace Falk. You ought to take a look at those biographies, just for the fun of reading those letters and pretending that you're doing historical research.

Reitman was an anarchist among anarchists. Because the other anarchists distrusted him because he was a total individualist and wouldn't go along with anything that anybody would do, insisted on doing everything his own way. They distrusted his relationship with Emma Goldman and feared for her—rightly—because she was so involved. But he had courage, too. They went out to San Diego, and there was a ferocious attack on them by all sorts of people in San Diego who saw anarchists as the devil. Ben Reitman was kidnapped, taken out into the countryside, tarred and feathered, and branded on his backside with the letters IWW—Industrial Workers of the World. He was the kind of guy who later, when they would appear on a platform, would suddenly turn his back to the audience and pull down his pants and show them what had been done to him, which horrified Emma Goldman. A lot of things horrified her, but it didn't stop their relationship. What stopped it was politics, and World War I. By then Emma Goldman had spent much time in prison. She had been imprisoned on Blackwell's Island in New York for speaking out during the economic crisis in 1893. There was a fierce economic situation in New York in 1893, and all over the country really. Huge numbers of people were unemployed. They did not have enough food to take care of their families. Emma Goldman gets up in front of this huge crowd in Union Square and says, "If you don't have food enough for your kids, go into the stores and take the food." It's called direct action. That's what anarchists believe in. You don't sign petitions. You don't lobby. You don't visit your legislator. You take direct action against the source of your problem. That's what workers do when they take direct action against an employer, what women do when they take direct action against men, or against the source of their oppression. So she was in jail for that. Her jail record was a very long one. And the FBI always had people following her, and the police were reporting on her speeches. There was one of her speeches that they couldn't record because, as the agent reported to his superiors, "Well, she spoke to this group of Jewish women on the Lower East Side, and I'm sorry I couldn't take down what she said because she spoke in Yiddish."

By the time WW I came on, they both had spent quite a bit of time in prison, she by now was a famous speaker, lecturer, and she began to speak against the war and against the draft. You may know, WW I was the occasion for a kind of hysteria that happens again and again in wartime, right? People who speak out against the war are looked on as a kind of traitor; the government induces an atmosphere of fear, and makes examples of a small number of people in order to intimidate everybody else. In this case, in WW I, they imprisoned about a thousand people for speaking out against the war. And when Emma Goldman and Alexander Berkman spoke at a big rally in Harlem against the conscription act, they were arrested and sent to prison and not released until the war ended. And when the war ended, that's when the Palmer raids took place, which some of you may know about. But not far off from what is going on now, with the treatment of immigrants and noncitizens—a wholesale roundup of people who are noncitizens; no due process, no trial, no hearing, and you put them on a boat and you deport them. And Emma Goldman and Alexander Berkman were deported, ironically enough back to Russia, where they had been born. That was Czarist Russia and now it was Soviet

Russia in 1919. But they were still anarchists. And even though they had first welcomed the overthrow of the czarist regime, they soon found themselves in Russia at odds with the new Bolshevik regime because they were anarchists. They were antiauthoritarian, antistate. Maxim Gorky was putting out a little dissident newspaper and it didn't last long because they were rounding up dissidents. So as opponents of the regime, they soon left the Soviet Union, settled in Western Europe. They picked a warm spot, the Mediterranean coast of France, and lived in very modest way there, separately, but still friends and still involved in things happening here. Berkman became sick and died in 1936. Emma Goldman died in fact when she was making a rare visit to the US in 1940. She died actually up in Canada.

I said I wanted to talk about something else, and that is about war and the present situation. Because wherever I go now, I have to talk about the war, and that's what's happening and what people are thinking about. People talk about terrorism, people are talking about war, and I have to talk about that or I'm not doing my duty to myself, that is to move from history in the past, into the present. And Emma Goldman was an absolutely incorrigible fighter against war, and spoke out against the Spanish-American War, against WW I, and anarchists in general, being antiauthoritarian and not trusting governments, I can't imagine why they don't trust governments, but they are instinctively antiwar. It's clear that people all over the country have been bombarded with the notion that we must support the war, support the president, we must have unity, we mustn't dissent, you're either for us or against us, if you raise questions about American foreign policy, the retort is "Oh, you're justifying the attacks on the Twin Towers." Or if you say that there are alternatives to war—and you probably know that people have been visited by the FBI for criticizing the war and the president. The incidents have been multiplied, multiplied around the country. A retired worker out in the West who made a remark critical of Bush at his sports club was visited by the FBI and asked, "Are you a member of the sports club? Did you make this remark about the president?" A young woman was visited by the FBI, who said, "We hear you have a poster on your wall with a picture of Bush in a very unflattering way," meaning: we must flatter Bush. This is scary. This is totalitarian. They passed the Patriot Act, in which terrorism is defined in such a way to enable them to pick up anybody for anything they say. You don't even have to do anything. We're at a time when it becomes even more important to dissent from the establishment and the president, when everybody's crying "We must unite behind the president"—it's exactly such a time when we need dissenting voices. And the irony is that it's exactly in times of war, that is when you're dealing with life-and-death matters, that you're not supposed to speak. So you have freedom of speech for trivial matters but not for life-and-death matters. That's a nice working definition of democracy, isn't it? But it shouldn't be that way. This is exactly when we need the most lively discussion, so wherever I go these days I try to contribute to that discussion. I spoke recently at North High School in Newton, just outside of Boston. I spoke to about five hundred students about the war, and afterward about four or five parents reacted angrily, showed up at a school committee meeting in Newton, saying, "Why did they invite him?" "Why would you let him speak?" I say this only to indicate that apparently to raise questions about the war is to engender a kind of ferocity that goes against democracy. So yes, I speak against the war, I'm writing against the war. I've written for *The Progressive* about the war.

On both pragmatic and moral grounds, I'm opposed to the war. Because pragmatic is simply, Is this very effective in doing something about terrorism? Because it seems to me very clear. We've carried on a war for four months, the president is asking for $50 billion more for the military budget, $45 billion more for home defense. It seems that people are still worried about terrorism. Have you noticed that people's fears about terrorism have diminished because of the war? Since the war? I don't see that. If anything, excitement is growing. And the measures taken presumably to guard us—Star Wars—from a pragmatic point of view, what are we doing against terrorism? We set out to say, "Well here are these terrorists. We're going to find Osama bin Laden." Well, we didn't, and even if we did, would that be dealing with terrorism? Well, we found this group, that group, we bombed the caves in Afghanistan, they said there were thousands of fighters in the caves. Well, they came up with a handful of people. Where are the others? As we learn from the government itself, there are terrorist networks in other countries—maybe forty, fifty—it changes from day to day, like the numbers of communists in McCarthy's State Department used to change from day to day, because the truth is that they don't know. So if you don't know, what are you doing bombing Afghanistan? There may be a network in the Philippines, in Syria, in Somalia in Africa, who knows where? Well clearly, we're bombing and bombing but we haven't done anything about terrorism. It's as if a crime had been committed, a mass murder, and you're looking for the perpetrators, and you hear that they are hiding out in Cambridge. Bomb Cambridge! Or the criminals in this neighborhood—you bomb the neighborhood! On the chance that this might result in killing the criminal. This is what we've been doing in Afghanistan—it's absurd, just from a pragmatic point of view. Then on the moral point of view—that rests on how many innocent civilians have we killed with our bombing? That's what my article in the current *Nation* is about. Those of you reading the *New York Times*, there is this page every day, with photos of the victims from the World Trade Center and the Pentagon—little photos and biographical sketches—it's very moving. They'll tell you about who these people were, what they did, what they cared about, what their hobbies were, who their families were—it's very moving. Suddenly the numbers—three thousand or whatever it was—become not numbers but human beings. And I thought, "Well, we haven't done the same thing to our victims in Afghanistan." They are just numbers, just as the victims in the Twin Towers were just numbers to whoever planned those attacks in New York and Washington. And I like to think, not specifically of the perpetrators of the attacks, but a significant number of people around the world who were sad about the attacks—"well, that's too bad"—but they weren't excited, they weren't repelled by it. I wonder if those people who didn't feel repelled by the attacks were deluded by the fact that they only knew about numbers—the people in the Twin Towers were just numbers to them. That if they had encountered them, seen their faces, talked to their families, a lot of these people would for the first time begin to recognize what had been done here in New York. And conversely, if American people could know, really know up close, and see the pictures and meet the families, and visit the hospitals of the victims of our bombing in Afghanistan, would the American people continue to support the bombing? I suspect that the reason the American people support the bombing is because they believe Rumsfeld, because we have no one else talking to us. You turn on the TV, there he is. You turn off the TV, and there he is. You can't escape him. And he is very calm and blithe. If there are questions about civilian casualties, he says, "Oh, well, we try our best. We don't really mean to kill any civilians. These things happen. Collateral damage, right?" Remember Timothy McVeigh, when he was asked about the Oklahoma bombing (he'd learned this during the Gulf War, because this was a phrase used by the US during that war to describe what happened to civilians in Iraq), Timothy McVeigh said of the children: "Collateral damage." So this is Rumsfeld. Collateral damage, an accident, unintentional. Or "They're deliberately putting civilians in military targets." That always gets to me. A village is destroyed. You mean they populated this village with ordinary people so that then it would become a propaganda weapon against the US, created a Hollywood set? No, there's something wrong with that. I remember back to the Gulf War. And here, history is important. When you're dealing with an event like this, what's happening in Afghanistan, if you don't have any history to American wars or American foreign policy, it's as if you were born yesterday. And then whatever people in authority tell you, you have no way of checking up on it. And it's important to remember the lies that were told to the people of this country during the war in Vietnam. Lies about "Oh, we're only bombing military targets"—and a million civilians die in Vietnam. I was in North Vietnam in 1968 and 1972 and saw the villages, a hundred miles away from a military target (as if there are that many military targets in Vietnam)—the village is totally destroyed by attacking jet planes. With some of that history, you know that the government lies all the time. These things are not accidents. When I say that, I don't mean that the government goes out to deliberately kill civilians. I mean that they don't care. Because it's inevitable. When something is neither deliberate nor an accident, and there's something in between, the something in between is inevitable. And so when you do the bombing on this scale, it's inevitable that you'll kill large numbers of civilians. And the numbers of civilians killed in Afghanistan, nobody knows. The Pentagon doesn't know, or won't tell, and some of their responses are "Well, we're not there on the ground; we don't know." And you can't believe the Taliban; you can't believe the Pentagon. But if you put together the dispatches in American newspapers and scattered on the back pages of the *Times*, the *Washington Post*, and the *Chicago Tribune*, and you read Reuters and Agence France Presse, and you read in England *The Guardian*, *The Independent*, and *The Times of London* and put those scattered pieces together, you come up with a horrifying picture of the human damage that we have done in Afghanistan. And that is a moral disaster. We've met terrorism with terrorism.

So I'm arguing it from both a pragmatic and a moral point of view that war is indefensible. And people ought to speak out and defy the admonitions to be patriotic, using a very distorted definition of patriotism, and create a discussion about what is going on, or else we become victims, as people all over the world have become victims to their governments, and have allowed wars to go on endlessly, one after the other.

11

Confronting Government Lies

General Assembly of the Unitarian Universalist Association, Boston, Massachusetts, June 28, 2003

In 2003, talk of empire had become fashionable again. In January, the United States had again invaded Iraq and begun an occupation that would last for years and lead to hundreds of thousands of deaths. Zinn spoke at numerous rallies and events to build opposition to the war and place it in the context of the long history of governments deceiving the public in the interests of US empire.

What we can learn from history? I start with the supposition that if you don't know any history, it's as if you were born yesterday. And if you were born yesterday, then anybody in authority can get up in front of a microphone and tell you "We must go to war" for this reason or that reason, and you have no way of checking up. But history can give you a perspective. History can't tell you definitely what is true or false about something happening today. There is always the possibility of something unique taking place. But history can be suggestive. It can tell you enough to make you look further than the latest presidential speech. It can suggest skepticism, and so it's very, very useful that way.

For instance, history can disabuse you of the notion that your interests and the interests of the government are the same. The political philosophers of the modern era have always made that clear. They were very, very honest about it, I mean, that's what governments are set up for. Rousseau said so. Governments are set up for a small number of people. Adam Smith said it. James Madison said it in the *Federalist Papers*. They're very clear. Government is not set up for the people. And if you know some American history, you would never believe that government was set up in order to serve the interests of all of us, despite the words in the preamble to the Constitution: "we the people of the United States." They weren't "we the people of the United States" who established the Constitution of the United States. They were fifty-five rich white men who gathered in Philadelphia, and they set up a government which they felt would serve the interests of the slaveowners and the merchants and the western land speculators.

They wanted a government that would be able to put down rebellions. They were very conscious of the fact that just a year before the Constitutional Convention, a rebellion of farmers had taken place in western Massachusetts. You probably know about that: Shays' Rebellion. You know it from those multiple-choice tests. But you will not learn of the connection between Shays' Rebellion of 1786 and the Constitutional Convention of 1787. You will not learn about that in your classes in school or in orthodox histories. But the fact is that when Shays' Rebellion took place, thousands of farmers gathering around the courthouses, many of them veterans of the Revolutionary War, because their farms were being taken away from them, their livestock, their land being taken away from them because they couldn't afford to pay the taxes levied on them by the rich who controlled the legislature of Massachusetts. So they surrounded the courthouses and wouldn't let the proceedings go on, the auctioning off of their farms.

This was democracy. That's when democracy comes alive, when large numbers of people gather to defy the state and declare what they really want and how people should live. And so that's what they did in western Massachusetts. You would have to read the letters that went back and forth between the founding fathers after Shays' Rebellion. The letters weren't about "Oh, let's set up a new government which will be for the people, of the people." No. That's not what they said. Their idea was "We're going to set up a government that will maintain law and order."

There was a guy—I shouldn't call him a "guy" because he was a general. He was a general under George Washington in the Revolutionary War: General Henry Knox from Massachusetts. We have all sorts of people in this state. And after Shays' Rebellion, Knox wrote to Washington, who had been his commander during the Revolutionary War. I don't have his exact language with me, he was very elegant, and so I'll give you sort of a rough translation of it. He said, "Look, George, these people out there in western Massachusetts, they think, because they fought in the Revolution, that they deserve an equal share of the wealth of this country." Knox was worried. Washington was worried, and the others were worried. So the Constitution was not set up in order to represent people like the embattled farmers of western Massachusetts, or the slaves, or the Native Americans, or the other people, propertyless people, who are left out.

If you don't know any history, you will not understand that, and you might actually think that our interests are the same as the government's. You might actually think that "national security," when it's used by the government, means "our security." You might think that "national defense" means "our defense." You might think that the phrase "national interest" means "our interest." But what history can teach you is that there are different interests in society. And we had better learn what "our interest" is, and how different that is from what the government's interest is, so that we can act as citizens in a democracy, and not as loyal, obedient servants to the elite who happen to be in power at this moment.

If you know some history, and you listen to the president, or the secretary of defense, or any of those guys, you will know the history of lies told by leaders of government, especially when it comes to going to war. That's when the most lies are told. And after all, when you think about it, if the interests of the government are not the same as the interests of the people, the government had better learn to lie because if it told the truth, it wouldn't be up there very long. And so governments learn to lie, and they especially lie about war. If you just look a little into history, you will see the kinds of things that were told to the people of the United States when they were exhorted to go to war.

You will hear James Polk saying how we must go to war against Mexico because "blood has been shed, American blood has been shed on American soil." Well, it was sort of like weapons of mass destruction, that is, it was not quite true. But it was a good way to get the American people roused up: "American blood has been shed on American soil." There was a young Congressman from Illinois who got up in Congress and said, "Where? Where was it shed? What is the spot? Show me the spot where this blood was shed." The young Congressman was Abraham Lincoln, who called the "spot resolutions." But Polk was just one in a long line of presidential liars when it came to war. I know you're not supposed to talk that way about presidents. Sometimes you hear people say "We must respect the president." Why?

President McKinley lied to the nation: "Why are we going into the Philippines? To civilize and Christianize the Filipinos." That's what he said. And you can go on. Woodrow Wilson: "We're going into WW I to make the world safe for democracy" or "This is the war to end all wars." Woodrow Wilson, a PhD. Now would a PhD lie? No, I find that hard to believe, but I guess when you've lived awhile you learn that there's no necessary relationship between higher education and morality.

The list of lies goes on. You've heard a lot of things about Truman and the dropping of the atomic bomb, but I doubt you'd have heard this. Truman told the nation, "We have dropped a bomb on Hiroshima, a military target." Once you see that, the next time you hear somebody in authority say, "We are only bombing military targets," it ought to suggest something to you.

Kennedy lied about American involvement in the invasion of Cuba in 1961. Johnson lied, again and again, about involvement in Vietnam, from the Gulf of Tonkin on. Eisenhower had lied when he said, "We don't have any planes going over the Soviet Union." And then one was shot down, and they captured the pilot. It was a little embarrassing.

I won't talk about Nixon's lies. No. Or Reagan's lies. No. By the way, not only Republican presidents lie. Lying is bipartisan. I'm very proud to say that. And now of course, I mean, Clinton lied too. No, I'm not talking about *that*! I'm talking about important things. Clinton bombed Iraq in 1998 around the issue of weapons of mass destruction. Bush was not the first one to deal with this issue of weapons of mass destruction and to use it as a way of excusing the bombing of other countries. Not at all.

So there's always some reason given for going into a war, whether it's "manifest destiny," or "civilizing people," or "we have to stop communism." Of course, now it's terrorism. And these are all very useful for mobilizing a country to go to war. But when you look behind all of the reasons, through the history of American foreign policy, given for going to war, and look for the real reasons, you find a common denominator. You find that the real reason is expansion. Economic expansion. Territorial expansion. Political expansion. Power. Imperialism. I don't like to use the word "imperialism" because only radicals use the word "imperialism." But I feel more emboldened these days to use the word, because now I find that defenders of American foreign policy are using the word "imperialism." They say, "Yes, we're imperialists, and we're happy." But yes, behind all those excuses was expansion. Taking half of Mexico, going across the country fighting all those wars against the Indians in order to secure this enormous expanse of land between the Atlantic and the Pacific.

And then going in to the Caribbean and making war, oh yes, to liberate the Cubans from Spain. The Spanish-American War. I remember that's what I learned in school. The Cubans were oppressed by Spain and we went in there because we were going to bring freedom to Cuba. Well, we liberated Cuba from Spain, but not from us. Spain was out. We were in. Spain was out of Cuba, and the American corporations were in. The railroads and the banks and the American military bases. And we write a clause into the Cuban Constitution giving us the right to intervene in Cuba anytime we feel like. We still have that base. Guantánamo. We still have that military base in Cuba. Yes, that expansion. All through. Behind the Cold War. Behind the war on terrorism. We go into Afghanistan, presumably to do something about terrorism. We don't really do anything about terrorism, but we manage to establish military bases not only in Afghanistan but also in those Central Asian countries north of Afghanistan: Uzbekistan, Turkmenistan, and all the other "-stans." That's what we managed to do. That's the common denominator behind all of the claims made about why we must go to war.

When you know that history, then you become very suspicious of what is being told to you today. The idea that American imperialism is different: kinder, gentler, . . . Really, really. There's a professor at the Kennedy School at Harvard who wrote, "The twentieth century sees a new invention, a global hegemony, whose grace notes are free markets, human rights, and democracy." A writer for the *New Republic*, Charles Krauthammer, says, "We are a unique, benign imperialism." And it made me go back to something that the secretary of war, Elihu Root, said at the time of the Spanish-American War and at the time of our conquest of the Philippines. He said, "The American soldier is different from all other soldiers of all other countries since the world began. He is the advance guard of liberty and justice, of law and order, and of peace and happiness."

All you have to do is read the headlines in today's newspapers and you get a very different picture of what is going on right now in Iraq. So when you know history you start—listening to the Bush administration, you start with skepticism. Oh, you're not sure the Bush administration is lying, but after you know some history you figure there must be a good chance of it.

And then you look closely in the newspapers and you listen to *Democracy Now!*, and you go outside the mainstream press. You read all those funny little magazines that have small circulations. You go to the Internet. You learn things. But then you even read things that break into the mainstream press, and so when you hear the Bush administration say, "We are going to bring order to Iraq. They will greet us like liberators"—well, it didn't take long for that to be revealed as a lie. There is no order in Iraq. There is chaos in Iraq. There are no crowds of cheering Iraqis, as they expected, but widespread hostility.

What are they shouting in these crowds in Iraq? "No to Saddam, no to Bush!" And that takes cares of the complication. Yes, we got rid of a tyrant, but we didn't get rid of the United States, which in fact was a supporter of the tyrant in his worst days. Saddam Hussein was ruthless and he killed a lot of people, but if you look closely at the chronology of it, you will see that his greatest killing and his worst atrocities took place when he was an ally of the United States. And so many of the mass graves that were dug up recently go back to 1991, when at the end of the Gulf War the United States really gave the go-ahead to Saddam Hussein to destroy the Shiite rebellion in the south, and that's when these mass graves in the south were created. So when they say, "No to Saddam, no to Bush!" they are thinking of their national historic treasures, which have been destroyed, in this so-called liberation of Iraq. They think of their destroyed homes and the graves of the dead. And that's one of the things that suggest to us that we'd better look very closely at the things that we are told. It turns out to be not a liberation but a very ugly occupation. And every day you see that. An American or two American soldiers killed, and more and more Iraqis killed.

And there was a bizarre reminder of Vietnam which I found in a Reuters dispatch. You very often have to read the foreign press in order to know what is going on. And if you ever wondered—I say "if people," I don't say "if *you* ever wondered," because, no, you don't wonder about those things. You know all those things. But there are people who wonder, "How is it that in the United States so many people declare their support for Bush, and the rest of the world is totally opposed to what we're doing in Iraq?" Well, it's a simple answer. The rest of the world doesn't watch Fox News.

You have to read Agence France Press, and Reuters, and the London *Observer*, and the *Guardian*. You have to read foreign newspapers to really know what is going on. So here is this dispatch from Reuters News Agency, from Baghdad: "U.S. troops psyched-up on a bizarre musical reprise from the Vietnam War film 'Apocalypse Now' before crashing into Iraqi homes. With Wagner's 'Rite of the Valkyries' still ringing in their ears, amid the clatter of helicopters overhead, soldiers rammed vehicles into metal gates and hundreds of troops raided houses in the western city of Ramadi after sunrise." Playing the music from *Apocalypse Now*.

So we have all these lies about weapons of mass destruction, which as they become more and more desperate about the administration trying somehow to weasel out of the things that they said. Remember Ari Fleischer? He said, "We know for a fact there are weapons there." Now how does he know? He spends all of his time briefing people. But "we know for a fact there are weapons there." Then Vice President Cheney, who occasionally shows up, was on *Meet the Press*. He said, "We believe Saddam has in fact reconstituted nuclear weapons." Now you know there is not an iota of evidence for that. On ABC, Rumsfeld says, "We know where they are." Well, then, why doesn't he tell us? You know, it's a secret. And then Bush, this . . . I started to say this is hard to believe . . . no, nothing is hard to believe anymore, right? Bush was speaking on Polish television. Maybe he thought, "Oh, I'm speaking on Polish television. I can say whatever I want." He said, on Polish television when the war ended: "We have found the weapons of mass destruction."

The only weapons of mass destruction in Iraq turned out to be the bombs and missiles that were raining down upon the Iraqi people by the thousands, and all the cluster bombs with their deadly pellets, the arsenal of the greatest military power in the world, visiting destruction on a country ruled by a murderous tyrant, but a country that was devastated by two wars, and ten years of sanctions, and that was militarily helpless. A great military victory. Almost as great as our victory over Grenada, or our victory over Panama. Only a nation that is concentrating on television could believe what the administration was saying, because it's all coming out now. "Oh, we have documents." The documents turn out to be forged. "Oh, there are drones of death in Iraq." They turn out to be model airplanes. Well, you know, when you look from a great distance up high . . . Colin Powell talked about "decontamination trucks." They turned out to be fire trucks. And then remember they talked about these "mobile germ labs" which turned out to be used for inflating balloons for the artillery. Nonsense. All of this.

We've learned from history that we can't trust the government, and yet at the same time we know that the government has the power. It can do what it wants. It can spend the wealth of the country the way it wants to spend the wealth of the country. It can send troops anywhere in the world it wants to send them. It can threaten twenty million Americans who happen to be noncitizens. It's just a kind of nice bureaucratic division between noncitizens and citizens, but I assume we're all human beings, whether we're citizens or noncitizens. And there are twenty million noncitizens who are subject to indefinite detention with no constitutional rights.

This is the power of the government. And the government has the power to affect public opinion by its connections with the major media. It's interesting to me what the polls show. Very often we're a little saddened. We see all the polls show that Bush has 60 percent support. But when I think that Bush has 90 percent of the media and only 60 percent of the population, there must be a lot of people with common sense.

I've always been skeptical of polls, especially when they say what I don't like them to say. But then I was reinforced. In the midst of the war, I read a column by Thomas Friedman in the *New York Times*. Thomas Friedman is for the war, always has been for the war. He wrote one column: "You know, you shouldn't believe the polls. I've been traveling around the country . . ." He also said, parenthetically, "My wife is opposed to the war." That heartened me. And didn't surprise me. But, he said, "I've been traveling around the country, and I find that 90 percent of the people I talk to are opposed to the war." Well, if I say that, I almost don't believe it myself. But if Thomas Friedman says it, I figure, yes, absolutely.

You also have to consider this about public opinion. Public opinion is very volatile. And this is where history comes in handy, too. You see how often public opinion changes. How amazingly public opinion can turn around in a very, very short time. Do you remember how there was large majority support for George Bush the First? George Bush the Wiser. I didn't say "Wise," I said "Wiser." And he had all that support, and you notice how all that support diminished very quickly after the Gulf War as people began to have second thoughts about the war, and as the veterans began to come home with their various illnesses, and as the economic situation deteriorated, and then Bush was out. Remember that. It's a good thing to keep in mind. Think about how at the start of the Vietnam War, two-thirds of Americans in 1965 were in favor of the war. Two years later, two-thirds of Americans were opposed to the war. What happened then? What caused people to turn around?

I think what happened in those years was a gradual realization of having been lied to by the government. A kind of information seeping through the cracks of the propaganda system. A kind of osmosis of the truth which began to reach more and more people in the country. And when people began to suspect they'd been deceived and lied to, as is always true, the government loses its legitimacy and loses its power. And we've seen this happen in recent decades. Actually we've seen it all around the world. How the leaders of a country seem to be totally in charge. They're in power. They have everything, and then suddenly there are a million people in the streets, and you see the leaders begin packing their bags and calling for a helicopter. We've seen this in the past thirty years in many places in the world. We've seen it in the Philippines. We've seen it in Indonesia. We've seen it in Portugal. We've seen it in Spain. We've seen it in Russia and East Germany and other countries in Eastern Europe. And think of Argentina. And South Africa, where it seemed that apartheid was all-powerful. And then it was gone, and Mandela was out of prison and Mandela was president of South Africa. Things can change.

The reason we are very often surprised when something suddenly happens in another country is we forget that the power of governments is superficial. And that under the surface there are always rumblings and rumblings and vibrations and the growth of consciousness. And suddenly one day that erupts, and something happens. And that can happen anywhere in the world, including the United States. It's not that we expect Bush to scurry off in a helicopter, except maybe to a baseball game. But he can lose the next election. I mean, after all, he lost the last one! And this time, not all the king's judges or all the king's men will be able to put Humpty Dumpty together again.

There are people around the country calling for Bush's impeachment. Some people think this is a daring thing to say. No, it's in the Constitution. It provides for impeachment. It's perfectly constitutional. Not that Congress is going to impeach Bush, I mean, this is a . . . I don't like to say this. No, I do like to say it. This is a craven Congress. It's not going to impeach Bush. Congress was willing to impeach Nixon for breaking into a building, but they're not willing to impeach Bush for breaking into a country. They're willing to impeach Clinton because of his sexual shenanigans, but will not impeach Bush for turning the country over to the super-rich. But I think it's healthy to talk about impeachment, because surely the constitutional requirement for "high crimes and misdemeanors" applies to sending the young people of the country halfway around the world to kill other people, to be killed in a war of aggression against a people who have not attacked us. I think that's a high crime and misdemeanor.

There's a long history of imperial powers that gloat over the victories, and then they become overextended and overconfident. And they don't realize, and very often even we in the peace movement don't even realize, that power does not simply come out of the barrel of a gun. Military power has its limits. And the limits are created by human beings. By human resistance. Think. The United States, with ten thousand nuclear weapons, could not win in Korea or Vietnam. The Soviet Union with also thousands of nuclear weapons had to retreat from Afghanistan and couldn't do anything to stop the Solidarity movement in Poland. So a country with military power, it can destroy, but it can't build. And what happens is that its citizens after a while begin to get uneasy, because their day-to-day fundamental needs are being sacrificed for military glory and the young are being sent to die.

And the uneasiness grows and grows, and the citizens gather in resistance in larger and larger numbers, and someday they become too many to control, and one day this top-heavy empire falls over. And this change in public consciousness starts with a kind of low-level discontent, which is at first vague with no connection being made between the discontent and the policies of the government, and then the dots begin to be connected, and indignation rises, and then people speak out, and they organize, and they act. And I think what's happening today all over the country is that there's a growing awareness that something is wrong and that what's happening to people here at home is connected to what we are doing to people abroad. Because people are becoming aware that we're spending billions and billions and billions for war, and there's a shortage of teachers. There's a shortage of nurses. There's a shortage of medical care, of affordable housing. There are budget cuts that are taking place in every state of the union and people are hurting because of this. Last week, a teacher wrote a letter to the *Boston Globe* and said, "I may be one of six hundred Boston teachers who will be laid off as a result of budget shortfalls." And then the letter writer connects this to the billions spent for bombs, as he puts it, "sending innocent Iraqi children to hospitals in Baghdad."

I think the connections will be made, between war and human needs. Money for war, not for medical care, not for children, not even for veterans. This is the irony. We send the young people overseas, and at the same time you look at Bush's budget: billions cut from money for veterans. And so the Veterans Administration finds itself already strapped for money, already in difficulty, finds it has less and less funds for the GIs who go over and then come back. Think of this. This is a persistency that goes back to Shays' Rebellion. The veterans of the Revolutionary War, coming back and finding that the country, the government, doesn't care about them. Think about the Gulf War. Think about the Vietnam veterans who came back and those suffering from Agent Orange. You cannot tell the consequences of war by looking at the casualty numbers. Because, you know, they talk about "Well, now, the government learned from Vietnam. Oh, it's not going to suffer huge casualties. Going to keep the casualties low. We're only going to have a couple of hundred casualties now in a war."

And so in 1991, in the first Gulf War, there were maybe two hundred and some casualties, maybe a hundred or so from battle and a hundred or so from sickness. By the way, I can't help going back into history, I remember that in the Spanish-American War we fought this nice quick war in Cuba. They called it a "splendid little war," a short war, very few American casualties. A few hundred American dead in the Spanish-American War. But the total number of dead was about five thousand. A few hundred dead from battle, and about five thousand dead from poisoned beef that was given to the soldiers, sold to the army by the big meat packinghouse companies in Chicago. And if you look at the Gulf War, only a few hundred dead, but then the Veterans Administration not long ago released a report which showed that in the ten years following the Gulf War, eight thousand Gulf War veterans died of various causes, of sickness. And 150,000 veterans of the Gulf War, after the Gulf War, filed for disability for medical problems that they had as a result of being in the Gulf. These are the human consequences, not only for the people that we bomb, but these are the human consequences for our soldiers. And I believe that this is going to become more and more clear to more and more people in this country.

I don't know if you've ever wondered why it is that the people in power very often are nervous. That is, they must be, because they will rush to squelch a little group of people. They will put nuns in prison. And what are they worried about? You go out on a picket line, and there's seven of you on a picket line, and soon there's twelve cops around. Why? Is it possible that they know something we don't know? Is it possible that they understand that small movements grow into large movements? Small acts become large social movements? Maybe they understand that if an idea takes hold in a population it may become indestructible.

Sure, they can control information and they can seduce people temporarily. Well, like Lincoln says, "You can fool all of the people some of the time, but not all of the people all of the time." Sure, they can fool people, and they can get people to support a war, and even to oppress others, but I don't think that's the natural inclination of people. I think that there's a natural desire to live in peace, to believe in the equality of people. I think there's a natural desire to believe that people in other countries are as important as people here, that the lives of children in other countries are as important as the lives of children here. I think that's a natural feeling.

I know there are people who talk about original sin and human nature is tainted and violent and aggressive and all of that. But I like what the writer Kurt Vonnegut said. He said, "I believe in original virtue."

Very often rebellion starts in the culture. It starts with the poets and the writers. I've always been heartened by the fact that the artists in society have almost always been on the side of peace and justice. Tolstoy and Victor Hugo. And in the United States, the Black poets, and the writers, have always been on our side. That's always been heartening. And we're seeing this now. We've seen the poets defying the White House. They wanted to go to the White House and read antiwar poetry. Well, you can't do that. And then they went ahead and they read their poetry all over the country. And then they put on *Lysistrata* simultaneously all over the world.

There's an Aeschylus play right now in New York, *The Persians*, in which they talk about, it's so apropos, how the Persian Empire at a certain point is seen to be hollow, and all of their boasting, and all of their triumphalism, is going to come crashing down. The Greek playwrights were against the war, and we've seen that poetic reaction against violence and war all through history.

And we're seeing now rap groups, and singers, the Dixie Chicks. I confess, I never thought that I would be talking about the Dixie Chicks. But they've become a kind of household word, and they're attacked for making statements against Bush, and they go on and they play to huge sellout crowds all over the country. Same thing for Pearl Jam and Eddie Vedder. I know about all these groups. And all these musicians and actors and writers signing thousands and tens of thousands of "Not in Our Name" statements, and spreading it all over the world. It's a rebellion that's first ignored by the media, and then it sort of breaks through, so then they can't ignore it again. We see Michael Moore winning an Academy Award. His documentary films are seen by millions of people. His book *Stupid White Men* is on the *New York Times* best-seller list for a long, long time. Look at Barbara Ehrenreich's book *Nickel and Dimed*, about poor, working people and the new welfare regulations. It has been on the best-seller list for several years.

This all to me is very encouraging. I guess it suggests something about the power of words, the power of books, the power of what art does. There are millions and millions of people in this country who are opposed to the war, and so when you see a statistic, "60 percent of the people support the war," it means that 40 percent of the people are opposed to the war. You can read that both ways. I'm encouraged when I see that 40 percent are opposed to the war, because I know that the 60 percent will get lower and the 40 percent will grow. Because the truth is going to come out. Truth has a power of its own. Art has a power of its own. When you combine the power of truth and the power of art, you have something that at some point becomes unstoppable. Something that guns cannot dislodge.

And we also should remember that we are not alone. That on February 15th something happened that had never happened before in the history of the world. We don't know how many, ten million, twelve million, fifteen million people around the world simultaneously demonstrating against the American war in Iraq. That's an amazing event. I think that's what the writer Arundhati Roy meant when she spoke of the "globalization of resistance." Every tiny act that we engage in, and those of us who have been in social movements know this: you do little things, and you think "It doesn't mean anything. Where's it going to go? Who's going to listen?" You do little things, and they don't seem to be working, and then more people do little things, and the little things multiply.

And at a certain point in history, millions of little, tiny, apparently inconsequential acts multiply. We saw this in the civil rights movement. We saw this in the antiwar movement and the women's movement, in the gay and lesbian movement, in the disabled persons movement. At a certain point all these little acts multiply and something changes. We should keep that in mind. Every little act that we engage in contributes to this world phenomenon.

Thank you.

12

History Matters

Cambridge, Massachusetts, February 6, 2004

In this speech, Zinn explores his reasons for teaching and writing about history.

I want to talk about history and how history might be useful. This is my claim. My claim is that history is useful. My claim is that if you don't know history, you become a victim of whatever anybody is telling you today or told you yesterday, because if you don't know history, you have no way of checking up on the daily headlines or on the daily pronouncements from the White House. And so anybody in authority can tell you anything, and tell you in a very authoritative voice, and they can tell it to you twelve times, on twelve different television channels, and it begins to have the ring of truth. And unless you know some history, you might be inclined to just believe it because there is no way of checking up on it. So I claim that history is useful for checking up on whatever is given to you at any moment of the present time. It's not that history can definitively and finally tell you what judgment to make about what is happening today, whether it's a president's budget or the war in Iraq. History can't give you a positive, clear, final answer to these questions, because there is always a possibility, whatever patterns there have been in history, of a unique event, there is always a possibility that something different has happened. And yet history, by showing you certain persistent kind of phenomena that have occurred again and again, even if it can't give you a final, definitive answer, can suggest something to you, can tell you enough to make you look further, can suggest, if not certainties, probabilities. And that's useful.

So this approach of mine, looking to history to deal with contemporary events, is, I think, probably different from the usual, traditional professional historian's approach. That is, a professional historian's approach is generally to be a little leery of dealing with immediate political issues. Let's be safe. It's safe to deal with the past. Let's practice safe history. My approach—it's not only my approach but maybe more and more the approach of new historians, maybe historians who were affected by the movements of the 1960s and who look to history to give them some guidance—but my approach and the approach of some of these newer historians, in my case comes out of, I suppose, my own circumstances, my own life, my own experiences in that I was not an academic all the way up to the point where I started to teach and write history. I didn't go straight through from high school to college to graduate school to teaching history and writing about history. A bunch of things happened to me in between. I had ten years between graduating from high school and going to college under the GI Bill of Rights. And in those ten years I think the experiences that I had, when I finally went to college at the age of twenty-seven, gave me a certain approach to education and to the study of history, and they made me want to study history, to put it very modestly, in order to try to change the world. Nothing more than that. No, let's not be modest.

What happened in between high school and college is that at the age of eighteen I went to work in a shipyard. I worked in a shipyard for three years. I grew up in a working-class family in New York. My father was a waiter, a member of Waiters' Union Local 2. Since I'm with trade union people, I have to bring out all of my trade union credentials. Waiters' Union Local 2. So I went to work in the shipyard. None of the kids that I grew up with went to college at the age of eighteen. Everybody went to work. I went to work in the Brooklyn Navy Yard and became an apprentice ship fitter. And I joined a union; I joined something with this terrible acronym of IUMSWA, the International Union of Marine and Shipbuilding Workers of America. I'm sure your unions have done better than that in figuring out something more pronounceable. It was a CIO union. At the time, the CIO and the AFL had not yet merged. And there was a CIO union trying to break into the unskilled ranks of the navy yard because the AFL had a monopoly on all the skilled workers, who were organized by crafts. There were the electricians and there were the shipwrights and there were the joiners and the boilermakers, all these. But no, we were trying to organize the unskilled. It didn't work very well. But I had three years of experience organizing, actually, the younger workers in the shipyard. And then I volunteered for the air force. It was World War II. I could have stayed in the shipyard, because I had an exemption. But I was all imbued with the idea of the good fight, the good war, fighting against fascism. And so I joined the air force, became a bombardier in the air force. I flew combat missions over Europe, I came back. I was married by this time. We had a kid or two. I'm very big about how many kids we had. I knocked around in various jobs, went back to the shipyard for a while, knocked around at terrible jobs. I worked in a brewery, and I worked as a waiter for a while. And finally I decided, "I'm going to do something that I might like." I went to school under the GI Bill of Rights and decided I would study history and become a teacher.

But I tell you about these experiences because I think they shaped my thinking about history. My growing up in that kind of atmosphere that I grew up in, the tenements of Brooklyn, and going to work gave me a kind of class consciousness, a phrase that's not used very often in the United States, because in the United States we're generally brought up to believe that we're not really a class society. It's all one big happy family. And in the culture we have the language that goes along with that, the language that tries to envelop us all into "we're all together in this." There is the flag, there is America. We all say the Pledge of Allegiance, we all sing "The Star Spangled Banner." And then the president tells us we've got to go to war for national security. National security. That must mean everybody's security. Nobody asks the question, "Whose security?" Or they say, "This is for national defense." And nobody asks the question, "Whose defense?" Or they say, "This is in the national interest." And nobody asks, "Whose interest?" But as soon as people throw out these phrases, you're expected to get into this great big pen in which everybody has the same interest. You and the president, me and Bush, Exxon and me, we all have the same interest. If any of you have read Kurt Vonnegut, he has this expression "granfalloon." If you read his wonderful little novel *Cat's Cradle*, a granfalloon is one of these abstractions like national interest or like America or like France or like England or like any artificial constellation of things. And they are artificial constellations of things in which people are put together and made to feel "we are all one and we all have the same interests." So I grew up with a kind of class consciousness, which meant that I came to the conclusion that no, we don't all have the same interests. There are people in this country who are very rich and people in this country who are really struggling, and they don't have the same interests. And sure, there are people in between, you might say, the famous great American middle class. And the people in the middle, they're not very rich and they're not very poor, but they're nervous. They don't know where they are, they don't know where they're going, they don't know if they're going up or down, they don't know if they're going to have a job tomorrow, they don't know if they're going to become rich tomorrow or they're going to descend into the lower depths tomorrow. But it's a class society. I came to that conclusion. And when I started to study history, I began to look at American history from a class-conscious point of view.

So when I read the preamble to the Constitution of the United States, which starts off with the words "We the people of the United States," and so on, there too, "we the people of the United States" got together in Philadelphia in 1787 and established this Constitution? No, it wasn't "we the people." It was fifty-five rich white men who gathered together in Philadelphia to form the Constitution, really. I was, like most other people, kind of awed by the Constitution. It's an awe that still goes on. The Constitution. A holy document. Some of you may remember that in the bicentennial of the framing of the Constitution, that is, two hundred years after 1787, 1987, there were celebrations around the country celebrating the bicentennial of the Constitution. And there was all this romantic discussion of that marvelous document put together by "we the people." In fact, I remember that in that year, 1987, Ronald Reagan, who was our president, you may recall, wrote an essay, believe it or not, for some scholarly publication, *Parade* magazine. And in this essay Reagan said that the Constitution of the United States was such a perfect document it could only have been written with the guiding hand of God. That's awesome. If God wrote the Constitution, then we'd better not criticize it, right? The very idea that he or she took time out just to concentrate on the Constitution of the United States. But we throw God around a lot, especially in politics. It's very useful and it's very heartwarming. During that year of the bicentennial, 1987, there was one dissenting voice in this chorus of hallelujahs about the Constitution. The one dissenting voice was the voice of the one Black member of the Supreme Court, Thurgood Marshall. And Thurgood Marshall made a speech in that year, and he said, "Why is everybody so excited about the Constitution? The Constitution legitimized slavery." The Constitution declared that a Black slave was equivalent to three-fifths of a human being. The Constitution provided that slaves who escaped from their masters would have to be brought back to their masters, a provision of the Constitution that was later reinforced by the Fugitive Slave Act of 1850. This has been historically true. It's still true, this deification of the Constitution.

Then I read a book by Charles Beard, whose name is not well known, but he was sort of a famous historian of the 1930s. Charles Beard wrote a book called *An Economic Interpretation of the Constitution*. And what he did was to examine the fifty-five men who were there in Philadelphia framing the Constitution, and he examined their economic interests and their political views. And he found that these people were all, almost all—you might find one person who was not wealthy—they were slaveowners, they were bondholders, they were merchants, they were land speculators. They were not "we the people of the United States." And they framed a Constitution that would benefit their interests. That's a very important insight, because what he was saying, and something that is resonant with us today: behind the political acts look for economic interests. It's funny, last night I was in a debate of sorts at Suffolk University in downtown Boston with somebody who teaches philosophy at Suffolk. And I guess he had read some of my stuff or he had heard me speak. And he said, "I don't know why Zinn talks about economic interests in our foreign policy. This is a Marxist point of view." It's really very funny. Who talks more about economic interests than the economic interests? Are they Marxists? Halliburton, what are they interested in? But behind politics is economics. And it's not only economics, it's more complicated than that, but economics is a very, very powerful factor. So Beard looks at the economic interests, and he saw, in fact, that they had set up—what did they set up? I remember going to school and learning about the Constitution and learning that this was good. Before the Constitution, we had the Articles of Confederation. This was the standard historical treatment. You may recognize this from your history classes, the standard treatment. There were the Articles of Confederation. After the Revolutionary War, the thirteen colonies were not really unified; they were unified loosely under the Articles of Confederation. But now the Constitution came along, and it gave us a country, it unified us, it created a strong central government. True. There is absolutely no question about that: the Constitution created a strong central government. But it's very important to look behind that and look at the motives behind that, to look at the class motives behind that. I hope you don't mind my going all the way back there to the Revolutionary War and the Constitution. That's what historians do. It's a disease. But my claim is that it's important in relation to today.

It's interesting to look at the year 1786, which is the year before the making of the Constitution, because that was the year that there was a phenomenon that took place in western Massachusetts, which some of you may recognize from some multiple-choice test you once took, Shays' Rebellion. When you mention Shays' Rebellion, people say, "Oh, yes, multiple-choice test, number B, Shays' Rebellion." Sometimes you even learn a little bit about Shays' Rebellion, a rebellion of farmers in western Massachusetts, many of them veterans of the Revolutionary War, who came back after the Revolution and found—this was standard treatment for veterans—that they were not given the things that they were promised, that the things that were said to them about fighting in the Revolution for liberty and equality and the right to the pursuit of happiness didn't really work for them, that they weren't treated like equals. No, these farmers in western Massachusetts, many of whom, as I say, were veterans, found, yes, they had their little piece of land, but their land was being taxed very heavily by the rich, who controlled the legislature of Massachusetts, taxed so heavily that they couldn't pay these taxes. And so the courts were foreclosing and taking away, auctioning off their farms and their land, their livestock. And they decided to organize and to rebel, under the leadership of a captain in the Revolution, Daniel Shays. So thousands of them gathered around the courthouses in western Massachusetts, in Springfield and Amherst and Great Barrington, and they surrounded the courthouses, would not let the courts proceed. And at one point the sheriff would call out the local militia, and the local militia would come, and one thousand militia would face five thousand farmers. And the judge would come out of the courthouse and look over the situation and say—this is what happened in one instance—"Let's take a vote of the militia to see"—militia don't usually take democratic votes—"Let's take a vote of the militia and see what they want to do in this case." He said, "How many are for the farmers and how many are for the state?" Most of the militia went over on the side of the farmers. That was the end of that proceeding. But the rebellions continued, and finally an army was brought out from Massachusetts to quell the rebellions, to crush them.

My point in bringing this up is simply to say that in our history classes, in traditional history, the connection is not made between Shays' Rebellion and the Constitution, although Shays' Rebellion occurred the year before. But there was an important connection between the two. And the connection is that after Shays' Rebellion, the messages went back and forth about Shays' Rebellion among the elite of the colonies, among the powerful people in the colonies; Jefferson was over in Europe, in Paris, and they told him about it. He wrote back, "Don't worry about it. A little rebellion now and then is a healthy thing." But he was there. These people were here. They were the ones facing the rebellion and the possibility of more rebellion. And one of these messages was from General Knox, one of Washington's aides in the Revolution. Knox formed a veterans' organization called the Order of the Cincinnati. It was like an early version of the American Legion. But it really was not a rank-and-file organization; it was a veterans' organization of the generals and the colonels. And Knox wrote to Washington—I have the quote somewhere in my notes but you have to take my word—this is roughly what he said: "Dear George"—I don't know exactly how he put it—"These people who have rebelled in western Massachusetts, they think that because they fought in the Revolution they are entitled to an equal share of the wealth of this country. No. Something has to be done."

The idea of the Constitution was to set up a government that would be able to handle rebellion of poor people, that would be able to handle slave revolts, that would be able to go out West and deal with the Indians who were going to refuse to let the white settlers move into their territory. The idea, in other words, was to set up a government strong enough to protect the interests of the land expansionists, of the slaveholders, of the merchants, the bondholders. That was the idea. It was a class document. I talk about that because that is the story of American history. Behind the laws, from the Constitution on, behind the legislation passed by Congress over all these years, there is class interest—and almost always the class interest of the rich. I say almost always, because there have been times in American history when Congress has passed laws to benefit the people at the lower levels. That has happened, those few times, when there have been upsurges, rebellions, in the United States.

The 1930s is a good example. The New Deal legislation was not simply an act of kindness on the part of Franklin D. Roosevelt, although, yes, he had a certain streak of warmth for people who did not come from his upper class. The reforms of the 1930s—the unemployment insurance and social security and the creation of jobs and subsidized housing and all of that—came as a result, to a large extent, of the great wave of strikes that swept this country in the 1930s, general strikes in San Francisco and Minneapolis, huge textile strikes in the Carolinas, upsurges of people, of tenants all over the country protesting against what landlords were doing to them, evicting them, councils of the unemployed meeting. A country in turmoil. In times like that, yes, the government will pass legislation that will benefit the poor or the lower middle class, working people. But in general, the history of legislation, from that very first economic program of Alexander Hamilton in the first Congress of the United States to benefit bondholders and tax the farmers, down to the oil-depletion allowances of today, or the great tax breaks for the corporations of today, the story has been the class interest of the people in power expressing itself through legislation. It's important to know that, because otherwise you approach every new development in politics as if there were no history to it, as if there were no pattern to it. The budget of the United States is a class document—this one, this budget particularly, more crass than other class documents. But it's important to know that. It's important to ask, when you're discussing politics and this politician and that politician, "What are the economic interests behind this politician? What are the economic interests behind that politician? How many of them are sensitive to the needs of working people and how many of them are not?"

So when I began to write history, yes, class consciousness pervaded my writing of history. I wasn't going to simply write about the economic miracle of the United States, which had been presented to me in high school. Wow, how proud we were, sitting there in my high school class. America, after the Civil War, becomes a great industrial power. The railroads are crisscrossing the country, the steel mills are going up, the gross national product is increasing. They didn't use that term in those days, "gross national product." I think they're more honest now: they call it gross. But this was the idea. And I remember feeling very proud looking at those figures. I didn't realize until I got out of school and began to read on my own, and began to read about labor struggles and began to read about working people, which I wasn't getting in my classes; not up through graduate school, not up through the PhD at Columbia University was I getting the story of working people. I had to get it on my own. I had to read about the railroad strikes of 1877 and the Lawrence textile strike of 1912 and the Ludlow, Colorado, massacre of 1914, because I wasn't getting that in my history classes. So I wanted to tell the story of America's economic miracle from the standpoint of the people who worked in Rockefeller's oil refineries, the Chinese and Irish immigrants who worked on the transcontinental railroad, which was always presented as, oh, what a marvelous thing. They never told me about those Chinese and Irish immigrants who worked by the thousands and thousands on those railroads, and who died in large numbers of sickness and heat and overwork, or the girls who went to work in the textile mills in New England at the age of twelve and died at the age of twenty-five. They didn't talk about brown lung disease. They didn't talk about mine safety regulations.

So I wanted to look at, yes, American economic history from the standpoint of working people and also tell the story of the struggles of working people and of the resistance that they put up and the strikes and the boycotts and the way working people faced off the sheriffs and the National Guard, because otherwise, if you don't know the history of those struggles, you think the eight-hour day came about simply because Congress passed a law in 1938, the Fair Labor Standards Act. That's the general story. When you see a reform coming out of Congress, you assume, oh, it came because Congress suddenly had an enlightenment and they thought, "Oh, we should help these people." No, these reforms usually come as a result of decades and decades of struggle. The eight-hour day—you probably know that better than I—did not come simply as a result of an act of Congress; it came as a result of a long, long period of struggle by working people, and risks and sacrifices by working people, starting with the great wave of strikes for the eight-hour day in 1886 and coming down to the present time. So yes, class interest dominated the history that I wanted to tell. And the fact that I was in the war affected my writing and thinking about wars and about American foreign policy. And I was in the "good war." As you know, there are good wars and bad wars. This is the conventional way of thinking: there are good wars and bad wars. It's a neat way of thinking, because then all you have to do is decide when a war comes along, is this a good war or bad war? And I was in the best. World War II is the best of wars. And that's why I volunteered for it, to fight against fascism, to fight for democracy. In a way, it's a test of the concept of good wars to take the best of wars and subject it to a little bit of scrutiny so that you don't simply say, "Oh well, this is a good war, period." I came out of that war, although I had volunteered for it and was an enthusiastic bombardier, very skeptical of the idea that war solves fundamental problems. Sure, at the moment it seems to. You get rid of Hitler, you get rid of Mussolini, you get rid of the Japanese military machine. A great victory. You've won.

But then, and I didn't begin to think about this until after the war, I began to think about the complications that accompany a so-called good war, the fact that in the so-called good war we had ourselves committed atrocities. The Germans had committed, of course, the great atrocities, the Holocaust. But we ourselves had committed atrocities—we who had denounced the German bombing of civilians at the beginning of World War II. This is awful, this is savage, this is horrible, imagine dropping bombs on cities with civilians. The Germans were doing this on Coventry and Rotterdam. Hundreds of people, maybe a thousand, died in Rotterdam. But as the war went on, *we* were bombing civilians. Deliberately, by the way. Don't let anybody ever tell you, "We would never deliberately bomb civilians." Nonsense. Deliberately bomb. Because what you do in war is try to destroy the morale of the other side. How do you destroy the morale? You kill as many people as you can. And it doesn't matter who they were. This was a deliberate decision by the Churchill war group, and agreed to by the US, to bomb the working-class populations of German cities. So Dresden—we don't know how many people died in that one night of bombing of Dresden. Fifty thousand? One hundred thousand? Nobody knows. Read Kurt Vonnegut's book *Slaughterhouse-Five*, a fascinating book, a novel based on his own experience as a prisoner of war in Dresden at that time. And the other cities. Thirty thousand in one night, Hamburg, Frankfurt. Tokyo, the spring of 1945. One night of firebombing Tokyo. One hundred thousand people died in one night in Tokyo. If you look at this new documentary, *The Fog of War*, about McNamara and Vietnam, you will see McNamara says, "Well, if we had lost the war, we could have been convicted of war crimes, as war criminals, because of that." What do you mean, if we had lost the war? You mean if you win the war, that changes the nature of your act? If you kill 100,000 innocent people and you lose the war, then you're a war criminal; but if you kill 100,000 innocent people and you win the war, then it's okay? It's an interesting way of thinking. And then, of course, Hiroshima and Nagasaki. And we can have a discussion, if you want, about that, because still most Americans believe that it was necessary to bomb Hiroshima and Nagasaki in order to win the war against Japan. We can talk about that. I did a lot of work on that, a lot of research on that. A lot of people have.

I came to the conclusion that war, as a means to achieve something, inevitably, in our time especially, with the modern technology of warfare, involves the massive killing of innocent people. That is certain in warfare. What is uncertain is the end, the result. You don't know really what will happen. You may see an immediate result—Hitler is gone, Mussolini is gone—but you really don't know what is going to happen after that. After fifty million people died in World War II, you're going to have a world now with peace? Oh. The war to end all wars? No. In fact, I looked around at the world after World War II, and what did I see? You call it fascism. Whatever word you use, what I saw was not a world—although we were free of Hitler and Mussolini and so on, we were not free of fascism in the world, we were not free of dictatorship, we were not free of poverty, of misery, of the rich controlling the resources of the world, and of war after war after war after war. And this was the "good war." It made me think, and it made me scrutinize very carefully all the wars that followed. So when the Vietnam War came along—wars just come along, as we know, just accidentally—I was a student of the history of American foreign policy. I knew the history of the Mexican War, and I knew the history of our wars against the Indians, and I knew the history of the Spanish-American

War and the war against the Philippines and the marine incursions into Central America. And nobody could tell me when we started the Vietnam War that the US just wants to bring democracy and liberty to the people of Vietnam. It took quite a number of years for the American people to realize, no, it wasn't what they were telling us it was.

And now, with this present war in Iraq, if you didn't know history, you might believe the president of the United States. He said, "Weapons of mass destruction, an imminent threat, terrorism. We've got to do this. We have no ulterior motives. No, no, it's not oil, no. We just want to establish democracy in Iraq. We want a regime change so we will have a good regime." If you knew the history of the United States when it comes to regime change, you would know how many regimes we've changed and whether those regimes turned out to be democracies or not, and you would know how many times the US had taken a democratically elected regime and changed it into a dictatorship. Look at Iran in 1953, Guatemala in 1954, Chile in 1973. So in the Iraq War history was very important to me in understanding the motives and being able to examine the claims of the US government against what I think are the realities in Iraq.

I'll just say one more thing. And that is, when I studied history and then finished my PhD and got my first teaching job, it was in Atlanta, Georgia, at a Black women's college, Spelman College, in Atlanta, Georgia. And my wife and I and our kids—by this time I knew how many kids I had—our two kids, went down and spent seven years in Atlanta between the years 1956 and 1963. I became involved in the movement, because my students were involved in the movement, and I couldn't possibly teach about constitutional rights and liberty and democracy and stay in the classroom while my students were out demonstrating, going to jail, and so on. So I became involved in the movement, writing about the movement and going from Atlanta to Albany, Georgia, and Selma, Alabama, and various towns in Mississippi. I'll just tell you one thing that I learned, aside from learning a lot more about the role of Black people in American history and the different view of history that Black people have from the traditional view. The one thing I learned was that when fundamental injustices need to be corrected in this country, they are not corrected by the initiative of the government, they're corrected by the initiative of citizens, of people who gather together, who organize, who take risks, and who create a situation where finally the government has to do something. That's what happened in the civil rights movement in the South. The federal government was not going to enforce the Fourteenth and Fifteenth Amendments. For almost one hundred years, no president enforced the Fourteenth and Fifteenth Amendments. Every president for almost one hundred years violated his oath of office. Democrat or Republican, it didn't matter. Everyone violated his oath of office, because he didn't enforce the Constitution. Only when Black people took to the streets and demonstrated and were beaten and went to jail and some of them were killed, only when a national and international commotion was created over this, only then did the government begin to act. So I learned something, something that the people in the labor movement learned a long time ago: If you want to get something done, you can't depend on politics, you can't depend on if we vote for this guy or this guy, everything will be okay. No. Ultimately, if you want to bring about important social change, it has to be through a citizens' movement. That's democracy. That's when democracy comes alive. Thanks.

13

The Myth of American Exceptionalism

Massachusetts Institute of Technology, Cambridge, Massachusetts, March 14, 2005

Zinn spoke on a number of occasions at MIT, where his longtime friend Noam Chomsky has taught since 1955 and which has long had a vibrant student movement. This speech appeared in a series of lectures organized by the Department of Urban Studies and Planning called "Myths about America."

The notion of American exceptionalism—that the United States alone has the right, whether by divine sanction or moral obligation, to bring civilization, or democracy, or liberty to the rest of the world, by violence if necessary—is not new. It started as early as 1630 in the Massachusetts Bay Colony when Governor John Winthrop uttered the words that centuries later would be quoted by Ronald Reagan. Winthrop called the Massachusetts Bay Colony a "city upon a hill." Reagan embellished a little, calling it a "shining city on a hill."

The idea of a city on a hill is heartwarming. It suggests what George Bush has spoken of: that the United States is a beacon of liberty and democracy. People can look to us and learn from and emulate us.

In reality, we have never been just a city on a hill. A few years after Governor Winthrop uttered his famous words, the people in the city on a hill moved out to massacre the Pequot Indians. Here's a description by William Bradford, an early settler, of Captain John Mason's attack on a Pequot village:

> Those that escaped the fire were slain with the sword, some hewed to pieces, others run through with their rapiers, so as they were quickly dispatched and very few escaped. It was conceived that they thus destroyed about 400 at this time. It was a fearful sight to see them thus frying in the fire and the streams of blood quenching the same, and horrible was the stink and scent thereof; but the victory seemed a sweet sacrifice, and they gave the praise thereof to God, who had wrought so wonderfully for them, thus to enclose their enemies in their hands and give them so speedy a victory over so proud and insulting an enemy.

The kind of massacre described by Bradford occurs again and again as Americans march west to the Pacific and south to the Gulf of Mexico. (In fact our celebrated war of liberation, the American Revolution, was disastrous for the Indians. Colonists had been restrained from encroaching on the Indian territory by the British and the boundary set up in their Proclamation of 1763. American independence wiped out that boundary.)

Expanding into another territory, occupying that territory, and dealing harshly with people who resist occupation has been a persistent fact of American history from the first settlements to the present day. And this was often accompanied from very early on with a particular form of American exceptionalism: the idea that American expansion is divinely ordained. On the eve of the war with Mexico in the middle of the nineteenth century, just after the United States annexed Texas, the editor and writer John O'Sullivan coined the famous phrase "manifest destiny." He said it was "the fulfillment of our manifest destiny to overspread the continent allotted by Providence for the free development of our yearly multiplying millions." At the beginning of the twentieth century, when the United States invaded the Philippines, President McKinley said that the decision to take the Philippines came to him one night when he got down on his knees and prayed, and God told him to take the Philippines.

Invoking God has been a habit for American presidents throughout the nation's history, but George W. Bush has made a specialty of it. For an article in the Israeli newspaper *Ha'aretz*, the reporter talked with Palestinian leaders who had met with Bush. One of them reported that Bush told him, "God told me to strike at al Qaeda. And I struck them. And then he instructed me to strike at Saddam, which I did. And now I am determined to solve the problem in the Middle East." It's hard to know if the quote is authentic, especially because it is so literate. But it certainly is consistent with Bush's oft-expressed claims. A more credible story comes from a Bush supporter, Richard Lamb, the president of the Ethics and Religious Liberty Commission of the Southern Baptist Convention, who says that during the election campaign Bush told him, "I believe God wants me to be president. But if that doesn't happen, that's okay."

Divine ordination is a very dangerous idea, especially when combined with military power (the United States has ten thousand nuclear weapons, with military bases in a hundred different countries and warships on every sea). With God's approval, you need no human standard of morality. Anyone today who claims the support of God might be embarrassed to recall that the Nazi storm troopers had inscribed on their belts "Gott mit uns" (God with us).

Not every American leader claimed divine sanction, but the idea persisted that the United States was uniquely justified in using its power to expand throughout the world. In 1945, at the end of World War II, Henry Luce, the owner of a vast chain of media enterprises—*Time*, *Life*, *Fortune*—declared that this would be "the American Century," that victory in the war gave the United States the right "to exert upon the world the full impact of our influence, for such purposes as we see fit and by such means as we see fit."

This confident prophecy was acted out all through the rest of the twentieth century. Almost immediately after World War II the United States penetrated the oil regions of the Middle East by special arrangement with Saudi Arabia. It established military bases in Japan, Korea, the Philippines, and a number of Pacific islands. In the next decades it orchestrated right-wing coups in Iran, Guatemala, and Chile and gave military aid to various dictatorships in the Caribbean. In an attempt to establish a foothold in Southeast Asia it invaded Vietnam and bombed Laos and Cambodia.

The existence of the Soviet Union, even with its acquisition of nuclear weapons, did not block this expansion. In fact, the exaggerated threat of "world communism" gave the United States a powerful justification for expanding all over the globe, and soon it had military bases in a hundred countries. Presumably, only the United States stood in the way of the Soviet conquest of the world.

Can we believe that it was the existence of the Soviet Union that brought about the aggressive militarism of the United States? If so, how do we explain all the violent expansion before 1917? A hundred years before the Bolshevik Revolution, American armies were annihilating Indian tribes, clearing the great expanse of the West in an early example of what we now call "ethnic cleansing." And with the continent conquered, the nation began to look overseas.

On the eve of the twentieth century, as American armies moved into Cuba and the Philippines, American exceptionalism did not always mean that the United States wanted to go it alone. The nation was willing—indeed, eager—to join the small group of Western imperial powers that it would one day supersede. Senator Henry Cabot Lodge wrote at the time, "The great nations are rapidly absorbing for their future expansion, and their present defense all the waste places of the earth. . . . As one of the great nations of the world the United States must not fall out of the line of march." Surely, the nationalistic spirit in other countries has often led them to see their expansion as uniquely moral, but this country has carried the claim farthest.

American exceptionalism was never more clearly expressed than by Secretary of War Elihu Root, who in 1899 declared, "The American soldier is different from all other soldiers of all other countries since the world began. He is the advance guard of liberty and justice, of law and order, and of peace and happiness." At the time he was saying this, American soldiers in the Philippines were starting a bloodbath which would take the lives of 600,000 Filipinos.

The idea that America is different because its military actions are for the benefit of others becomes particularly persuasive when it is put forth by leaders presumed to be liberals or progressives. For instance, Woodrow Wilson, always high on the list of "liberal" presidents, labeled both by scholars and the popular culture as an "idealist," was ruthless in his use of military power against weaker nations. He sent the navy to bombard and occupy the Mexican port of Veracruz in 1914 because the Mexicans had arrested some American sailors. He sent the marines into Haiti in 1915, and when the Haitians resisted, thousands were killed.

The following year American marines occupied the Dominican Republic. The occupations of Haiti and the Dominican Republic lasted many years. And Wilson, who had been elected in 1916 saying, "There is such a thing as a nation being too proud to fight," soon sent young Americans into the slaughterhouse of the European war.

Theodore Roosevelt was considered a "progressive" and indeed ran for president on the Progressive Party ticket in 1912. But he was a lover of war and a supporter of the conquest of the Philippines—he had congratulated the general who wiped out a Filipino village of six hundred people in 1906. He had promulgated the 1904 "Roosevelt Corollary" to the Monroe Doctrine, which justified the occupation of small countries in the Caribbean as bringing them "stability."

During the Cold War, many American "liberals" became caught up in a kind of hysteria about the Soviet expansion, which was certainly real in Eastern Europe but was greatly exaggerated as a threat to Western Europe and the United States. During the period of McCarthyism the Senate's quintessential liberal, Hubert Humphrey, proposed detention camps for suspected subversives who in times of "national emergency" could be held without trial.

After the disintegration of the Soviet Union and the end of the Cold War, terrorism replaced communism as the justification for expansion. Terrorism was real, but its threat was magnified to the point of hysteria, permitting excessive military action abroad and the curtailment of civil liberties at home.

The idea of American exceptionalism persisted as the first President Bush declared, extending Henry Luce's prediction, that the nation was about to embark on a "new American Century." Though the Soviet Union was gone, the policy of military intervention abroad did not end. The elder Bush invaded Panama and then went to war against Iraq.

The terrible attacks of September 11 gave a new impetus to the idea that the United States was uniquely responsible for the security of the world, defending us all against terrorism as it once did against communism. President George W. Bush carried the idea of American exceptionalism to its limits by putting forth in his national-security strategy the principles of unilateral war.

This was a repudiation of the United Nations charter, which is based on the idea that security is a collective matter and that war could only be justified in self-defense. We might note that the Bush doctrine also violates the principles laid out at Nuremberg, when Nazi leaders were convicted and hanged for aggressive war, preventive war, far from self-defense.

Bush's national-security strategy and its bold statement that the United States is uniquely responsible for peace and democracy in the world has been shocking to many Americans.

But it is not really a dramatic departure from the historical practice of the United States, which for a long time has acted as an aggressor, bombing and invading other countries (Vietnam, Cambodia, Laos, Grenada, Panama, Iraq) and insisting on maintaining nuclear and non-nuclear supremacy. Unilateral military action, under the guise of prevention, is a familiar part of American foreign policy.

Sometimes bombings and invasions have been cloaked as international action by bringing in the United Nations, as in Korea, or NATO, as in Serbia, but basically our wars have been American enterprises. It was Bill Clinton's secretary of state, Madeleine Albright, who said at one point, "If possible we will act in the world multilaterally, but if necessary, we will act unilaterally." Henry Kissinger, hearing this, responded with his customary solemnity that this principle "should not be universalized." Exceptionalism was never clearer.

Some liberals in this country, opposed to Bush, nevertheless are closer to his principles on foreign affairs than they want to acknowledge. It is clear that 9/11 had a powerful psychological effect on everybody in America, and for certain liberal intellectuals a kind of hysterical reaction has distorted their ability to think clearly about our nation's role in the world.

In a recent issue of the liberal magazine *The American Prospect*, the editors write,

> Today Islamist terrorists with global reach pose the greatest immediate threat to our lives and liberties. . . . When facing a substantial, immediate, and provable threat, the United States has both the right and the obligation to strike preemptively and, if need be, unilaterally against terrorists or states that support them.

Preemptively and, if need be, unilaterally; and against "states that support" terrorists, not just terrorists themselves. Those are large steps in the direction of the Bush doctrine, though the editors do qualify their support for preemption by adding that the threat must be "substantial, immediate, and provable." But when intellectuals endorse abstract principles, even with qualifications, they need to keep in mind that the principles will be applied by the people who run the US government. This is all the more important to keep in mind when the abstract principle is about the use of violence by the state—in fact, about preemptively initiating the use of violence.

There may be an acceptable case for initiating military action in the face of an immediate threat, but only if the action is limited and focused directly on the threatening party—just as we might accept the squelching of someone falsely shouting "Fire!" in a crowded theater if that really were the situation and not some guy distributing antiwar leaflets on the street. But accepting action not just against "terrorists" (can we identify them as we do the person shouting "fire"?) but against "states that support them" invites unfocused and indiscriminate violence, as in Afghanistan, where our government killed at least three thousand civilians in a claimed pursuit of terrorists.

It seems that the idea of American exceptionalism is pervasive across the political spectrum.

The idea is not challenged because the history of American expansion in the world is not a history that is taught very much in our educational system. A couple of years ago Bush addressed the Philippine National Assembly and said, "America is proud of its part in the great story of the Filipino people. Together our soldiers liberated the Philippines from colonial rule." The president apparently never learned the story of the bloody conquest of the Philippines.

And last year, when the Mexican ambassador to the UN said something undiplomatic about how the United States has been treating Mexico as its "backyard," he was immediately reprimanded by then–Secretary of State Colin Powell. Powell, denying the accusation, said, "We have too much of a history that we have gone through together." (Had he not learned about the Mexican War or the military forays into Mexico?) The ambassador was soon removed from his post.

The major newspapers, television news shows, and radio talk shows appear not to know history, or prefer to forget it. There was an outpouring of praise for Bush's second inaugural speech in the press, including the so-called liberal press (*The Washington Post*, *The New York Times*). The editorial writers eagerly embraced Bush's words about spreading liberty in the world, as if they were ignorant of the history of such claims, as if the past two years' worth of news from Iraq were meaningless.

Only a couple of days before Bush uttered those words about spreading liberty in the world, *The New York Times* published a photo of a crouching, bleeding Iraqi girl. She was screaming. Her parents, taking her somewhere in their car, had just been shot to death by nervous American soldiers.

One of the consequences of American exceptionalism is that the US government considers itself exempt from legal and moral standards accepted by other nations in the world. There is a long list of such self-exemptions: the refusal to sign the Kyoto Treaty regulating the pollution of the environment, the refusal to strengthen the convention on biological weapons. The United States has failed to join the hundred-plus nations that have agreed to ban land mines, in spite of the appalling statistics about amputations performed on children mutilated by those mines. It refuses to ban the use of napalm and cluster bombs. It insists that it must not be subject, as are other countries, to the jurisdiction of the International Criminal Court.

What is the answer to the insistence on American exceptionalism? Those of us in the United States and in the world who do not accept it must declare forcibly that the ethical norms concerning peace and human rights should be observed. It should be understood that the children of Iraq, of China, and of Africa, children everywhere in the world, have the same right to life as American children.

These are fundamental moral principles. If our government doesn't uphold them, the citizenry must. At certain times in recent history, imperial powers—the British in India and East Africa, the Belgians in the Congo, the French in Algeria, the Dutch and French in Southeast Asia, the Portuguese in Angola—have reluctantly surrendered their possessions and swallowed their pride when they were forced to by massive resistance.

Fortunately, there are people all over the world who believe that human beings everywhere deserve the same rights to life and liberty. On February 15, 2003, on the eve of the invasion of Iraq, more than ten million people in more than sixty countries around the world demonstrated against that war.

There is a growing refusal to accept US domination and the idea of American exceptionalism. Recently, when the State Department issued its annual report listing countries guilty of torture and other human-rights abuses, there were indignant responses from around the world commenting on the absence of the United States from that list. A Turkish newspaper said, "There's not even mention of the incidents in Abu Ghraib prison, no mention of Guantánamo." A newspaper in Sydney pointed out that the United States sends suspects—people who have not been tried or found guilty of anything—to prisons in Morocco, Egypt, Libya, and Uzbekistan, countries that the State Department itself says use torture.

Here in the United States, despite the media's failure to report it, there is a growing resistance to the war in Iraq. Public-opinion polls show that at least half the citizenry no longer believe in the war. Perhaps most significant is that among the armed forces, and families of those in the armed forces, there is more and more opposition to it.

After the horrors of the First World War, Albert Einstein said, "Wars will stop when men refuse to fight." We are now seeing the refusal of soldiers to fight, the refusal of families to let their loved ones go to war, the insistence of the parents of high-school kids that recruiters stay away from their schools. These incidents, occurring more and more frequently, may finally, as happened in the case of Vietnam, make it impossible for the government to continue the war, and it will come to an end.

The true heroes of our history are those Americans who refused to accept that we have a special claim to morality and the right to exert our force on the rest of the world. I think of William Lloyd Garrison, the abolitionist. On the masthead of his antislavery newspaper, *The Liberator*, were the words "My country is the world. My countrymen are mankind."

14

Just War

Rome, Italy, June 23, 2005

Zinn became a friend of Dr. Gino Strada, who cofounded the international humanitarian group Emergency and wrote the introduction to the English edition of his book on cluster bombs, Green Parrots. *In 2005, Strada invited him to Italy to speak at a conference organized by Emergency and to work with him on a project with the modest aim to end all wars. Zinn had once taught at the University of Bologna and spoke of his fond memories of his time there.*

Thank you for inviting me to Italy. And special thanks to Dr. Gino Strada and Rossella Miccio for arranging this trip, and to them and the whole staff of Emergency for the magnificent work they are doing to bring a bit of sanity into the madness of war.

I come from a country which is at war, as it has been almost continuously since the end of World War II. The United States has not been invaded for almost two hundred years, not since the year 1812, but it has invaded other countries again and again, as it is doing at the present, in Iraq, and for that I feel shame. The world has been at war again and again all through the twentieth century, and here it is a new century, and we still have not done away with the horror of war. For that we should all feel ashamed.

That shame should not immobilize us. It should provoke us to action.

I want to talk tonight about the persistence of war and suggest what it is that we might be able to do. Of course we can try to help the victims of war, as Emergency has done so heroically. It has cared for a million patients in the last ten years, saving the lives of countless children. But as Gino Strada writes in the final pages of his book *Green Parrots*, our mission must go beyond helping the victims of war to abolishing war itself. He asks the question "Is it monstrous to think about how to create the possibility of human relationships based on equality, on social justice, and on solidarity, and relationships from which the use of violence, terrorism and war is excluded by common accord?"

So let us think together about that possibility.

We must recognize that we cannot depend on the governments of the world to abolish war, because they and the economic interests they represent benefit from war. Therefore we, the people of the world, must take up the challenge. And although we do not command armies, we do not have great treasuries of wealth, there is one crucial fact that gives us enormous power: the governments of the world cannot wage war without the participation of the people. Albert Einstein understood this simple fact. Horrified by the carnage of the First World War in which ten million died in the battlefields of Europe, Einstein said: "Wars will stop when men refuse to fight."

That is our challenge, to bring the world to the point where men will refuse to fight and governments will be helpless to wage war.

Is that utopian? Impossible? Only a dream?

Do men go to war because it is part of human nature? If so, then we might consider it impossible to do away with war. But there is no evidence, in biology, or psychology, or anthropology, of a natural instinct for war. If that were so, we would find a spontaneous rush to war by masses of people. What we find is something very different: we find that governments must make enormous efforts to mobilize populations for war. They must entice soldiers with promises of money, land, education, skills. And if those enticements don't work, government must coerce. It must conscript young people, force them into military service, threaten them with prison of they do not comply.

But the most powerful weapon of governments in raising armies is the weapon of propaganda, of ideology. It must persuade young people and their families that though they may die, though they may lose arms or legs, or become blind, that it is done for the common good, for a noble cause, for democracy, for liberty, for God, for the country.

The Crusaders of the Middle Ages fought for Christ. The Nazi storm troopers had on their belts "Gott Mit Uns" (God is with us). Young Americans today, asked why they are willing to go to Iraq, will answer: "I owe something to my country." God, liberty, democracy, country—these are all examples of what that great novelist Kurt Vonnegut called "granfaloons," abstractions, meaningless terms that say nothing about human beings.

The idea that we owe something to our country goes far back, to Plato, who puts into the mouth of Socrates the idea that the citizen has an obligation to the state, that the state is to be revered more than your father and mother. He says: "In war, and in the court of justice, and everywhere, you must do whatever your state and your country tell you to do, or you must persuade them that their commands are unjust." There is no equality here: the citizen may use persuasion, no more. The state may use force.

This idea of obedience to the state is the essence of totalitarianism. And we find it not only in Mussolini's Italy, in Hitler's Germany, in Stalin's Soviet Union, but in so-called democratic countries like the United States.

In the United States, every year at the end of May, we celebrate Memorial Day, which is dedicated to the memory of all those who have died in the nation's wars.

It is a day when bugles blow, and flags are unfurled, and you hear politicians and editorial writers say, again and again: "They gave their lives for their country."

There is a double lie in that short sentence. First, those who died in war did not give their lives—their lives were taken from them by the politicians who sent them to war, politicians who now bow their heads on Memorial Day.

Second, they did not give their lives for "their country" but for the government—in the present instance for Bush and Cheney and Rumsfeld and the corporate executives of Halliburton and Bechtel—all of whom are profiting, either financially or politically, from the military action that has killed over seventeen hundred Americans and countless Iraqis. No, they did not die for their country. The ordinary people who make up the country get no benefits from the blood shed in Iraq.

When the United States was born, in revolt against British rule, it adopted a Declaration of Independence, which states the fundamental principle of a democracy, that there is a difference between the country, the people, on one side, and the government on the other side. The government is an artificial creation, established by the people to defend everyone's equal right to life, liberty, and the pursuit of happiness. And when the government does not fulfill that obligation, it is the right of the people, in the words of the Declaration of Independence, to "alter or abolish" the government.

In other words, when government acts against life, liberty, the pursuit of happiness, disobedience to government is a necessary principle of democracy. If we care about democracy, we must remind young people of that principle, especially when they are asked to go to war.

It is a tribute to the natural instincts of people, to preserve life, to care for other people, that governments must use all the powers at their command—bribery, coercion, propaganda—to overcome those natural instincts and persuade a nation that it must go to war.

When the United States government decided, in 1917, to join the slaughter that was taking place in Europe, it did not find a population eager for war. Indeed, Woodrow Wilson, running for president in 1916, promised that the United States would remain neutral in the war, saying: "There is such a thing as a nation being too proud to fight."

But the economic ties with England, the huge loans of American bankers to England which would be jeopardized by defeat in war, pushed Wilson after he was elected to ask Congress to declare war on Germany.

The American people did not rush to support the war. A million men were needed, but in the first six weeks after the declaration of war by Congress only seventy-three thousand volunteered. And so the government turned to coercion. It instituted conscription, and now young men would be compelled, by the threat of imprisonment, to join the military.

But coercion would not be effective if the nation could not be convinced that this was a just war, a war, as President Wilson said, "to end all wars," a war "to make the world safe for democracy." And so the government launched the most massive propaganda campaign in history to persuade the American people that the war in Europe was worth fighting, even if it meant sacrificing the lives of their sons, their brothers, their husbands. A Committee on Public Information was established, which sponsored seventy-five thousand speakers who roamed the country, giving 750,000 speeches in five thousand American cities and towns.

Opposition to the war was widespread. The Socialist Party, which at that time was a major force in American life, immediately called the declaration of war "a crime against the people of the United States." There were antiwar rallies all over the country and acts of resistance against the draft. In New York City, of the first hundred men drafted for military service, ninety claimed exemption. In Florida, two Negro farmhands went into the woods with a shotgun and mutilated themselves to avoid the draft. Hundreds of thousands of men evaded the draft.

The government used all its powers to suppress opposition. It passed an Espionage Act which made it a crime to discourage enlistment in the armed forces. Two thousand people were prosecuted under this act, and a thousand sent to prison, including the leader of the Socialist Party, Eugene Debs.

But when the war ended in 1918, the horror of it all slowly came into the consciousness of people all over the world. Ten million men had died on the battlefields of Europe. In one battle early in the war, there were 500,000 casualties on each side. In the first three months of the war, almost the entire original British army was wiped out. Battles were fought over a few hundred yards of earth, leaving the earth strewn with corpses.

After the war, with twenty million wounded, with the war veterans visible everywhere, shell-shocked, without arms or legs, blinded, the full picture of the war began to be known. A literature of disillusionment appeared. Erich Maria Remarque wrote that while men by the thousands were being blown apart by machine guns and shells, the official dispatches were telling the German people back home, "All quiet on the Western Front." The bitter war poems of Wilfred Owen, who fought and died in the British army, were published. Ernest Hemingway wrote *A Farewell to Arms.*

The idea of a just war, a good war, a war for democracy, for liberty, a war to end all wars, seemed, in 1918 to be thoroughly discredited. War had been revealed in all its ugliness, and no one could point to any good that had come out of the sacrifice of all those human beings.

All over the world, more and more people recognized that the Great War of 1914–18, which had pretended to be a war against the tyranny of the German Kaiser, a war, as Wilson had put it "to make the world safe for democracy," had in reality been a struggle among imperial powers, at the cost of millions of young lives. Indeed, the general revulsion against war was great enough to cause sixty-two nations to sign the Kellogg-Briand Pact, which declared that war could not be accepted as "an instrument of national policy."

But already fascism was on the march in Europe, The first sign of its aggressiveness toward other countries came with the Italian bombardment and conquest of Ethiopia in 1935. Hitler was now in power in Germany, and soon he had taken over Austria. Hitler and Mussolini together enabled Franco to take power in Spain; then the Nazis marched into Czechoslovakia in 1938, invaded Poland in September 1939, and World War II had begun.

Now the idea of the just war, the good war, received its most powerful support.

What could be more justifiable than a war against fascism, which was ruthlessly crushing dissent at home, and taking over other countries, while proclaiming theories of racial supremacy and promoting a spirit of nationalist arrogance? When Japan, which was committing atrocities in China, allied itself to Italy and Germany and then attacked the US fleet at Pearl Harbor, it seemed to be clear—it was the democratic countries against the fascist countries.

Let me tell you a little about myself, because I grew up in the 1930s, and I want to tell you how my own thinking about war changed over the years. As a young boy growing up in the United States, I read adventure novels about the First World War which presented it as a story of military heroism and comradeship. It was war clean and glorious, without death or suffering.

That romantic view of war was totally extinguished when, at the age of eighteen, I read a book by a Hollywood screenwriter named Dalton Trumbo. In later years he would be imprisoned for refusing to talk to a Congressional committee about his political affiliations. Trumbo's book was called *Johnny Got His Gun*. Written some years after the First World War, it is, perhaps, the most disturbing antiwar novel ever written.

Here was war in its ultimate horror. On one of the battlefields of the First World War they had found a slab of flesh in an American uniform, with no legs, no arms, no face, blind, deaf, unable to speak, but still alive, the heart still beating, the brain still functioning, able to think about his past, ponder his present condition, and wonder if he will ever be able to communicate with the world outside. For him, the oratory of the politicians who sent him off to war—the language of freedom, democracy, and patriotism—is now seen as the ultimate hypocrisy.

He is a mute, thinking torso on a hospital bed, but he finds a way to communicate with a kindly nurse, and when a visiting delegation of military officials comes by to pin a medal on his body, he taps out a message. He says: "Take me into the workplaces, into the schools, show me to the little children and to the college students, let them see what war is like. Take me wherever there are parliaments and diets and congresses and chambers of statesmen. I want to be there when they talk about honor and justice and making the world safe for democracy. . . . But . . . before they give the order for all the little guys to start killing each other let the main guy rap his gavel on my case and point down at me and say here gentlemen is the only issue before this house and that is are you for this thing here or are you against it."

That novel, *Johnny Got His Gun*, had a shattering effect on me when I read it. It left me with a bone-deep hatred of war. This was reinforced by a class consciousness which came from my growing up in a poor working-class family. I agreed with the judgment of the Roman biographer

Plutarch, who said, "The poor go to war to fight and die for the delights, riches, and superfluities of others." I agreed with the Socialist leader Eugene Debs, who told a crowd of Americans in 1917: "Wars throughout history have been waged for conquest and plunder. . . . The master class has always declared the wars; the subject class has always fought the battles."

And yet in early 1943, at the age of twenty, I volunteered for the Army Air Force.

Bombing raids were going on every day and night over Europe. I wanted to make my contribution to the defeat of fascism. Yes, I had learned to hate war, but this war, I thought, was not for profit or empire, it was a people's war, a war against the unspeakable brutality of fascism.

I had been reading about Italian fascism in a book about Mussolini, by journalist George Seldes, called *Sawdust Caesar*. I was inspired by his account of the Socialist Matteotti, who stood in the Italian Chamber of Deputies to denounce the establishment of a dictatorship. The black-shirted thugs of Mussolini's party picked up Matteotti outside his home one morning and shot him to death. That was fascism.

Mussolini's Italy, deciding to restore the glory of the old Roman Empire, invaded the East African country of Ethiopia, a pitifully poor country. Its people, armed with spears and muskets, tried to fight off an Italian army equipped with the most modern weapons and with an air force that, unopposed, dropped bombs on Ethiopians towns ad villages. It was a slaughter. The American black poet Langston Hughes wrote, in bitterness: "The little fox is still—The dogs of war have made their kill."

I was thirteen when this happened and was only vaguely aware of headlines: "Italian Planes Bomb Addis Ababa." But I later read about this and about the rise of Hitler, the attacks on the Jews, the beatings and murders of opponents, the shrill oratory of the little man with the mustache, the monster rallies of hysterical Germans shouting "Heil Hitler!"

I became part of a crew on a B-17, a heavy bomber that flew out of England over the Continent. I dropped bombs on Berlin, on other cities in Germany, Hungary, Czechoslovakia, and even on a small town on the Atlantic coast of France. I never questioned anything I did. Fascism had to be resisted and defeated. I flew the last bombing missions of the war, received my Air Medal and my battle stars, and was quietly proud of my participation in the great war to defeat fascism. I had no doubts. This was a just war.

And yet when I packed up my things at the end of the war and put my old navigation logs and snapshots and other mementos in a folder, I marked that folder, almost without thinking, "Never Again."

I'm still not sure why I did that, but I suppose I was beginning unconsciously to do what I would later do consciously: to question the motives, the conduct, and the consequences of that crusade against fascism. It was not that my abhorrence of fascism was in any way diminished. But that clear certainty of moral rightness that propelled me into the air force as an enthusiastic bombardier was now clouded over by many thoughts.

Perhaps the doubts started in the midst of my bombing missions in my conversations with a gunner on another crew. To my astonishment he spoke of the war as an "imperialist war," fought on both sides for national power. Britain and the United States were opposing fascism only because it threatened their own control over resources and people.

Yes, Hitler was a maniacal dictator and invader of other countries. But what of the British Empire and its long history of wars against native peoples to subdue them for the profit and glory of the empire? And the Soviet Union—was it not also a brutal dictatorship, concerned not with the working classes of the world but with its own national power? And what of my own country, with its imperial ambitions in Latin America and Asia? The United States had entered the war not when the Japanese were committing atrocities against China but only when Japan attacked Pearl Harbor in Hawaii, a colony of the United States.

These were troubling questions, but I continued to fly my bombing missions. Ironically, my radical friend, who called it an imperialist war, was killed in a mission over Germany not long after our conversation.

When the war in Europe ended, my crew flew back to the United States in the same plane we were in for our bombing missions. We were given a thirty-day leave and then were supposed to go to the Pacific to fly bombing missions against the Japanese. My wife and I had been married before I went overseas. We decided to spend some time in the countryside before I had to go to the Pacific. On the way to the bus station we passed a news stand. It was August 7, 1945. There was a huge headline: "Atomic Bomb Dropped on Hiroshima, City Destroyed." I had no idea what an atomic bomb was, but I remember my feeling at the time, a sense of relief: the war would be over soon, I would not have to go to the Pacific.

Shortly after the war ended, something important happened to cause me to think differently about Hiroshima and also to rethink my belief that we had been engaged in a "just war." I read the report of a journalist, John Hersey, who went into Hiroshima shortly after the bombing and talked to survivors. You can imagine what those survivors looked like—some without arms, others without legs, others blinded, or with their skin so burned that you could not look at them. I read their stories, and for the first time I realized the human consequences of bombing.

For the first time it came to me that I had no idea what I was doing to human beings when I was dropping bombs on cities in Europe. When you drop bombs from six miles (perhaps eight kilometers) in the sky, you do not see what is happening down below. You do not hear screams or see blood. You do not see children torn apart in the explosions of your bombs. I began to understand how in times of war atrocities are committed by ordinary people, who do not see their victims up close as human beings, who only see them as "the enemy," though they may be five years old.

I thought now about a bombing raid I had flown just weeks before the end of the war. Near a little town on the Atlantic coast of France, called Royan, there was an encampment of German soldiers. They were not doing anything, just waiting for the war to end. Our crew and a thousand other crews were ordered to drop bombs on the area of Royan, and were told we would be using a new type of bomb called jellied gasoline. It was napalm. Several thousand people were killed, German soldiers, French civilians, but flying at high altitude I saw no human beings, no children burned by napalm. The town of Royan was destroyed.

I did not think about that until I read later about the victims of Hiroshima and Nagasaki. I visited Royan twenty years after the war, did some research, and realized that people had died because someone wanted more medals, and someone on high wanted to test what napalm would do to human flesh.

I then began to think about the Allied bombing of civilian populations all through the war. We had been horrified when the Italians bombed Addis Ababa, when the Germans bombed Coventry and London and Rotterdam. But when the Allied leaders met at Casablanca in early 1943, they agreed on massive air attacks to undermine the morale of the German people. Winston Churchill and his advisers, with the knowledge of the American high command, decided that bombing the working-class districts of Germany would accomplish that.

And so the saturation bombing began, of Frankfurt, Cologne, Hamburg, killing tens of thousands in each city, in February 1945. It was terror bombing. The German city of Dresden was attacked in one day and one night of bombing by British and American planes, and when the intense heat generated by the bombs created a vacuum, a gigantic fire storm swept the city, which was full of refugees at the time. Perhaps fifty thousand or a hundred thousand people were killed. No one knows exactly how many.

I studied the circumstances of the bombing of Hiroshima and Nagasaki and concluded, as did the most serious scholars of those incidents, that all the excuses given for those horrors were false. Those bombings were not necessary to bring the war to an end, because the Japanese were on the verge of surrender. One motivation for them was political—they were the first acts of the Cold War between the United States and the Soviet Union, with several hundred thousand innocent Japanese people as guinea pigs. Even before the atomic bombing, in the spring of 1945, there was a night attack on Tokyo which set the city afire. There was no pretense of precision bombing, and perhaps a hundred thousand men, women, children died.

I gradually came to certain conclusions about war, any war, even a so-called good war, a "just war" to defeat fascism. I decided that war corrupts everyone who engages in it, that it poisons the minds and souls of people on all sides. I realized there was a process by which I and others had become unthinking killers of innocent people. A decision is made at the start of a war that your side is good and the other side is bad, and once you make that decision you don't have to think anymore; anything you do, no matter how horrible, is acceptable.

I also realized that the idea of just war is based on several logical fallacies. One of them is that if the other side is evil—as fascism certainly was—then it means that your side must be good. Another fallacy involves a jump in logic which happens unconsciously, but which should be examined. The jump is this: that a cause may indeed be just—a country has been invaded, a tyrant is in power, something wrong has taken place—but then the reality of a just *cause* blends almost imperceptibly into the idea of a just *war*. In other words, a cause may be just, an injustice may have taken place, but that doesn't mean that the use of war to remedy that injustice is itself just. It is time to consider an idea which is not part of conventional thinking about international relations—that if there are injustices in the world, whatever they are, we must search for a way to remedy them without war.

We must recognize something else. That in going to war against a nation which is ruled by a tyrant, the people you kill are the victims of the tyrant. Gino Strada points out in his book that as wars have developed in the twentieth century, the ratio of civilian deaths to military deaths has changed radically. In the First World War, there were ten times as many deaths of soldiers as civilians. By the time of the Second World War, 65 percent of the dead were civilians.

And when we come to our time, the wars in Vietnam, Afghanistan, Iraq, 90 percent of the victims are civilians. In Afghanistan, Dr. Strada, studying four thousand patients who were operated on, found that 93 percent were civilians, and 34 percent were children less than fourteen years of age. In the other war zones he has been in, he found it was no different.

War, we must realize, is the massive and indiscriminate killing of human beings. War is always fundamentally a war against children. And therefore, whatever just cause is presented to us, whether true or invented, whatever words are thrown at us about fighting for liberty or democracy or against tyranny, we must reject war as a solution. In 1932, Albert Einstein was in Geneva, where delegates from sixty nations had gathered to draw up rules for the conduct of war. Einstein was horrified. He did something he had never done, called a press conference, and said the gathering was mistaken. War, he said, cannot be humanized. It can only be abolished.

The idea of a just war begins to disintegrate when you extend your time frame beyond the immediate consequences of the war—which may seem a great victory for humanity over evil—and look at the long-term consequences. In the Second World War, which is the model for the idea of a just war, there was great joy over the defeat of Germany, Italy, Japan. I remember vividly May 8, 1945, the day called V-E Day, Victory in Europe, when our air crew drove to the town of Norwich in England, and the city, which had been dark for five years in fear of air raids, was ablaze with light and everyone was out in the street, singing and shouting for joy.

Yes, we were right to celebrate. Hitler was dead, the Japanese military machine was destroyed, Mussolini was hanging in a town square. But, looking at the world after the war, was fascism really defeated? The elements of fascism—totalitarianism, racism—were still alive all over the world. Was militarism defeated? No, there were now two superpowers, armed with thousands of nuclear weapons, which if used, would make Hitler's holocaust look insignificant. And after fifty million died in World War II, was this the end of war? No, wars continued over the next decades, and tens of millions of people died in these wars.

When I was discharged from the air force, I received a letter from General George Marshall, commander of all the armed forces, congratulating me and the sixteen million other Americans who had served in the military and telling me it would now be a different world. But as the years went it became more and more clear that it was not a different world. I came to realize that war, even a victorious war over an evil enemy, as in the war against fascism, is a quick fix, like a drug, which gives you a rush of euphoria, but when it wears away you are back in the depths and you must have another fix, another war. Yes, war is an addiction which we must decide to break, for the sake of the children of the world.

I want to point to a characteristic which is true of all wars, even so-called just wars, like the Second World War, or humanitarian wars, as some people described the bombing campaign in 1999 in Kosovo and Yugoslavia. We need to think about the moral equation of means and ends. Both Catholic theologians and moral philosophers talk about "proportionality." They argue that if the end, the goal, is important enough, then it is morally acceptable to use war as a means of achieving that end. But I believe we have reached the point in human history where the technology of war has become so horrendous—the cluster bombs, the napalm, the land mines—that no conceivable end can justify their use. Furthermore, when you go to war, there is certainty about the awfulness of the means but always uncertainty about what will be the result, what will be the end.

I have spent some time talking about World War II because it is the classic example of the just war, the good war, the humanitarian war. I insist on talking about it also because its immoral elements have not been examined. And if, on examination, we find disturbing questions about this best of wars, this most humanitarian of wars, then what can we say to justify any other war? There was a moral core to the Second World War, which makes the issue of a just war complicated. But where is the moral core in any of the wars fought in the second half of [the twentieth] century? They have shed the blood of millions of human beings, have mutilated the bodies of old people and children, have driven millions of people out of their homes, have left a hundred million land mines buried around the world, killing more thousands every year.

Examine the wars fought by my government, the United States. In Korea, three million people dead, after ferocious bombing and the use of napalm. In Vietnam, Cambodia and Laos, another three million dead. The idea of just war, discredited by World War I, had been revived by the Second World War. But the experience of the Vietnam War once again gave war a bad name, as more and more Americans realized they had been deceived by the government and decided they could not justify a war that killed fifty-eight thousand Americans and millions of Vietnamese.

After Vietnam, the US government tried desperately to eliminate what was called "the Vietnam syndrome." The word "syndrome" suggests a disease. And the disease was the American people's loss of faith in the government, and the unwillingness of the citizenry to support a war. The United States decided it must make war acceptable once more, and it would do this by fighting wars only against weak opponents, where the wars would end quickly, with few US casualties, and without giving enough time for an antiwar movement to develop. Also, the government decided it must control the public's information more tightly, to be able to persuade the citizens of the necessity for war.

You can see this strategy at work in Ronald Reagan's administration with the ridiculous attack on the tiny island of Grenada, in the Caribbean Sea. You can see it in George Bush Sr.'s invasion of Panama in 1989, which destroyed entire neighborhoods, killed hundreds, perhaps thousands of people. You can see it in the first Gulf War against Iraq in 1991. Where was there even an ounce of justice in these wars? Lies were told to the American public to justify them. But they were soon discredited: Was tiny Grenada a threat to the United States? Did we invade Panama to stop the traffic in drugs? The drug trade is flourishing there more than ever. Did we invade Iraq because George Bush Sr. was heartbroken about the Iraqi invasion of Kuwait? That is hard to believe. Oil seems a much more plausible reason.

In all of these cases, few American casualties, information strictly controlled, and large numbers of Iraqi civilians killed. When General Colin Powell, at the end of the first Iraq war, boasted about the quick victory and only a few hundred US casualties, he was asked about Iraqi casualties and he responded: "That is not a matter I am terribly concerned with."

The new Bush administration came into office under a cloud. Though he received less votes than his opponent, Bush was made president only because a 5-4 vote of the Supreme Court refused to allow a recount of the votes in the state of Florida. He desperately needed to give his presidency some credibility. And he knew that historically, whenever the nation went to war, the people immediately rallied to the support of the president. Add to these motives what was at the heart of US policy in the Middle East ever since the end of World War II—the desire to control the oil resources of that region.

The events of September 11, 2001, the destruction of the Twin Towers in New York and the deaths of three thousand people, gave the Bush administration what it needed, a justification for going to war. Bush announced a "war on terrorism" and immediately ordered the bombing and invasion of Afghanistan. The justification was that Afghanistan was harboring Osama Bin Laden, who was considered responsible for the attacks of 9/11. It was not known exactly where Osama Bin Laden was hiding. But the entire country of Afghanistan was now a target. It was a strange way of thinking. If a criminal is hiding in a neighborhood and you don't know in which house he is hiding, you destroy the whole neighborhood.

What could be more just than a war on terrorism?. The horrors of 9/11 created an atmosphere of fear in the United States. This was magnified by the government and the media into a kind of hysteria which prevented people from realizing that a war on terrorism contains an internal contradiction, because war itself is terrorism. Indeed, war is the extreme form of terrorism. No group of terrorists anywhere in the world can match the capacity for mass murder possessed by nations.

Every day during the bombing of Afghanistan, the *New York Times* showed the photos and biographies of victims of the 9/11 attacks. It was an important thing to do, to see the victims as human beings. But the press did nothing like that for the Afghan people who were dying in the war. The control of information by the government, with the cooperation of the media, allowed the United States to present the war as a just war, a war against terrorism, and thus gain popular support. It was a "short" war, with few US casualties, with the public kept ignorant of the fact that more Afghans had died in the US bombing campaign than were killed in the Twin Towers, that hundreds of thousands had been terrorized, driven from their homes.

The success of the US government in getting public support for the war in Afghanistan encouraged it to do what we now know, from the testimony of officials close to the White House, it wanted to do even before the attacks of 9/11, to invade Iraq.

And so it set out to persuade the public that Iraq was a danger to the world, that it had weapons of mass destruction. The major newspapers and television networks dutifully reported, without criticism, what the government was saying. When Colin Powell appeared before the United Nations and presented a detailed list, which turned out to be completely false, of Iraq's weapons, the *New York Times*, considered the nation's leading liberal newspaper, praised his presentation.

The United Nations refused to go along with the plans for war on Iraq, but the United States prepared for war. On February 15, 2003, something happened that had never happened before in human history: simultaneously, on that one day, ten to fifteen million people all over the world protested against the war. In the United States, hundreds of thousands of people, in towns and cities all over the country, demonstrated against the coming war. The day after that worldwide protest, a *New York Times* reporter wrote: "There are now two superpowers—the United States and world public opinion."

A ferocious bombing of Iraq began—the phrase "shock and awe" was used proudly by the officials of the US government as thousands of innocent Iraqis were dying in the attack and hundreds of thousands fled the cities to become homeless refugees. The US Army entered Baghdad and President Bush proudly proclaimed: "Mission Accomplished." But as we know, the war did not end with the taking of Baghdad, or even with the capture of Saddam Hussein. It is still going on, two years later. The major media have been reluctant to criticize the war and the Bush administration. When Bush earlier this year delivered his inaugural address, the *New York Times* gave it a huge headline: "BUSH, A 2ND INAUGURAL, SAYS SPREAD OF LIBERTY IS THE CALLING OF OUR TIME." The *Times* editorial admired his speech.

Despite this, the truth about the war has been coming through to the American public even in the major media. Every day there is a report of one or two or six US military who were killed in Iraq. And though the

Bush administration, with the cooperation of the press, has not publicized the ten thousand or more Americans who have been wounded in the war—some blinded, some with legs or arms amputated—the information is beginning to come through. Whatever idea there was in the minds of many Americans that this was a "just war" has begun to fall apart.

The American public has been mostly kept ignorant of what this war has done to the Iraqi people—very few know that a prestigious international team of researchers has concluded that anywhere from 25,000 to 100,000 Iraqis have died in this war. Occasionally, a glimpse of the horror comes through even in the media. Two days before Bush's inaugural speech, there was, on an inside page of the *New York Times*, a photo of a little girl, crouching, covered with blood, weeping. The caption read: "An Iraqi girl screamed yesterday after her parents were killed when American soldiers fired on their car when it failed to stop, despite warning shots . . ."

More and more, the lies of the Bush administration have been exposed—the lies about weapons of mass destruction, the lies about Iraq's connection to al-Qaeda, the covering up of the Bush's secret plans, even before 9/11, for the invasion of Iraq. More and more Americans have become aware that Iraq has been invaded not just by soldiers but by American corporations, by Halliburton and Bechtel, who have been awarded billions of dollars in contracts to support the occupation. Americans are much more class conscious than is realized by people in other parts of the world. They understand that our society is dominated by the wealthy classes and that wars bring huge profits to some. During the Vietnam War, one of the most effective posters of the antiwar movement, made by a well-known artist, said simply, chillingly: "War is good for business. Invest your son."

There has been a slow seeping of information to the public, some of it even through the major media, much of it through alternative literature: books, progressive radio programs, documentary films (Michael Moore's preelection film was seen by millions). The Internet has been an important source of information not available in the mainstream media, and also a useful organizing tool, making it possible for groups around the country to communicate with one another instantly.

Let us go back to Einstein, who said, "Wars will stop when men refuse to fight." This is beginning to happen in Iraq. Thousands of soldiers have deserted. Some have spoken out publicly against the war. The Pentagon reports that it has trouble recruiting new soldiers. Families of people in the military—some of them have lost sons or daughters—are criticizing the war. In March, marking two years of war, there were antiwar protests in eight hundred communities across the United States. In one small city, Fayetteville, North Carolina, near an important military base, there was a demonstration of thousands, listening to veterans from Iraq and a mother whose son was killed, all of them calling for an end to the war.

According to the latest public opinion surveys, Bush no longer has majority approval for his policies. Two years ago, only 20 percent of the public disapproved of the war in Iraq. As of last week, 60 percent of those polled said they did not believe in the war.

We have learned from historical experience that people can change their opinions dramatically if they get new information. At the start of the war in Vietnam, 60 percent of the American people supported the war. A few years later, 60 percent opposed the war. The reason for that turnaround in public opinion is that the truth about the war gradually emerged. The numbers of dead and wounded kept growing. And people slowly became aware that atrocities were being committed in Vietnam, that US bombers were destroying peasant villages. Photos appeared of the My Lai Massacre, when US soldiers executed four hundred to five hundred peasants, mostly old people, women, and children, in a small village. There was a photo of a young Vietnamese girl running along a road, her skin burned and shredding, from napalm.

That suggests to us what we must do if we are to rid the world of war, not just this particular war, but war in general. We need, all of us, to become teachers, to spread information. We need to expose the motives of our political leaders, point out their connections to corporate power, show how huge profits are being made out of death and suffering.

We need to teach history, because when you look at the history of wars, you see how war corrupts everyone involved in it, how the so-called good side soon behaves like the bad side, how this has been true from the Peloponnesian Wars all the way to our own time.

And most important, we have to show, in the most graphic way, as Gino Strada has done in his book *Green Parrots*, the effect of war on human beings. And how wars, even when they are over, leave a legacy of death in the form of land mines, and a legacy of mental disturbance in the soldiers who return from war.

We need to point to the reckless waste of the world's wealth in war and militarism, while a billion people in the world are without clean water and a hundred million suffer from AIDS and other deadly illnesses. Dr. Strada reminds us that nine million people die of hunger every year. A fraction of the money spent on war and preparations for war would save the lives of tens of millions of people.

We need to hold out a vision of a different world, in which national borders are erased and we are truly one human family, in which we treat children all over the world as our children, which means we could never engage in war.

The abolition of war is of course an enormous undertaking. But keep in mind that we in the antiwar movement have a powerful ally. Our ally is a truth which even governments addicted to war, profiting from war, must one of these days recognize: that wars are not practical ways of achieving their ends. More and more, in recent history, the most powerful nations find themselves unable to conquer much weaker nations. The United States, with the most deadly military machine in the world, could not win in Korea. It could not win in Vietnam. The Soviet Union, with all its power, was forced finally to withdraw from Afghanistan. And the American victory in Afghanistan has turned out to be a sham, as the warlords are back in power in most of the country.

As for Iraq, we can see what is happening. What looked like a victory in Iraq is turning out to be a disaster, as the insurgency against the US occupation not only continues but grows. There was an embarrassing moment last week when reporters pressed the White House press secretary about Vice President Cheney's recent remark that the insurgency was "in its last throes." Where is the evidence for that? he was asked. He stumbled and stumbled and could not answer the question.

Perhaps it will take a combination of factors to end war. It will become intolerable for the people and impractical for the establishment. And the crucial factor making it impractical will be, as it was for the Soviet Union in Afghanistan and the United States in Vietnam, that the citizens of warmaking nations will no longer tolerate the deaths of their offspring and the theft of their national wealth.

There is still time to make this twenty-first century different from the last century. But we must all play a part.

15

Overcoming Obstacles

University of Colorado at Boulder, November 30, 2006

In 2006, many felt despair over the direction of US and global politics. The "war on terror" had contributed to a widespread sense of powerlessness. But Zinn remained hopeful that people could challenge those in power and open up new possibilities for change.

I'd like to talk about the situation we face today and what are the obstacles to doing something about it. In a certain sense I don't have to tell you what our situation is. Why beleaguer you with those suicidal bits of news, the things that depress your friends and drive them to distraction? We all know the country has been taken over by a group of aliens. They are ruthless. They don't care about human rights, they don't care about freedom of expression. And, yes, I wake up in the morning and I feel I live in an occupied country. Iraq is occupied, we're occupied. These people—you know who I mean, I don't really have to name names—are alien to me.

The human beings who come across the border from Mexico into Arizona and California, those people are not aliens to me. They're human beings who are doing what people have always done all through history—people moving from one part of the globe to another part of the globe to seek a better life. It's ironic that we're building a wall along the southern frontier of California and Arizona to keep Mexican families out of the land that we stole from Mexico in the Mexican War of 1846–48. I haven't heard any Congressman or Senator point that out. What do they read? But I guess it's asking too much of the members of Congress to learn history.

So that's the situation. Our problem is what to do about it. Our problem is that we have a huge number of people in this country who in some way recognize that that's the situation but have not yet created a force necessary to change it.

I want to talk about some of the ideological obstacles in our culture that stand in the way of changing this. I say the obstacles in our culture. The obstacles are not in human nature, they are not in human beings. Human beings naturally don't want war. Human beings naturally don't want people to be treated as subhumans. Human beings don't naturally want to erect walls all over the globe and separate people from one another. These are cultural things; these are things we learn. So I want to talk about some of the things we learn which stand in the way of understanding, which stand in the way of coming together, which stand in the way of bringing about change.

One of the obstacles is the idea of neutrality or objectivity or "I'm this, I'm that. I'm a businessman, I'm a lawyer, I'm a professor, I'm an engineer, I'm a this, I'm a that, and I don't have to take a stand or I shouldn't take a stand on the things that are going on in the world today." If everybody who has a different profession or job doesn't take a stand on the things that are happening, then that leaves it to the people who do take a stand, the people in Washington. My argument is there is no point even trying to be neutral, because you can't. When I say you can't be neutral on a moving train, it means the world is already moving in certain directions. Children are going hungry, wars are taking place. In a situation like that, to be neutral or to try to be neutral, to stand aside, not to take a stand, not to participate, is to collaborate with whatever is going on, to allow that to happen. I never wanted to be a collaborator, and I wanted always to intercede into this moving world and see if I could deflect it by even the slightest of degrees.

We all face that problem. We all go into professions where you're supposed to be professional. And to be professional means that you don't step outside of your profession. If you're an artist, you don't take a stand on political issues. If you're a professor, you don't give your opinions in the classroom. If you're a newspaperman, you pretend to be objective in presenting the news. But, of course, it's all false. You cannot be neutral. If you're a historian and you've been brought up to believe that you're objective as a historian, you're not taking a stand, you're just presenting the facts as they are, you're deceiving yourself, because all the history that's presented in books or in lectures and so on is a history that's selected out of an enormous mass of data. When you make that selection, you've decided what you think is important. That comes out of your point of view. So, one, it's impossible to be so-called objective and neutral. Two, it's not desirable, because we need everybody's energy, we need everybody's intervention in whatever's going on.

There is another obstacle I find to understanding and to action, and it has to do with the notion that we live in a democracy. That could deceive you. Because if you believe we live in a democracy, it gives you a certain confidence that what is going on can't be too bad. A democratic country can't do terrible things. If it does terrible things, it may be just temporary. We're a democratic country, but we may have our little faults, like slavery. But basically this confidence that we're a democratic country allows us to do all sorts of things that are very far from democratic but to rest on this confidence: "Well, we're a democratic country, so it's okay," or, "What's wrong is only a mistake which has been made and which will be corrected very quickly"—just like slavery was corrected, after two hundred years or so.

I came across a book written by a man who was at the Nuremberg Trials after World War II. He was a psychologist. Remember the Nazi leaders who were put on trial at the end of World War II in Nuremberg. And they were in their jail cells while the trial was going on, and this man was given the job of interviewing these Nazi leaders while they were awaiting trial. He took notes on all of these interviews and then wrote a book about it shortly after the war called *Nuremberg Diary*. If you want to look it up, his name was Gustav Gilbert.

He interviewed Hermann Göring. Hermann Göring was second in command to Hitler, head of the Luftwaffe. And I don't know whether he interviewed him in German or English, because actually Göring spoke very good English. A lot of those Nazi leaders were well educated in the sense that No Child Left Behind calls for education; that is, they got high scores on tests. So, yes, they were highly educated, and Göring was. The psychologist asked Göring, "How come the German people were led into this disastrous war for Germany, a war which killed so many Germans and which led to its defeat, a war which made Germany contemptible before the whole world? How were you able to get the German people to go along with this?" These are his notes from what Göring said. "Of course the people don't want war. Why would some poor slob on a farm want to risk his life in a war? But, after all, it is the leaders of the country who determine the policy. The people can always be brought to the bidding of the leaders. All you have to do is tell them they are being attacked and denounce the pacifists for lack of patriotism and exposing the country to danger. It works the same way in any country."

It was that last sentence that interested me. "It works the same way in any country." You mean it works the same way in a democratic country as in a totalitarian country? You mean when it comes to preparing the citizens for war, it works the same way in a country like ours as in a country like Germany or any kind of fascist country? Then what happens to the notion of democracy being so different or the notion of our being a democracy? It makes you ask the question, can we really consider ourselves a democracy if on that very existential level of life and death and war and peace we resemble the Nazis? That's a sobering, sobering thought.

No, it doesn't lead you to think we are just like the Nazis. No, we are different. But we're not that different, to put it another way. It isn't simply that you're either a democratic country or a totalitarian country. There is a range, there is a spectrum. And we are not at the democratic end of the spectrum. We're somewhere in between. We ought to recognize that. We have a ways to go before we can consider ourselves a democracy. So I think it's important to have that kind of self-examination, that awareness of yourself, that awareness of your limitations, so you won't get too arrogant about who you are and what you're able to do.

So, yes, people can be fooled, just as the American people were fooled at the onset of this war, just as they were fooled at the onset of the so-called war on terrorism right after 9/11. People can be fooled at least for some of the time. You remember Lincoln: "You can fool some of the people all of the time, and all of the people some of the time, but you can't fool all of the people all of the time." That's always a comforting thought. Just wait a little, have patience, work a little.

Why are the people so easily fooled? Don't they have sources of information that can enable them to know really what's going on, enable them to challenge the government, to check up on the government, on what the government is doing? What about the press? What about the media? In a democratic country, in a country that's well informed, the media play the role of gadfly, the media play the role of representing the public. Since they're professionals, it's their professional job to gather information, then we have to depend on them to give us the news and the information and the insight and the background and the criticism that will enable us, the public, to be able to challenge what is happening. That's the way it would work in a democracy, in a country where we had a democratic media. But we don't. We have a media which is controlled by a very small number of very powerful corporations, and basically the same story is given out on the major networks every night. You've all had that experience. You see a story, you turn to the next network, the same story, the next network, same story. Turn it on. There is Bush on television. You quickly turn to another channel. There he is again. You quickly turn to another channel. There he is again. You turn off the TV. He's still there.

After all, the media have not done their job. If they had done their job, they might have brought to the public the memory of Nuremberg. When the United States invaded Iraq, the media might have reminded the public that it is a violation of the UN Charter to attack another country when that country hasn't attacked you. It's a violation of international law, a violation of that basic charter that was drawn up after World War II.

In fact, it is a war crime. That's what the Nazi leaders were accused of: they were accused of war crimes. They were accused of the crime of aggressive war because Italy had waged an aggressive war in Ethiopia, the Germans had waged an aggressive war on virtually every country in Europe. At Nuremberg the leaders were accused of this. The leaders were hanged for waging aggressive war.

The Bush administration has waged aggressive war. I don't believe in capital punishment. And I wouldn't even ask jail terms for Bush administration officials. I would just ask that they be removed from power and then maybe assigned community service. Maybe we'll give George Bush a year working in a homeless shelter so he can find out that not everybody in America lives on a ranch. And then we can assign Dick Cheney to be in the same shelter so he can tell Bush what to do. But at least that way we would recognize that they have committed war crimes. But the press didn't point that out.

You may remember that just before the invasion of Iraq Colin Powell appeared before the UN to lay out before the world all the weapons of mass destruction that Saddam Hussein possessed. And he did. Wow, that was so impressive. How many gallons of this, how many gallons of this. And when he finished, the newspapers the next day were so admiring. Of course, it was all lies. It was probably the greatest single set of falsehoods uttered in one speech before the United Nations in its history. But the American press, which might have asked questions like "Where did you get that information? Who are your intelligence sources?"—no, they didn't ask those questions. Instead, the *New York Times* just was absolutely overcome with admiration for Colin Powell. The *Washington Post* editorial was entitled "Irrefutable," and said, "After Powell's talk, it is hard to imagine how anyone could doubt that Iraq possesses weapons of mass destruction." That's the press we have. It's very important to understand that. We don't have a press that operates the way a press should operate in a democratic country.

Of course we're not a totalitarian country, so we have resources: we have alternative newspapers, we have alternative radio stations. We have *Democracy Now!* We have David Barsamian here in Boulder—*Alternative Radio*. Boulder is one of the world centers of alternative information, really. And I only say this because I'm in Boulder. If I were in Hoboken, I'd say Hoboken. So you can't depend on the press. That's a fundamental problem that we have in knowing what is going on.

And there is no opposition besides the press. That is, you would think in a democratic country you would have an opposition party. We don't have an opposition party. We have a slightly opposition party, we have a whispering opposition party, but we don't have a real opposition party. Congress passed recently a military appropriations bill of $500 billion, the largest military appropriations bill in history. The vote in the Senate was 100 to zero. That's how much opposition we have. There are some Democrats who have taken courageous positions. Barbara Lee of California, a lone voice speaking out against the war. We've had some intrepid people in Congress and the Senate occasionally speaking up, but we don't have a real opposition party.

So if we don't have a press that informs us, we don't have an opposition party to help us, we are left on our own, which actually is a good thing to know. It's a good thing to know we're on our own. It's a good thing to know that you can't depend on people who are not dependable. But if you're on your own, it means you must learn some history, because without history you are lost. Without history, anybody in authority can get up before the microphone and say, "We've got to go into this country for that reason and this reason, for liberty, for democracy, the threat." Anybody can get up before a microphone and tell you anything. And if you have no history, you have no way of checking up on that.

If you have some history—when I say some history, I don't mean the history we get in traditional history. I don't mean the history of the founding fathers. I'm sorry, I know the founding fathers are holy and they're our fathers, and you mustn't say anything. But look at all the books published about the founding fathers and compare that to the books published about the dissenters in American history. Look at the books published, the biographies of presidents: twenty-one volumes on John Adams, his writings, and so on and so forth; and the history in which Andrew Jackson is a hero—Andrew Jackson the slaveowner, the racist, the

Indian killer; in which Theodore Roosevelt is a hero. You look on any list of presidents. They're always drawing up lists. "Who are the greatest presidents?" Who cares? It's interesting: the list itself is a sign of a lack of objectivity, the very fact that you would concentrate on a list of presidents.

On this list of great presidents, Theodore Roosevelt is always near the top. Why? What did he do? He loved nature. He passed a few pieces of legislation in his tenure, like the Meat Inspection Act. You notice how good our meat is these days? He was a hero of the Spanish-American War, rode up San Juan Hill. He's our hero. Theodore Roosevelt was a war lover. Theodore Roosevelt congratulated an American general for committing a massacre in the Philippines in the early part of the twentieth century. Woodrow Wilson, the idealist, sent warships to bombard the Mexican coast in 1914. Why? Because the Mexicans had arrested some American sailors, charged them with drunkenness, which is hard to believe. So we bombard the Mexican coast, under Wilson. Then Wilson sends an occupying army into Haiti in 1915, an occupying army which is going to stay in Haiti until 1934. Haitians resist, they rebel. Thousands of Haitians are killed in the resistance. The following year Wilson sends an occupying army into the Dominican Republic, and they stay there for years and years. So here he is, Wilson the idealist. That's the kind of history we get.

Not very much on the Vietnam War. Interesting. I've discovered this. Maybe you have had a different experience. But in just going around, I find that amazingly little is talked about with regard to the Vietnam War. I was in an honors history class. There were one hundred students there in the room. I said, "How many students here have heard of the Ludlow Massacre—of the My Lai Massacre?" If I had asked about the Ludlow Massacre, forget it. But the My Lai Massacre, which is more recent, a Vietnam War event. Not a single hand was raised. No, not that kind of history.

A history of lies. Lies around World War I. And of course we know, more recently, lies around the Vietnam War, the Gulf of Tonkin. Lies about Panama. "Oh, we're going in to stop the drug trade in Panama." We really have stopped the drug trade in Panama, yes. "We're going into

Grenada because Grenada poses a threat to the United States." It's amazing what people believe if they have no history of governmental lies told in the past. Those lies, of course, continue up to the present day.

Here's another obstacle to our learning, understanding, acting, something that our culture is full of from the time we go to kindergarten. That is the idea that we are the greatest, we are number one, we are the best. In the language of the social scientists, it's called American exceptionalism. We are an exception to all the things that plague other countries. We are the good guys of the world. We are the Boy Scouts of the world. We help other countries across the street. That's what we do. It starts very early. It starts with the pledge of allegiance to the flag and "with liberty and justice for all" and singing "The Star Spangled Banner." Kids, before they even know what those words mean, are uttering and pledging and singing those words and singing "The Star Spangled Banner" or singing "God Bless America." I wondered about that. When you go to a ballgame, "God Bless America." Why us? Why is God just blessing us? Why is God singling us out for blessing? Why isn't he blessing everybody? Do they sing "God Bless the Yankees"? No. God is not a baseball fan. He treats all baseball teams equally. But he doesn't treat all countries equally, because he only blesses America. But this idea of American exceptionalism starts right from the beginning, from the Puritans of New England. We are the "city on a hill," et cetera, et cetera.

You can see it in the statements of our leaders again and again, where a lot of it has to do with God choosing us. In the middle of the nineteenth century, when we were going into Mexico, there was this idea of manifest destiny, that it was the destiny of the US, given to us by providence, that is, really by God, to move across the continent and take possession of the entire continent. Again and again presidents have invoked God. God intended the United States to do this and intended the United States to do that.

Of course, Bush brought this to its peak. With Bush, almost anything he does is approved by God or suggested by God. No, really. This was a report in *Ha'aretz*, an Israeli newspaper, after a Palestinian leader had met with Bush. The Palestinian leader reported that Bush said to him, "God told me to strike al-Qaeda, and I did. And God told me to go into Iraq, and so I did. And now God is asking me to transform the Middle East." Like God is a Mideast expert, you see. Again and again in the speeches of our leaders of the past there is the idea, we represent civilization, we are the best. When Bush gave his inaugural address in January of 2005, he said, "Spreading liberty around the world is the calling of our time." "Spreading liberty around the world is the calling of our time." The next day, *The New York Times*, that bastion of liberalism, called the speech "striking for its idealism." The *Times* had not read its own newspaper. The day before, on the front page of *The New York Times*, there was a photo of a small Iraqi girl who was crouching, bloody. Her parents had been killed in a car which had been blown up by American soldiers just the day before. And now Bush talks about "spreading liberty around the world," and the *Times* congratulates him for it.

This is a very important thing for Americans to understand. We are not different. This empire is not different. There are some American intellectuals who said, "Yes, this is an American empire, but this is different." They say, "This is empire lite, like a beer." Empire lite. No. We're empire heavy. In fact, we're taking the notion of empire and carrying it beyond what the English and the Dutch and the French and the Russians and the others were doing. We're bringing empire to its farthest reaches, every part of the world.

I believe that the part of the American population that is less vulnerable to this claim of "We're the greatest" and "We're the best" is the African Americans. I think Black people are very often in the best position to be skeptical about all the claims of democracy and liberty and spreading liberty around the world. The great African American poet Langston Hughes. Some of you may know his work during the Harlem Renaissance, the 1920s, 1930s, 1940s. Langston Hughes, in the 1930s, even before the US had expanded in the way it has expanded now—by the 1930s, the US had already expanded into the Caribbean, into the Pacific, sent marines into Central America on twenty different occasions—wrote this poem called "Columbia," Columbia representing the United States:

Columbia,
My dear girl,
You really haven't been a virgin so long
It's ludicrous to keep up the pretext.
You're terribly involved in world assignations
And everybody knows it.
You've slept with all the big powers
In military uniforms,
And you've taken the sweet life
Of all the little brown fellows
In loin cloths and cotton trousers.
…
Being one of the world's big vampires,
Why don't you come out and say so,
Like Japan, and England, and France
And all the other nymphomaniacs of power

Another obstacle to understanding and activism: the idea, also deeply embedded in our culture, that we Americans have a common interest and we have a common history. We all fought in the Revolution against England, we all et cetera, et cetera. The founding fathers represent all of us. The Constitution starts off with the words "We the people of the United States," pretending that it was we the people who established the Constitution of the United States and not fifty-five rich white men who got together in Philadelphia to establish the Constitution of the United States. The idea is we're one family, we have the same interests.

This is a very important concept, because if we're one family and we have the same interests, it means the government of the US has our interests at heart. It may make a mistake from time to time, but if it makes a mistake, it's sort of an honest mistake because they really care about us. That's where history comes in, because if you know some history, you will see from the beginning that there was no common interest in this country. The leaders of the country never did have a common interest with the people of the country. This goes back to before the American Revolution, where there was class conflict all through the colonial period before the

Revolution: tenants against landlords, slaves against slaveowners, riots in cities of poor people for bread, and understanding that the authorities were not on their side, that their interests were different.

This is a very important thing to understand. Otherwise you will accept these phrases that are thrown out in our culture to bind us together—national interest, national security, national defense—as if we all have the same notion of national security and national defense.

All through American history there has been this conflict, this difference of interest, represented in the Constitution. Who did the Constitution represent? Sure, I know the Constitution was an advance in many ways over monarchy. Yes, we had three branches of government and, yes, people voted. The voting was very limited, as you know, at that time. They didn't have popular election of the president or of the Senate, and not everybody could vote for the House of Representatives because there were property qualifications in almost every state, and so on. But still, it was certainly more democratic than the autocracies of Europe and tyrannies in other parts of the world. But it was not really a democratic document designed to help everybody, because it was a document designed to please the slaveowners and the merchants.

If you look at the history of legislation in this country, from that point to now, it's class legislation. It's legislation generally that has benefited the upper classes, tax legislation benefiting the upper classes, subsidies and franchises given to big business, huge amounts of free land given to the railroads, subsidies to merchant marines and corporations, armies sent out to stop break up strikes, the government doing the job of the upper classes all through American history.

There are a few breaks in that. The breaks in that come in the 1930s and the 1960s, when you have popular movements, labor struggles, strikes, general strikes. You finally get some legislation under the New Deal. You get social security, unemployment insurance, and under Lyndon Johnson you get Medicare and Medicaid. Finally you got some legislation. But aside from those exceptions, you can see it today in the legislation passed by Congress, you can see it in the results of the tax system that we have, where the wealth flows up and up, into the richest 1 percent of the population. So it's very important for people to understand that our interests and the interests of the government are not the same. If you don't understand that, you will not be prepared.

There are so many things I want to talk about. Next year, maybe. Patriotism. When you start criticizing, when you start talking the way I have been talking, criticizing what the government does and being skeptical, you are accused of being unpatriotic. This is another obstacle in the way of being a sharp and bold and unabashed critic. Oh, is this unpatriotic? Nonsense. Patriotism does not mean supporting the government. Patriotism means supporting the principles for which the government is supposed to stand. Read the Declaration of Independence. That tells you governments are artificial creations. They're set up by the people to ensure certain things, an equal right to life, liberty, and the pursuit of happiness. And according to the Declaration, when governments become destructive of those ends—these are its words—"it is the Right of the People to alter or abolish" the government. The Declaration of Independence is a patriotic document.

Do I want to talk about terrorism? No. You all know about terrorlsm. You know it's a scam. How can you have a war on terrorism? War is terrorism. And war increases terrorism. It should be so clear. 9/11 takes place. Al-Qaeda is somewhere in Afghanistan, Osama bin Laden is somewhere in Afghanistan. We don't know where he is. We'll bomb Afghanistan. It really makes a lot of sense. It's an absolute scam. And remember that governments are capable of terrorism on a much larger scale than the IRA, al-Qaeda, the Palestinian suicide bombers. Governments have enormous resources of military weaponry at their command, and the terrorism that governments engage in far outstrips the terrorism of bands of people. Both are immoral, both are fanatical, but the scale of it is so much greater when governments engage in it.

I want to say something about war. We're going to get out of Iraq one way or the other. We have to. We don't belong there. It's not our country. We're not wanted there. There will be complaining and—I started to use a military phrase, pissing and moaning, but we'll get out. We have to. But the question is, what about beyond Iraq? Are we going to learn from that? Are we going to hold on to that history? Or are we then going to go into another war? Okay, Iraq is put to the side, like Afghanistan was put to the side and "now we'll go into Iraq." We didn't make out in Iraq? We'll make out in Iran, or Syria, or—who knows? Maybe Grenada again. We'll find a place.

This is my hope. Is it possible that we can abolish war? Not just this war or that war. We don't want to have another antiwar movement. We don't want to have an antiwar movement and another antiwar movement. No. We want to abolish war. Is it possible that the people of the world, people of the US, are, despite war after war, getting sick of war and coming to the conclusion that war solves nothing? Coming to the conclusion that I came to when I left the air force after being a bombardier, after dropping bombs on cities in Europe, and then thinking about what I had done and looking around at the world? And this was the best of wars, right? The war against fascism and so on. I was giving war the ultimate test: taking the best of wars and finding it wanting, finding it morally much more complicated than it looked at the beginning, when I said, "We're the good guys, they're the bad guys." We became the bad guys, too. They were committing atrocities, and we bombed Hiroshima and Nagasaki and Dresden and killed 600,000 civilians in Japan, 100,000 of them in one night of firebombing in Tokyo. War poisons everybody, corrupts everybody. I came to the conclusion that no, war cannot be accepted as a way of solving any problem in the world.

So we have to think now about what we're going to do about our resources. I think we have to think globally, that is, not globalization in the sense of capital going across, but a global society, a world society of no borders and no passports and no visas. It's sort of ridiculous when you think of it. In this age, in this century, after all we've gone through, to have the world divided up by all these frontiers and regulations and immigration quotas? It's ridiculous. People should be able to move across the earth. People should be taken care of wherever they go. People whose jobs are displaced should be taken care of. Nobody should suffer as a result of this. But we need to think about the fact that while we don't have a common interest with our governments, we have a common interest with people in other parts of the world.

There were several beautiful months during the Paris Commune of 1871 when democracy ruled. But they needed the support of the peasantry out in the countryside, because they were most of the population. They had just invented the balloon, so they sent a balloon up over the countryside and they dropped messages, leaflets, to the peasants around France. The leaflets had one simple statement: "Our interests are the same." That's the idea that we need to spread all over the world, to people in other countries and people of other races and people in Africa and Asia. Our interests are not the same as the interests of our political leaders. Our interests are the same, and we are going to act that way.

It's important not to become persuaded that you don't have any power. This is one of the great obstacles to people acting, a sense of futility: "They have it all. They're in charge. What can we do? Who are we? What do we have?" It's important to understand. That's when history comes in handy, too. Because you find that these concentrations of power, at certain points they fall apart. Suddenly, surprisingly. And you find that ultimately they're very fragile. And you find that governments that have said "we will never do this" end up doing it. "We will never cut and run." They said this in Vietnam. We cut and ran in Vietnam. In the South, George Wallace, the racist governor of Alabama, spoke to a huge crowd in Alabama: "Segregation now, segregation tomorrow, segregation forever." Enormous applause. Two years later, Blacks in Alabama had in the meantime begun to vote and Wallace was going around trying to get Black people to vote for him. The South said never, and things changed.

And the reason these very apparently invincible constellations of power at the top fall is that ultimately they depend on the obedience of everybody in the population. When people withdraw their obedience, they have no power. Ford Motor Company said, "We will never let anybody organize Ford." General Motors said, "We will never let anybody organize the workers at General Motors." When the workers went out on strike and factories shut down, Ford capitulated and General Motors capitulated. The fruit growers out in California, they're powerful. And there are these farmworkers with nothing. But the farmworkers organized a boycott—many of you remember that—a boycott of grapes, and the boycott caught on around the country. The corporations depend on consumers to buy their products. When these consumers stop buying their products, they're helpless, and then they have to give in. When governments face soldiers who don't want to fight anymore, when they face mutinies in the ranks, when they face desertions, as happened in Vietnam—a huge number of desertions from the war in Vietnam, and veterans coming back and turning against the war, protesting against the war, at a certain point, and I really believe this was decisive for the US getting out of Vietnam—the US decided, we cannot carry on this war with this total loss of morale in the military.

So yes, they depend on our obedience. When we withdraw it, their power disappears. It's important to know that. It's important to know that every little thing we do helps. We don't all have to do heroic things. All we have to do is little things. And at certain points in history, millions of little things come together and change takes place.

I want to end with a poem by Marge Piercy called "the low road." It's from her book *The Moon Is Always Female*.

> What can they do to you?
> Whatever they want.
> They can set you up, they can bust you, they can break your fingers,
> they can burn your brain with electricity,
> blur you with drugs until you can't walk, can't remember,
> they can take your child, wall up your lover.
> They can do anything,
> you can't stop them from doing it.
> How can you stop them?
> Alone, you can fight, you can refuse,
> you can take what revenge you can, but they are all over you.
> But two people can keep each other sane, can give support, conviction,
> love, massage, hope, sex.

Three people are a delegation, a committee, a wedge.
With four you can play bridge and start an organization.
With six you can rent a whole house,
eat pie for dinner with no seconds and hold a fund raising party.
A dozen make a demonstration.
A hundred fill a hall.
A thousand have solidarity and your own newsletter;
ten thousand, power and your own paper;
a hundred thousand, your own media;
ten million, your own country.

It goes on, one at a time,
it starts when you care to act,
it starts when you do it again after they said no,
it starts when you say We and know who you mean,
and each day you mean one more.

Thank you.

16

Civil Disobedience in the Twenty-First Century

University of Colorado at Denver, October 9, 2008

Here Zinn discusses in detail the kinds of civil disobedience we need to successfully challenge the wars fought in our name. He gave this address at the Anatomy of War conference.

I'll talk about war. And when you talk about war, you have to talk about civil disobedience, because the only way you get out of war is by civil disobedience. I say this to those people here who want to get out of war, to think about what you might do next, make your plans for tomorrow.

I don't want to say a lot about the present war in Iraq. The reason I don't want to say a lot about the present war in Iraq, I assume that everybody knows it's a disaster. Everybody knows it was one of the most stupid wars we've ever engaged in—and we've engaged in a number of them. It's a disaster not because we're losing. What if we were winning? What would that mean? People talk about winning and losing. You don't win in wars. You don't win in wars. That's a very important thing to keep in mind. So when I hear McCain talk about "we're going to win, I want us to win in Iraq," and, frankly, when I hear Obama talk about "we don't have to win in Iraq, we have to win in Afghanistan," please, no. We don't want to win.

We don't belong there. Just a very simple moral point before you get into the specifics of exactly what's happening there and what should we do, the sort of basic moral statement: We do not belong in Iraq, we do not belong in Afghanistan. Our troops do not belong in any place in the world where people do not want us and where we are doing harm. It's as simple as that.

I wrote a book early in the Vietnam War, the first couple years of the escalation of the war. I wrote a book called *Vietnam: The Logic of Withdrawal.* Mine was the first book, actually, to call for withdrawal from Vietnam. And there were responses and people said, "We can't withdraw. There will be a bloodbath." So we stayed for five more years. In those five years another thirty-five thousand Americans were killed and another million Vietnamese were killed. And then in the end we withdrew, and there was no bloodbath.

I say this because people scare you into sticking with a terrible situation by telling you, "If you don't stick with a terrible situation, there will be a more terrible situation." It's a very common thing to do. We must bomb Hiroshima and Nagasaki, we must kill several hundred thousand innocent people in Japan, because if we don't, something more terrible will happen. Actually, just from a factual, historical point of view, all those things they said about "Oh, we'll have to invade Japan and we'll save a million lives" were just untrue. The fact is, we did not have to drop the bombs. But nobody knew what would happen if we didn't drop the bombs on Hiroshima and Nagasaki, although the Japanese were very, very close, on the brink of surrender. Nobody knew what would happen. But we knew what would happen when we dropped the bombs on Hiroshima and Nagasaki.

There is a sort of principle involved there, there is a kind of theory you can come out with there. And that is that in war the horror of the means is certain, the outcome is uncertain. So when people tell you, "We must bomb Afghanistan in order to win the war on terror" or "in order to get the terrorists," the truth is, you don't know if you're going to get the terrorists, but in the meantime, with the means you are using—you are bombing Afghanistan, you are invading Afghanistan, you're killing in Afghanistan more people than were killed in the Twin Towers by those terrorists—you're engaging in terrorism. You're engaging in terrorism now on the supposition that you are going to do something useful against terrorism in the future. But in fact the result of bombing and invading Afghanistan is we've created more terrorists, we antagonized more people, we aroused more hostility. And where does terrorism come from? It comes from a great reservoir of hostility that comes out of our foreign policy.

By the way, although this sounds like a dissonant view, it's a view that you will find in the official report of the 9/11 Commission. Nobody will read the report of the 9/11 Commission. Who reads reports, right? Who reads reports that take up hundreds of pages? No. But this is the official report. These are very conservative people. This is Lee Hamilton, these are Congress people. But they're reporting on 9/11 and the causes of 9/11, and in reporting on it they say, "The critical reason for the terrorist acts on 9/11 was opposition to American military presence in the Middle East."

When people at the time said that, when people dared to say at the time of 9/11, "You know, it might be that that terrorist act was caused by the fact that the United States has been doing a lot of meddling in the Middle East, including military meddling, including sending troops and maintaining troops in Saudi Arabia, which happens to be Osama bin Laden's home country," when people said that, "Hey, let's look at what the United States has been doing," the response was saying, "What? You're justifying 9/11?" Of course not. Nobody is going to justify terrorist acts. But when terrorist acts are committed, it behooves an intelligent person not to immediately rush to bomb the first country you can possibly bomb without retaliation. It's no big deal, it's not a very risky thing to bomb Afghanistan. We are generally a no-risk bombing country. We bomb places that cannot retaliate against us. But no, instead of rushing to bomb Afghanistan, not knowing where al-Qaeda was, not knowing where Osama bin Laden was but, by God, we've got to do something, if instead of doing that they had sat down and said, "Hey, maybe we ought to examine the root motives of these terrorists. What's behind it? Let's take a look at that," that might have been an intelligent thing to do. But intelligence is one of the last things you can expect to come out of the White House.

I want to talk not just about the war in Iraq, because the war in Iraq will come to an end at some point, we're going to have to leave at some point. It's interesting, they say there will be civil war when we leave. Well, how do we know if we leave in five years or ten years or fifteen years, there won't be civil war when we leave? And in the meantime, many, many, many more people will die, just as happened in Vietnam, that many, many more people died after we said we wouldn't leave because there will be trouble. One of the important things when you take arguments like that into consideration, when they say, "Oh, we must stay for this reason," one of the things you must take into account is whether the people who tell you this care about the things they tell you they care about. Do they really care about human life? Do they really care about democracy? The people in Washington who talk about "we're going to bring democracy to Iraq," do you think Bush cares about democracy in Iraq? Do you think Cheney cares about democracy in Iraq? It's laughable.

One of the first principles that anybody studying history or studying political science or studying sociology or studying the world around you, one of the first principles you should understand is that the interests of the government are not the same as your interests. It's a very important principle to understand. If you think that the government has the same interests as you, then it seems natural for you to believe the government. They care about the same things you do. What if the government doesn't have the same interests? Is the interest of George Bush the same as the interest of the GI he sends to Iraq? I don't think so. Here's where history comes in. When you study the history of the United States or study the history of any country, you will find that the interests of the government are not the interests of the people. This is true not just in totalitarian states but in so-called democratic states. When you start with that understanding, it will clear up a lot things for you and will make you very wary of the things that you hear that come out of the seats of authority. Then you will understand why governments lie.

Did you know that governments lie? All the time. Not just our government. It's just the nature of governments. Why do they lie? Because they have to lie in order to keep power. If they told the truth, they would be out of power in two weeks. So there is a connection between the difference of interest between the government and the people and the deceptions continually carried on by governments.

Yes, I want to stop and talk about principles and theories and ideas about war and about governments and about people, because I want us to think beyond the war in Iraq. Because what happens when the war in Iraq ends and then they wait ten years or so, until the American people have subsided in their anger against war, and get us into another war? Maybe they won't even wait that long, if they can conjure up another enemy, if they can create another Hitler. Hitler was very useful to us, especially after the war, because then anytime you could find a Hitler somewhere or somebody who we could say was Hitler, boom, we can go to war. Noriega in Panama is Hitler. Go to war. Panama is a big, threatening country. Saddam Hussein is Hitler. Saddam Hussein is a tyrant, but is he Hitler? But Hitler is useful. So we have to think, what happens when they try to get us into the next war? So we have to not just get us out of Iraq, we have to have think about war in general.

For that it helps to know some history. If you don't have history, it's as if you were born yesterday. If you were born yesterday, you're a blank slate, you're an infant in the world. If you don't have any history, then anybody in power can say anything to you and you have no way of checking up on it. Then the president can come up to the microphone and say, "We've got to go to war in order to do something about terrorism," or "We've got to go to war to bring democracy to the Middle East," or "We've got to go to war because someday this little beleaguered, ruined nation may attack us." If you don't know any history, well, you have no cause for being skeptical. If you know some history, if you know how many times governments have lied, if you know the history of American foreign policy, if you know how many times the nation has gotten into war on the basis of deceiving the public and telling them things about how we're doing this to save civilization, how we're doing it for democracy.

Look at the history of the Mexican War. We're going into Mexico. First of all, we were going into Mexico because there was some clash on the border and they fired at us. All these little incidents that presumably are occasions for war. The Gulf of Tonkin incident. They fired at our ships in the Gulf of Tonkin. Where is the Gulf of Tonkin? It must be off the coast of San Francisco. Those Vietnamese must have been firing at our ships off the coast of San Francisco. No. Did Americans know where the Gulf of Tonkin was? "They fired at us." It turns out they were lying about all of that. They were lying about the occasion for starting a war in the Philippines. "Oh, the Filipino soldiers fired at us." What were we doing in the Philippines? It's not New Jersey. "So we're going into Mexico to bring civilization to the Mexicans." No.

That's where the business of interests comes in. The government tells you they're doing this for one thing. No, the government has its own interests. The slaveholders of the 1840s had their interests. They wanted more slave territory. President Polk had his own interest—expanding the nation. People who are leaders of countries always love expansion. It's true of any institution. Institutions love to expand. And, of course, some of the expansions are rather peaceful and other expansions are violent and deadly. Generally, the expansions of nations are violent and deadly, as our expansion.

So we took half of Mexico and therefore got all this beautiful territory in the Southwest. Why do we have all these Spanish names around? Why is California full of Santa Cruzes and Santa this's and Santa that's? That's Mexican territory, which we stole from them in an aggressive war, lying to the American public. And now we have to build a wall along the southern border to keep the Mexicans out of the country that we stole from them.

History. History at the turn of the century. History of the war in Cuba, the great Spanish-American War. Teddy Roosevelt, the Rough Rider. I remember those things. I don't know how much of that they still teach in school. They always taught a lot of nonsense in school, and they probably still teach a lot of nonsense in school. Heroism. Military heroism. Theodore Roosevelt, the Rough Rider. What in the world were we doing in Cuba? What are we still doing in Cuba? What are we always doing in Cuba? They're too close to us, they threaten us. Cuba is dangerous. Actually, we were going into Cuba to save the Cubans from Spain. And it's true. Very often there is a half-truth. Sometimes it's not a total lie, let's grant that. Sometimes it's a half-truth. We're going into Cuba in 1898 to save the Cubans from Spanish tyranny. And it's true. Spain was a tyrannical ruler of Cuba. So we go into Cuba and we free the Cubans from Spain.

But not from us. Spain is gone, we are in. Spain is gone, United Fruit is in. Vanderbilt and the railroads are in. American corporations are in. And from now on Cuba is basically ours. They don't call it a colony, but it acts like a colony. We support every dictator in Cuba. Until one. It's interesting. We loved all those dictators in Cuba but this guy. We loved the dictators who loved us. When you have a dictator who doesn't love us, that's bad. We went into Cuba and killed a number of people.

People died. Our soldiers died. Actually, more of our soldiers died from poisoned beef that was given to the soldiers than died in battle. Did you know that? Thousands of American soldiers died as a result of eating poisoned beef given to them by the meat-packing houses of Chicago. War profiteering, it's always gone on. You make a profit. You don't care what happens to the soldiers.

So we took Cuba. And in the course of it, in the midst of it, we decide we're going to go over and take the Philippines. Cuba is close to us, the Philippines is far away. But it doesn't matter. It's a small world. The Philippines are going to be useful: they're just off the coast of China. It's a nice place to have. So we fight a war, President McKinley said, "to bring civilization and Christianity to the Filipinos." God, he said, told him to take the Philippines. It's getting to be a habit, presidents saying that God told them to do this and God told them to do that. God is a registered member of the Republican Party. After all, we sing "God Bless America." God is on our side. Hey, doesn't God care about other people? Doesn't he care about the other people that we invade? Why does he only care about us?

God told McKinley to take the Philippines and bring civilization and Christianity to them. So we go into the Philippines.

And while the war in Cuba was a short war, three months—one of our diplomats called it a "splendid little war"—the war in the Philippines lasted for years. Hundreds of thousands of Filipinos were killed in that war. Atrocities on our side, the killing of children. That's what happened in the Philippines. It's interesting that in our history books, the Spanish-American War—this is what I learned about it when I was going to school; I don't know if it's still true—and Cuba took a lot of space, the war in the Philippines, very little. But the war in the Philippines was a very long and brutal war, a kind of precursor of the war in Vietnam, with all its massacres and so on. And so on and on and on. And all these recent wars.

And, of course, the war in Vietnam. It's amazing how much people have forgotten about the war in Vietnam. If people really remembered the history of the war in Vietnam, they would never have agreed to go into Iraq. The lies told about Vietnam: we're going to bring democracy to the Vietnamese, we believe in self-determination. It's interesting. You believe in self-determination. In other words, you believe those people should determine their destiny. Therefore, you send a force of 500,000 troops into their country.

Yes, history can put you on guard. Maybe that's why we're not getting a lot of really good, intelligent, and critical history, because the guardians of our culture get nervous when you get critical. And sometimes when you start talking about this history and you talk about the United States as an expansionist power, first we expanded across the continent. All benign, right? We just expanded. It's like a biological thing: you expand. I remember the maps in the schoolroom. Oh, the Louisiana Purchase, Mexican Cession. Nothing about a war. Mexican Cession, Louisiana Purchase. We just bought these territories. What about the violence? What about the fact that in the Louisiana territory there lived hundreds of Indian tribes which we had to expel and annihilate in order to do that? That was our expansion, you see.

If you start talking about that and talking about the Mexican War and about this war and that war and all the wars in which the American people were deceived, people say, "Wow, you're putting down our country." No, we're not putting down our country. We're putting down these rascals who have run our country for too long. That's who we're putting down. People are not making the distinction between country and government. People say, "You're being unpatriotic because you're criticizing the government." Be prepared for that, right?

Unpatriotic? What is patriotism? Does patriotism mean "support your government"? No. That's the definition of patriotism in a totalitarian state. The definition of patriotism in a democracy is Mark Twain's definition of patriotism. He said, "I'll support my government when it does right. I'll support my country all the time." The country and government are not the same.

When you hear a young fellow speaking in the microphone and he's going off to Iraq and the reporter asks him, "Why, young man, are you going? Why have you enlisted?" and he says, "To fight for my country," sorry, the man has been deceived. He's not fighting for his country. If he dies, he's not dying for his country. He's dying for Bush and Cheney. He's dying for those corporations that are making huge sums of money in the war, Blackwater.

So that's a very important distinction, between government and country. If people really read and understood the Declaration of Independence, they would understand that distinction, because the Declaration of Independence says governments are set up by the people to ensure certain rights. The governments are artificial creations; they're not given by God. They're set up by the people to give the people certain rights, to protect the equal right of everybody to life, liberty, and the pursuit of happiness. According to the Declaration of Independence, when governments become destructive of these ends—and these are the words of the Declaration—"it is the right of the people to alter or abolish" the government. The Declaration of Independence is a manifesto for civil disobedience.

That's what civil disobedience is. The laws are made by the government. Some of the laws might be good. But when the law violates basic moral principles or when the law protects somehow the violation of those basic principles, then it is your duty as a citizen, as a person who believes in democracy, to violate that law and to stand up not for the government but for the principles that the government is supposed to stand for. So yes, we have to think about basic principles in connection with war. And we have to think about the relationship between the government and the citizen.

My own attitude toward war came out of two things. It came out of my study of history and my own experience in war. I was in the air force in World War II and I dropped bombs on various cities in Europe: on Germany, on Czechoslovakia, on Hungary, on France. I enlisted because this was the good war, this was the war against fascism. And it's true, you can make out a better case for World War II, although now I don't believe there is such a thing as a good war, a just war. But you can make out a better case for World War II than any other, because there was this terrible evil, fascism, and we must do something about it.

People didn't think, "Is this the only way to do something about it? Is killing 600,000 ordinary people in Germany through our bombing, is killing 100,000 people in one night in Dresden, is killing several hundred thousand people in Hiroshima and Nagasaki, is incarcerating 120,000 Japanese in our country, is engaging in a war that will kill fifty or sixty million people, is this the only possible way to resist fascism?" Or is it that after something has happened—this is an interesting phenomenon—after something has happened a certain way in history, it's very hard to imagine it happening any other way, it's very hard to imagine another scenario. The thing that has happened, if it's happened in a certain way, has a certain look of inevitability, of "this is the only way."

But if we are human beings with ingenuity and imagination, we have to begin thinking of different ways of solving problems. This is the conclusion I came to only after the war, because during the war I was an eager bombardier. During the war I dropped bombs on people and didn't think about it. I was dropping bombs from thirty thousand feet. I didn't see people, I didn't see human beings dying, children, their limbs torn off. I didn't see that. So much of modern war has that aspect. So much of modern war is killing people at a distance. The pilots come back from Iraq and happily say, "Mission accomplished." Did they know who they killed? With even the most sophisticated of bombing devices, do they really know who they killed? They don't. No way.

The technology of war has reached the point, certainly ever since World War I, where war is indiscriminate killing of innocent people and, to a large extent, children. And when war has become that, when war has become the indiscriminate killing of innocent people, then you mustn't engage in it no matter what you're told about democracy and terrorism and this and that, no, because in your reaction to and your support of this, you will be supporting an atrocity, you will be supporting terrorism.

War is terrorism. This is an important thing to keep in mind when you think we're fighting against terrorists. *War* is terrorism. I see Bush as a terrorist. Seriously. Terrorism is the willingness to kill large numbers of people for some presumably good cause. That's what terrorists are about. And governments—and this is a troubling thought—are capable of far larger-scale terrorism than bands of terrorists like al-Qaeda or the IRA or the PLO. Those terrorists can do terrible things, but governments can do much more terrible things.

We need to think about war as something that cannot be acceptable anymore, for any reason. That's a conclusion I came to after the war and after I looked at Hiroshima and Nagasaki and after I looked at missions that I had been on where I had no idea what I was doing. I began to think about certain things, certain ideas and certain principles, and I began to think about "how is it that people get inveigled into war?"

I recently came across this quote—I always claim I have something that I'm going to show you. I'll paraphrase it. We who are great scholars love exact quotations, which doesn't mean much, because they can be taken out of context. But I'll paraphrase it. After World War II, Hermann Göring—you remember Hermann Göring? A good guy. Hitler's second in command. He and other Nazi leaders were in prison in Germany awaiting trial in the Nuremberg war crimes trial. The Allies hired a psychologist (G. M. Gilbert). I guess he was trying to figure out what motivated them, peer into their minds, what made them do these things. You never think of hiring a psychologist to look into your own mind, but look into their minds. And the psychologist who interviewed Göring took notes and then wrote a book, *Nuremberg Diary*, about his interviews. One of the things he asked Göring was, how were the German people led into this war, which was so disastrous for them? And Göring said, "It's simple, really. It's not a problem. People don't really want to go to war, but you tell them that some terrible thing will happen to them if they don't go to war. You tell them that you're fighting against some evil. Just tell it to them enough times and they will believe it and you will go to war."

One of the things that happen in war—this is what I began to think about as I thought about my own trajectory from being a warrior, being a bombardier, to being antiwar—I realized that what happens is that if the other side is evil, which it often is, you assume, then, that your side must be good. It may not be so. The other side might be evil and you might also be evil. Maybe they're a little more evil. But the point is that you're not suddenly blessed with purity because you are fighting against something evil. It may be that the people on your side are really not good. When you think about it, who fought against Hitler? The British Empire, the French Empire, Stalin's Russia, the American Empire. I know I'm calling names, empires, but that's what they were. So you go through this psychological trick—they're bad, therefore we're good—forgetting that war corrupts everybody.

This is one of the conclusions I made. War corrupts everybody who engages in it. It doesn't matter. You go back to the Peloponnesian Wars. There are the Spartans and they're the bad guys, and there are the Athenians and they're the good guys, Athenian democracy and all of that. They get into the Peloponnesian Wars, and soon the Athenians are behaving like the Spartans. That's what happened in World War II. And that's the nature of war.

I want to look at some of the ideas that come out of the experience of war. One of the things to get accustomed to is the idea, these people who run our country are not wiser than we are. There are a lot of people who think—and this is a very obsequious attitude in what is supposed to be a democracy—"Who are we to know those things? Those people up there in the White House, they know what they're doing." No, they don't know what they're doing. We've seen this again and again. But they have experts around them. Yes, they have experts around them. They have experts with PhDs and Phi Beta Kappa keys. Kennedy had them, Johnson had them. They were called the best and the brightest, and they were engaged in the most stupid war that we had waged up to that time. We have tried to exceed it since then. But no, these people up on top are not necessarily smarter than you are.

There is such a thing as common sense. Aside from facts and figures—and maybe these people up there know more facts and figures, at least their facts and figures—there is such a thing as common sense. Like when Bush was telling us to go to war in Iraq five years ago and talked about weapons of mass destruction, and we didn't really know, do they really have weapons? Bush is telling us, Cheney is telling us, Condoleezza Rice is telling us "mushroom cloud," "working on a nuclear weapon." Common sense might have suggested, "What if they do have weapons of mass destruction? What are they going to do with them? You mean Iraq is going to attack the United States?" What do you think? Iraq is surrounded by enemies. What about this nuclear thing that they might be developing in five years? The United States has ten thousand nuclear weapons. So why are we excited? Is it possible that they're just trying to build up fear in us to get us to go to war? You have to be very wary of thinking that these people know a lot, and you have to have some faith, yes, in common sense.

We have to stop wars. We have to stop this war. And we have to get out of the habit of war. It's more than a habit. It's an addiction. You have a problem? Send the troops. You have a problem? Bomb them. We have to get out of that way of thinking. We have to get out of thinking that we must be a military superpower. We must get out of thinking that we must have military bases, as we have, in a hundred countries. Is it possible that having military bases in a hundred countries arouses a lot of antagonism? Is it possible that it provokes terrorism when your soldiers and your sailors are all over the world, occupying this country, occupying that country? Is it possible? How come there are countries that don't worry about terrorism? Could it be because they're not bothering anybody? Could it be that we're bothering too many people in too many countries? Shouldn't we stop thinking we have to be number one? Why should we be number one? Let's be modest. Let's be number twelve. Why do we have to be a military superpower? Why can't we be a humanitarian superpower? Instead of sending planes to bomb, why don't we send planes with food and medicine?

In order to turn things around, you've got to create a social movement. The people in the White House are not going to do it. Even if you change the leadership in the White House, that won't do it. Here again, history comes in handy. Whenever important things had to be done and injustices had to be rectified, that initiative did not come from Washington, it came from social movements. It was the antislavery movement more than Abraham Lincoln that was responsible for the end of slavery. It was the labor movement more than FDR that was responsible for the minimum wage and all of that. So we need a new social movement. We need more protests, we need more acts, we need more citizen involvement, yes, and we need civil disobedience. We need dramatic actions. In Vietnam, acts of civil disobedience were very important. It was very important when these priests and nuns and other people went into draft boards and broke the law and were put on trial for trespassing and breaking and entering. They weren't doing violence to people but they were breaking the law. You mustn't break the law. The president can break the law. A thousand times he can break the law. You cannot break the law. But breaking the law is important because it dramatizes your protest.

That's what happened during the Vietnam War. There were many dramatic acts of civil disobedience which aroused people to think more about the war. And probably the most important acts of civil disobedience were by the soldiers, the soldiers who came back from Vietnam and formed Vietnam Veterans Against the War. They exposed atrocities to the public. And the soldiers who remained in Vietnam and would not go out on patrol or the B52 bomber pilots who at a certain point said, "I'm not going to go over and do any more bombing," unlike McCain, who went over and bombed. I know McCain was a prisoner and he suffered torture, and he deserves credit for enduring torture. But he does not deserve credit for what he did in Vietnam. He was part of the American aggressive force of bombing peasants in Vietnam. That's not heroism. The protests of Vietnam veterans and soldiers were perhaps a crucial, crucial element in getting the United States to realize that it could not continue that war. That kind of civil disobedience is needed today.

Keep in mind, the people who have the power—and very often you're so daunted by the people in government who have that power—have that power only because everybody else obeys. When people stop obeying, their power disappears. When soldiers start disobeying, the power to carry on war disappears. Just as when workers stop obeying, the power of a great corporation disappears. When consumers boycott a product, the manufacturers that make that product are helpless. People have power if they organize, if they act, sometimes within the law and sometimes without the law, in acts of civil disobedience. But people have to know they have that power. It will take that to stop the war and to make our country a different kind of country—a peace-loving country, a country that uses its wealth not for war but for health and education and to take care of people.

In order for that to happen, all of us have to start doing something, anything. Little things. You don't have to do heroic things. There are some people who will do heroic things. Little things. The little things add up. That's how social movements develop. Somebody does something small, somebody else does something small, somebody else does something small. You get a million small acts, and they merge at some points in history into a great force that brings about change.

Thank you.

17

The State of the Union

Waltham, Massachusetts, November 18, 2008

Zinn gave this talk at Back Pages Books a little more than a week after the election of Barack Obama as the nation's first African American president. Though it was a time of euphoria, with many hoping that the new president would put an end to the disastrous policies of the Bush administration, Zinn raised questions that would soon prove prescient.

I was happy with the election. I wanted Obama to win. I am glad he won. It is historic. If nothing else, to break through in this country, to have enough white people to vote for a Black president, shows that we have made some progress in this country. Thirty years ago you would not have had so many whites vote for a Black president. It would not have happened. Having said that, I want to look at something Obama said in the course of his campaign which struck me at the time and still strikes me. At one point he said, "I don't want to just end the war, but I want to end the mindset that got us into war in the first place."

What is the mindset that brought us into Iraq? It is the mindset that has brought us everywhere else in the world. It is the imperial, aggressive mindset. It is the mindset that has made the United States an expansionist imperial power.

The Constitution begins, "We the people of the United States," and if we have a common interest and if the government's interests are the same as ours, then we have good reason to believe the government when it tells us something. If you think that the government's interests and ours are at odds, then you become suspicious of what the government tells you. I would argue that one of the elements of the mindset that gets us into wars is the notion, the very common notion, that the government's interests and ours are the same.

From the very beginning this country has not been a country of common interests. We have been a country riven by class conflict, by racial conflict. It was not *we the people* who created the Constitution of the United States, it was fifty-five rich white men in Philadelphia who did. They did not do it for the benefit of the majority of the people in the colonies, they did it for the benefit of the elite who were going to replace the British elite in running this new independent government. They did it for the benefit of the bondholders, the slaveowners, the merchants, and the land expansionists.

Before the Revolution there were food riots and slave rebellions, servant uprisings and tenant uprisings. From 150 years before the Revolution this country has been filled with these conflicts between rich and poor. During the Revolution, which is presented in schools as unified colonists fighting heroically for independence against England, the country was divided.

There were people in this country who were not going to benefit from the Revolution and they knew it. As the Revolutionary War progressed it became clear that Blacks were not going to gain anything. It was not the Americans who welcomed Blacks into the armed forces and promised them freedom, it was the British. Indians had nothing to gain from the Revolution, and as soon as the English left, the line they had drawn along the western border prohibiting colonists from going westward into Indian territory was obliterated. American colonists were free to move into Indian territory.

Many working people and farmers enlisted, but many others did not. In the South they were very disgruntled, not patriotic, and unenthusiastic about the rebellion. General Washington had to send General Greene to coerce and threaten people in order to get them into the military. During the battles themselves there were mutinies of soldiers against Washington and the officers.

Farmers rebelled because they saw that the Constitution had set up a government to protect against them. The Constitution that was adopted in 1787 came right after Shays' Rebellion in 1786. I have never seen any history course that has marked the juxtaposition of Shays' Rebellion and the Constitution, but the founding fathers meeting in Philadelphia were very worried about the rebellion, and they wanted a strong central government so they could deal with uprisings of all kinds.

A government was set up initially that would benefit a wealthy elite, and the government has fundamentally done that ever since, down to this moment. This notion of a common interest is very dangerous. It drives and seduces people into thinking that the government is being honest with them. That is one element that I would point to that is very important to keep in mind and to overcome if we are truly going to have change in this country.

Another element in this mindset is that the United States is uniquely beneficent in its dealings with the rest of the world—that we are good guys. We do good things. If we send armies into other places it is to bring democracy and liberty. In the academic world the phrase for that idea is "American exceptionalism." The notion that we are not just different, we are better. It does not take much history to explode that idea.

The history of American expansion into other countries is not a history of bringing democracy and liberty. Of course if you give that history and depress people by telling them the things we have done to the Cubans, the people of Latin America, Hawaii, the Philippines, and lately the people in the Middle East, then you are accused of being unpatriotic. Which is another element in the mindset—that patriotism means obedience to government and praise for what the government does.

That certainly was not Mark Twain's definition of patriotism. Mark Twain made a distinction between government and country. Patriotism is support of your country, not your government. Emma Goldman made the same distinction. The Declaration of Independence made that distinction because it made clear that governments are artificial things set up to ensure certain rights; equality, life, liberty, and the pursuit of happiness. When governments become destructive of those rights, it is the right of the people, as the Declaration put it, "to alter or abolish their government." The belief that patriotism means obedience to government is the kind of thing that gets people to support a war.

There is also the idea that our economic system is by and large a good system—that it works, and that the free market, the capitalist system, the market system, is in general a good thing. To believe this does not prepare you for the economic crisis that we are experiencing. It did not prepare people for the 1930s. It does not prepare you for looking at the economic history of the United States, in which the system, while doing huge amounts of good for the rich people on top and for corporations, has always kept a large number of struggling, impoverished people down. In between the upper crust and the poor down below, there is a stratum called the middle class who are always nervous about what is going to happen to them economically.

The mindset sees free-market capitalism as the best system we can have because the only other thing we can think of as a system is Stalinism. If you have a choice—if you are given a limited multiple-choice test between the free market and Stalinism, it is an easy test. But if your mind is expansive enough to take in the fact that there might be other options besides the free market and Stalinism, then you are considered dangerous.

There is of course simply the idea that military force is necessary in order to solve problems and that war, while bad, is often required. Once you entertain the idea that war is acceptable, you open the way for the president of the United States to get up before you and say, *Well, they just attacked the Twin Towers. Here's a case where war is the thing to do.*

The question is about Obama, who told us to watch out for this mindset. The question arises—has he escaped this mindset? Has he repudiated the elements of this mindset? I do not see that he has. That worries me even though I am happy with his election. Look at the faces on television when he was elected. Think how long it has taken for Black people to get this kind of recognition in the political sphere. But Obama has not escaped the mentality. Obama sees military force as part of his agenda. We are going to take troops out of Iraq, but we are going to send troops to Afghanistan. That is a very serious defect in his thinking. Part of the mentality that I was talking about is that if faced with a terrorist attack, as we were on 9/11, the proper response is to go to war. There are still many people, even people who are opposed to the war in Iraq, like Barack Obama, who consider themselves liberals and critics of the war in Iraq who say, "But Bush was right to go into Afghanistan." They make that distinction.

Paul Krugman, whom I admire as one of the best journalists we have, made the distinction between a bad war in Iraq and a good war in Afghanistan. I cannot understand that. To me it is the same as saying, "You are faced with a terrorist attack. What do you do? You don't know where the attackers are. Well, al-Qaeda. Where might al-Qaeda be? It looks like they're in Afghanistan. Where are they in Afghanistan? We don't know so we'll bomb the country. We'll invade the country. Like a police chief, right? Facing a criminal hiding out in a neighborhood. Don't know where in the neighborhood the criminal is hiding out? Destroy the neighborhood."

It is amazing to me that people would accept this, and still accept it. It is amazing to me that Obama would say, "Let's have more troops in Afghanistan." What is it? What is behind this? Is he worried about being considered unpatriotic? I think so. It is the only reason I can think of, because surely he must know that the war in Afghanistan is a horror, that we have brought nothing good to the people of Afghanistan, we have just continued their long history of misery. Killing thousands of innocent people and driving hundreds of thousands of them from their homes—he must know this.

I think again it is this belief that if you do not go for military force you are weak. If you do not counter terrorism with war, then it shows a lack of spine, a lack of courage. Obama calls for beefing up the military and a larger army. He does not talk about any severe cuts in the military budget, which is now $600 billion a year. Terrorism has to be met with military force. That belief is dangerous.

I was recently doing an interview with a radio station from home, and someone called in and said I had said something about dismantling military bases. She said, "If we dismantle our military bases, how will we defend ourselves against terrorism?" I said, "9/11 took place—an act of terrorism. When 9/11 took place, we had military bases in a hundred countries, we had ten thousand nuclear weapons, we had aircraft carriers and battleships on every sea. We were the most powerfully armed country in the world and 9/11 happened. How in the world are more aircraft carriers and more bases going to protect us against terrorism? This is the time to begin to think about getting at the *roots* of terrorism." I cited to her something from the official 9/11 Commission report. In the report, Lee Hamilton and the other authors say that a very significant cause of the terrorist attack was American occupation in the Middle East. This was buttressed by one of the chief investigators in the report, who said that the 9/11 attack was occasioned by hostility against American foreign policy. If that is so—and here it has been documented by establishment figures—then military force is not going to work. You have to reconsider the foreign policy of the United States. That is what nobody has wanted to do. Certainly the Republicans did not want to reconsider foreign policy, and now the Democrats seem not to want to reconsider our foreign policy. I am worried that Obama will not want to reconsider our foreign policy.

This mindset Obama spoke of exists. How is it going to change? There is a possibility, at least with Obama, of it changing. There was hardly any possibility while Bush and his gang were in power. But with Obama in office there is at least the possibility of change. There might be an aperture there, a sensitivity, in the way there was a sensitivity that FDR had. FDR came into office not planning to do anything drastic or bold about the Depression, but was pushed into action by turmoil in the country. Strikes—general strikes—by tenants organizations and unemployment groups caused agitation that said to him he had better do something.

If we are going to get rid of the mindset that gets us into war and maintains an economic system which is both inefficient and unjust, then it will take all the people who enthusiastically supported, voted for, and campaigned for Obama. It is an unusual collection of people. We have not had such an enthusiastic group of supporters for a presidential candidate in a long time. You did not see this kind of enthusiasm for Kerry, Gore, or Clinton, but this is an unusually energized, large number of people, and a lot of young people. If that same constituency holds Obama to this promise of altering this mindset, to the promise of change; if that same constituency does not simply sit back, watch, and then become disgruntled or cynical; if that constituency organizes, acts, becomes a social movement like the social movement that rose in the 30s or that rose in the 60s, and acted upon Johnson and Kennedy, who were very reluctant to do anything about racial segregation in the South; if that constituency should go into action, then there is the possibility of the change that Obama spoke about.

You might believe we can have domestic reform under Obama even if they do not change foreign policy, but that is the problem. FDR was not saddled with a $600 billion military budget. We are in a situation now where domestic and foreign policy are tied together. You cannot give everybody free health care in this country, create jobs, and clean up the environment so long as you are devoting an enormous amount of your wealth to preparing for or waging a war.

Perhaps that is why Obama's domestic policies are as limited as they have been. Perhaps that is why Obama has not come out for the single-payer health system. The public opinion has been in favor of such a system for years and years. It has been proven efficient in other countries. What stops him?

It would take a lot of money, and where is that money going to come from? If you are going to have a bold domestic program, a New Deal, and even go beyond the New Deal in getting people jobs, health security, and old age security, it is going to cost a lot of money. Where is that money going to come from? It can come from two sources. It can come from this huge sum that we pour into war—the military budget—and it can come from a more progressive tax structure.

Obama has promised he will raise taxes on the rich and lower taxes on everybody else, and that is a good start. He can go even further because the richest 1 percent of the country has gained trillions of dollars over the last decades, not just with Bush but also with Clinton and Carter. They have gained trillions of dollars as the result of a favorable tax structure. Not only should we have a progressive income tax, we should have a wealth tax—a tax on accumulated income. The people at the very top have been the beneficiaries of a very unequal, unfair tax structure.

The fact that we are facing such a severe economic crisis is an opportunity for us to reexamine the way our economic system has functioned. It is an opportunity to ask if corporations have had too much power, if profit motives as the chief factor in organizing the economy need to be reconsidered, and if regulation should take place with a view toward human needs before corporate profit. Crisis can cause you to reexamine the premises on which you have operated for a long time. I do not know if that will happen, but the possibility is there. The other possibility is that we will not take advantage of this moment and we will settle back into cycles in which we go from ordinary misery to extreme misery and back.

I am not a total pacifist. The idea of being absolutist in anything does not strike a chord with me. I think it is conceivable that there are situations where a small show of force, as might have happened in Rwanda in the 1980s, could avert an enormous tragedy. Clinton sent a very small force into Haiti and the military leaders collapsed. What happened after that is another story. I am using those examples to indicate that there might be such possibilities, but not with wars.

If I had to describe the elements of justified use of force, the elements would be small, limited, and focused directly on the evil that you are trying to stop. That is the opposite of what wars are. Wars are indiscriminate killing of huge numbers of innocent people.

Ever since World War I, war has killed more civilians than soldiers. In World War I the ratio was 90 percent military dead, 10 percent civilian dead. In World War II it was more like 50 percent military, 50 percent civilian. In Vietnam it was 70 percent civilians, and by the time we get to these recent wars, Iraq and Afghanistan, it is 80–85 percent civilians. We also talk about innocent civilians as if the soldiers who die in war are guilty. But who are the soldiers? They are also innocents. They are young people who get corralled and coerced and seduced into the military. At this point in our history I cannot see any reason for going to war.

World War II is morally very complicated to me. I volunteered for World War II. I enlisted in the air force and I was a bombardier. I bombed cities in Europe. I was an enthusiastic bombardier. To me it was a good war, a just war.

However, at the end of the war I began to rethink the whole question of World War II, just as there were other people who began to rethink it. It was hard and is still hard to say anything negative about World War II. It is "the good war," it is "the just war." This belief is understandable. What could be more important than getting rid of fascism? What could be a greater evil? However, I came to the conclusion that a certain psychological distortion takes place in the minds of people in a situation where there is a vicious enemy abroad. The psychological trick that is played on us is the notion that they are evil (and the fascists were), therefore we are good.

It is not that simple. They are evil. We are not good. All we have to do is look at our actions and our motives. Were our motives to save the Jews? Were our motives to save the Chinese? No. It took the Japanese to bomb Pearl Harbor, one of our colonies—remember that, Pearl Harbor was one of our *colonies*.

We did not go to war against the Japanese because they were committing massacres in Nanking. What were the motives of these imperial powers—France, England, the United States? What were the motives of Stalin's Russia? Were they motives of democracy and liberty? Was that why they were fighting against fascism? They may have been the motives of the guys like me and of a large part of the population, but the fact that their motives were not motives of peace, freedom, and democracy is shown by the way the war was carried out—with a ruthless abandonment of moral principles. With the bombing of Hiroshima and Nagasaki. And not just Hiroshima and Nagasaki, all over Japan, bombings, bombings, bombings, and the bombings of civilian populations in Germany.

I began to rethink the whole question of World War II. This is not to say we should have simply lain down in the face of fascism. I did not give up the idea that fascism has to be countered and resisted. But I gave up the idea that the way to deal with it is war. I looked at our war and saw how we committed atrocities that almost equaled—not quite, because nothing could equal—the atrocities of the Germans. War brutalizes everybody. And after war the promises of victory are not fulfilled.

When I was discharged from the air force I got a letter from the general of generals—General Marshall. The letter was sent to sixteen million people in the armed forces and said, "We have won the war. It will be a new world." It was not a new world. We just waited a little while to see what kind of a world it was. Not a new world. It did not do away with fascism. It did not do away with racism or militarism. It did not do away with war. War after war after war. Fifty million people dead. It made me think—there are evils in the world. Fascism. Whatever it is. Evils in the world. Fundamentalism. We have to find ways of countering that, resisting that, but without the killing of large numbers of people. Even if you seem to have won, the victory is pyrrhic, the victory is short term. It is a quick fix.

You wait a little while and you see you have not won. You have not changed fundamental things in the world. War and violence are quick and easy. They are like drugs. They give you a high momentarily, and then you settle. In a sense we are all experienced drug addicts. We have all been subject to the addiction of war.

I have contact with some of the people I was involved with in the southern movement. I have contact with Marian Wright Edelman, who is the head of the Children's Defense Fund. I have contact with Bob Moses, who was a very important figure in the movement in Boston. I am in touch with Alice Walker, who was a student of mine. I run into Student Non-Violent Coordinating Committee (SNCC) people from time to time, and I saw several of them a few months ago.

All these people welcomed the result of this election. That does not mean that all of these people uncritically accept Obama. I spoke recently to Vincent Harding. Vincent Harding is not as well known as some of the people who got a lot of publicity in the movement. I knew him in Atlanta. He is a Black man who came to Atlanta as a Mennonite minister and worked with Martin Luther King. He wrote King's 1967 Riverside Church speech in which King came out publicly against the Vietnam War. Vincent Harding is one of the wisest people in the Black movement in this country. He and I very much agree in our complicated feelings about Obama, welcoming his election as a historic moment, but understanding that he is not going to go very far unless he is pushed by a movement that grows up around him. I heard Harding recently and he said something about Obama—instead of seeing himself as a commander-in-chief he should see himself as a community-organizer-in-chief.

The socialist movement of the early twentieth century was the movement of Eugene Debs, Helen Keller, Jack London, Emma Goldman, and Clarence Darrow. There were socialist-elected members of state legislatures all over the country. There were fourteen socialist chapters in Oklahoma. Debs was put in prison for his opposition to World War I, but he ran for president and got a remarkable number of votes. Socialism had quite a good name in this country despite all the obstacles put in its way.

Then the Soviet Union came along, and for a long time it gave socialism a bad name. I do not think that what they had in the Soviet Union was socialism, but that is what people associated with socialism. It was not hard, then, to simply denigrate socialism. The media and the culture collaborated in all this, and they distort or forget the history. There is a good sense of the term. There is a bad sense of the term in the Stalinist model but a good sense of the term in what was represented in this country in the beginning of the twentieth century.

Socialism represented a kind of economic democracy—equalization of wealth and opposition to corporate power. I think that now that the Soviet Union is gone it might be easier to restore the good name of socialism, or at least make people open to the idea. If you have free medical care for everybody, that is socialism? Fine. The military has free medical care. I guess the military has socialized medicine.

I believe there is opportunity for the good name of socialism to be restored. It is the direction in which we have to move, because capitalism has been a failure. The failure is shown not just by these economic crises that come from time to time but by the way people live in between these crises. In between economic crises, in the richest country in the world, one out of five children is born into poverty. There is something wrong with that. Two million people are in prison. There is desperation and poverty. There is something wrong here. A system that has two million people in prison cannot count itself as a successful social system.

How have grassroots movements worked in the past? Or not worked? Obviously they have not worked in any overwhelming way, because we have not significantly changed our foreign policy. Still, we have had successes. The history of those successes should be instructive to us. History shows that when we have had successes, they have ameliorated the worst working conditions of people. They have not ended poverty and distress, but they forced the enactment of the eight-hour day. They have not ended child labor but have ensured regulation in the workplace which did not exist before. There has been some progress.

Progress did not come about through government initiative. There is nothing in the Constitution that says you cannot work sixteen hours a day. There is no economic bill of rights. Change happened because workers organized around the country. The trade union movement in the 1880s had a series of strikes which resulted in the eight-hour day. Labor legislation, the minimum wage, unemployment insurance, and social security in the 1930s were the result of grassroots movements creating commotion in the country. You might say they threatened the political and economic structure with something akin to revolution if government and corporations did not make some concessions. The economic benefits that have accrued to working people show what grassroots movements can do.

And what about the history of Black people in this country? The Emancipation Proclamation and the Thirteenth, the Fourteenth, and the Fifteenth Amendments did not come from the top. Ending slavery was not Lincoln's first priority. The antislavery movement became a massive movement in the country. From the 1830s when it was just a handful of bedraggled and set-upon people, to 1860, the antislavery movement became a movement which put enormous pressure on Lincoln and Congress. Out of that movement came the Emancipation Proclamation and the Thirteenth, the Fourteenth, and the Fifteenth Amendments.

One hundred years later, when it seemed that Blacks had gotten rid of slavery but not racism and segregation, again change did not come from the top. It did not come from Congress or Kennedy or Johnson. Support of racial segregation in the South was a bipartisan affair, and it took the growth of a movement in which hundreds of thousands of people participated and created commotions all over the country.

It is dangerous to look just to Obama. This has been part of our culture, looking to saviors. Saviors will not do it. We cannot depend on the people on top to save us. I hope that people who supported Obama will not simply sit back and wait for him to save us but will understand that they have to do more than this. All of these are limited victories. They are suggestive, because we cannot point to anything that was a total victory. If we could we would not have to talk about doing something now. But history shows that you have to build up. It takes time, and you must not get discouraged. It starts with small actions and small groups. It takes time, sometimes decades, for a movement to build into a force strong enough to change things.

18

Standing Up for Justice in the Age of Obama

Washington, DC, February 2, 2009

Zinn spoke on a number of occasions at the arts and culture venue Busboys and Poets, a combination bookstore, bar, restaurant, and performance space run by the remarkable Iraqi American activist Andy Shallal. So many people showed up for the talk that Busboys and Poets had to set up speakers for those outside who couldn't get in.

It's impossible now to come to Washington, DC, without being cognizant of how different the atmosphere is today—an amazing difference. When Obama's victory was announced, the overwhelming feeling was a sense of relief: Wow, they're gone. The only thing that remains is to put them in jail.

We're making this documentary based on *Voices of a People's History of the United States,* which Anthony Arnove and I put together, and we have these actors who are reading historical documents—a wonderful array of stars with social consciences, who are happy to do this, because they believe in it and are so glad not to be doing the usual Hollywood stuff.

We've had a number of these events around the country, and of course, the point is that it's the people who are important. Not the people up there; it's the people down here. The point is resistance, not acceptance, and disobedience, not obedience.

One of our readers is Viggo Mortensen. We were in the green room, and Viggo Mortensen says, "I'll be back in a minute." And when he comes back, he's taken a magic marker and written three words in big letters on the T-shirt that he's going to wear onstage to read. The three words are "IMPEACH, REMOVE, JAIL." We're not at that point yet, but who knows?

And who could not feel some sense of wonderment that this has happened? How moving it was, watching on television and seeing the faces of people in the crowd when Obama's victory was announced. To see Jesse Jackson weeping, to see the face of John Lewis, to see the faces of people who have been involved in the struggle for a long time.

For me, there was an especially poignant moment when they showed students at Spelman College. That's where I taught for seven years during the era of the civil rights movement. They showed those students at Spelman College, and the looks on their faces and their shouts of joy were overwhelming.

I felt all of that, and I have to say all of that before I discuss Obama soberly. Coming off that high and that amazing intoxication, you get to a point where you say it's a wonderful thing that happened, but now let's see what needs to be done.

And so I'm going to talk about Obama and his administration—what's going on, and what there is for us to do.

Because we are citizens, and Obama is a president. Obama is a politician. You might not like that word. But the fact is he's a politician. He's other things, too—he's a very sensitive and intelligent and articulate and thoughtful and promising person. But he's a politician. We have to remember that. Lincoln was a politician, and Roosevelt was a politician.

If you're a citizen, you have to know the difference between them and you—the difference between what they have to do and what you have to do. Although there are things they *don't* have to do, if you make it clear to them they don't have to do it.

From the beginning, I liked Obama. But the first time it suddenly struck me that he was a politician was early on, when Joe Lieberman was running for the Democratic nomination for his Senate seat in 2006. You may recognize that name with the same amount of distaste that I utter it—Joe Lieberman, who says he's a Democrat, who's really a Republican, and who's actually worse than both.

Lieberman—who, as you know, was and is a war lover—was running for the Democratic nomination, and his opponent was a man named Ned Lemont, who was the peace candidate. And Obama went to Connecticut to support Lieberman against Lemont.

It took me aback. But I say that to indicate that, yes, Obama is a politician. We have to understand that, and understand therefore that we must not be swept away into an unthinking and unquestioning acceptance of what Obama does. He will do some good things—he has already done some good things. He will do some bad things, and has done some bad things already.

Our job is not to give him a blank check or simply be cheerleaders. It was good that we were cheerleaders while he was running for office, but it's not good to be cheerleaders now. Because we want the country to go beyond where it has been in the past. We want to make a clean break from what it has been in the past. We want to go farther than where another liberal Democratic president will carry us.

I had a teacher at Columbia University named Richard Hofstadter, who wrote a book called *The American Political Tradition*, and in it he examined presidents from the founding fathers down through Franklin Roosevelt. There were liberals and conservatives, Republicans and Democrats, and there were differences between them.

But he found that the so-called liberals were not as liberal as people thought—and that the difference between the liberals and the conservatives, and between Republicans and the Democrats, was not a polar difference. There was a common thread that ran all through all American history, and all of the presidents—Republican, Democrat, liberal, conservative—followed this thread.

The thread consisted of two elements: one, nationalism; and two, capitalism. If you study American history, you see that these priorities run through the most liberal presidencies, like Franklin Roosevelt's:

nationalism and capitalism. And Obama is not yet free of that powerful double heritage.

We can see it in the policies that have been enunciated so far, even though he's only been in office a short time. Some people might say, "Well, what do you expect?" And the answer is that we expect a lot. People say, "What, are you a dreamer?" And the answer is, yes, we're dreamers. We want it all. We want a peaceful world. We want an egalitarian world. We don't want war. We don't want capitalism. We want a decent society.

Are we dreaming? We better hold on to that dream—because if we don't, we'll sink closer and closer to this reality that we have, and that we don't want.

Obama basically believes in a capitalist system. And he's not simply another president coming at any period in American history. Obama has become president at a very special time, when the American capitalist system is falling apart. And good! I'm glad it's falling apart, because unless the system falls apart, we're not going to do anything about it. We're not going to fix it.

We have to do something different. We have to have fundamental changes in the economic system. And Obama has been too ready to yield to corporations and the market.

The market system—be wary when you hear about the glories of the market system. The market system is what we've had. "Let the market decide," they say. "The government mustn't give people free health care; let the market decide."

Which is what the market has been doing—and that's why we have forty-five million people without health care. The market has decided that. Leave things to the market, and there are two million people homeless. Leave things to the market, and there are millions and millions of people who can't pay their rent.

You can't leave it to the market. If you're facing an economic crisis like we're facing now, you can't do what was done in the past. You can't pour money into the upper levels of the country and into the corporations and hope that it somehow trickles down. That's a trickle-down theory.

You know about the trickle-down theory? If the money does trickle down, it will be a trickle, and that's all.

What was one of the first things that happened when the Bush administration saw that the economy was in trouble? A $700 billion bailout, and who did we give the $700 billion to? To the financial institutions that ruined us—that caused this crisis.

This was when the presidential campaign was still going on, and it pained me to see McCain and Obama standing there, both of them endorsing this huge bailout to the corporations.

What Obama should have been saying was "Hey, wait a while. The banks aren't poverty stricken. The CEOs aren't poverty stricken. But there are people who are out of work. There are people who can't pay their mortgages. Let's take $700 billion and give it directly to the people who need it. Let's take $1 trillion, let's take $2 trillion. They spend that on bombers.

"Let's take this money and give it directly to the people who need it. Give it to the people who have to pay their mortgages. Nobody should be evicted. Nobody should be left with their belongings out on the street."

And yes, I'm going to keep telling Obama what he should be saying. He may not be listening. But if all of you listen, and then tell other people, and they listen and tell other people, and they listen, and you write your Congressman and tell them this is what you want, that's what happens—the listening reaches more and more and more people.

Obama now wants to spend hundreds of billions of dollars as part of his economic stimulus plan. Which is good—the idea of a stimulus is good. But if you look closely at the plan, too much of it goes through the market, through corporations, through private enterprise.

It gives tax breaks to businesses, hoping that they'll hire people. No—if people need jobs you don't give money to the corporations, hoping that maybe jobs will be created. You give people work immediately.

A lot of people don't know the history of the New Deal of the 1930s. The New Deal didn't go far enough, but it had some very good ideas. And the reason the New Deal came to these good ideas was because there was huge agitation in this country.

There was turmoil in the country, and Roosevelt had to react. So what did they do? They took billions of dollars and said the government was going to hire people. You're out of work? The government has a job for you. No matter what you do, no matter what your line of work, the government has work for you.

As a result of this, lots of very wonderful work was done all over the country. Several million young people were put into the Civilian Conservation Corps. Instead of sending them overseas to fight in a war, they were given money—for subsistence, and enough to send home to their parents—and they went around the country building bridges and roads and playgrounds, and doing remarkable things.

The government created a federal arts program. It wasn't going to wait for the markets to decide that—the government set up a program and hired thousands of unemployed artists: playwrights, actors, musicians, painters, sculptures, writers. What was the result? The result was the production of thousands of pieces of art. Today, around the country, there are thousands of murals painted by people in the WPA program. Plays were put on all over the country at very cheap prices, so that people who had never seen a play in their lives were able to afford to go.

And that's just a glimmer of what could be done. The government has to represent the people's needs. The government can't give the job of representing the people's needs to corporations and to the market, because they don't care about the people's needs. They only care about profit.

In the course of his campaign, Obama said something which struck me as very wise—and when people say something very wise, you have to remember it, because they may not hold to it. You may have to remind them of that wise thing they said.

Obama was talking about the war in Iraq, and he said, "It's not just that we have to get out of the war in Iraq." He said that, and we mustn't forget it. We must keep reminding him: out of Iraq, out of Iraq, out of Iraq—not next year, not two years from now, but out of Iraq.

But he also said, "It's not enough to get out of Iraq; we have to get out of the mindset that led us into Iraq."

What is that mindset—the way of thinking that got us into Iraq? It's the mindset that force will do the trick. Violence, war, bombers—they will bring democracy and liberty to the people.

It's a mindset that has been part of the history of this country from the very beginning: We will bring civilization to the Mexicans in 1846. We will bring freedom to the Cubans in 1898. We will bring democracy to the Filipinos in 1900. You know how successful we've been at bringing democracy all over the world.

The mindset is we'll do it by force of arms. It's a militaristic mindset. And Obama has not gotten out of that militaristic mindset. He talks about sending tens of thousands more troops to Afghanistan.

I took a cab from—do you call it Reagan National Airport?—and I like to get into conversations with cab drivers. And if I think the cab driver has a foreign accent, I will say, "Where are you from?" I asked this cab driver, and he said, "Afghanistan." I told him the truth—that I'd never had a cab driver from Afghanistan before.

I saw that I didn't have a lot more time left, so I had to get to the heart of the matter. I said, "What do you think of President Obama's idea of sending thirty thousand more troops to Afghanistan?" He shook his head. He said, "What they need is food. They need health care. They need houses. That's what they need."

Obama is a very smart guy, and surely he must know some of the history. You don't have to know a lot to know the history of Afghanistan has been decades and decades of Western powers trying to impose their will on Afghanistan by force: the English, the Russians, and now the Americans. What has been the result? The result has been a ruined country.

This is the mindset that sends thirty thousand more troops to Afghanistan, and that says, as Obama has, that we've got to have a bigger military. My heart sank when Obama said that. Why do we need a bigger military? We have an enormous military budget. Has Obama talked about cutting the military budget in half or some fraction? No.

The mindset is that we're a tough nation and we have to remain the most powerful. That's the kind of mindset that leads to having weapons in space. Did you know that we have a program—had one for years—for weapons in space?

We have military bases in a hundred countries. We have fourteen military bases on Okinawa alone. Who wants us there? The governments. They get benefits. But the people don't really want us there. Right now, there are huge demonstrations in Italy against the establishment of a US military base. There have been big demonstrations in South Korea and on Okinawa.

The governments may want us, but the people don't want us there. So what do you do? You have to look for a place where you can have a military base and there are no people to oppose you. And where is that? Space.

They want to have platforms in space, where they can aim their weapons to hit wherever they want. It's pretty scary, unless you believe them when they say, "Oh, we're very precise. We have the latest equipment. We can target anywhere and hit just what we want." This is what they've been saying all along, right?

But then you notice that with all the sophisticated equipment and so on, they can actually decide that they're going to bomb this one house. But there's one problem: They don't know who's in the house. They can hit one car with a rocket from a great distance. Do they know who's in the car? No.

And later—after the bodies have been taken out of the car, after the bodies have been taken out of the house—they tell you, "Well, there were three suspected terrorists in that house, and yes, there's seven other people killed, including two children, but we got the suspected terrorists."

But notice that the word is "suspected." The truth is they don't know who the terrorists are.

We have to get out of that mindset. And Obama has to be pulled by the people who elected him, by the people who are enthusiastic about him. We're the ones who have to tell him, "No, you're on the wrong course with this militaristic idea of using force to accomplish things in the world. We won't accomplish anything that way, and we'll remain a hated country in the world."

Now, Obama talked about having a vision. You have to have a vision, and now I want to tell Obama what his vision should be.

The vision should be of a nation that becomes liked all over the world. I won't even say loved—it'll take a while to build up to that. A nation that is not feared, not disliked, not hated, as too often we are.

A nation that is looked upon as peaceful, because we've withdrawn our military bases from all these countries. Why do we need military bases in other countries? They're not defending us.

The word "defense" is one of the most misused words in the English language. "We bombed this country in self-defense." "The Israelis pulverize and destroy Gaza in self-defense." This isn't defense. This is aggression. And we want a country that doesn't commit aggression anymore.

We don't need to spend the hundreds of billions of dollars on the military budget. Take all the money allocated to military bases and the military budget, and—this is part of the emancipation—you can use that money to give everybody free health care, to guarantee jobs to everybody who doesn't have a job, guaranteed payment of rent to everybody who can't pay their rent, build child care centers.

Let's use the money to help other people around the world, not to send bombers over there. When disasters take place, they need helicopters to transport people out of the floods and out of devastated areas. They need helicopters to save people's lives, and the helicopters are over in the Middle East bombing and strafing people.

What's required is a total turnaround. We want a country that uses its resources, its wealth, and its power to help people, not to hurt them. That's what we need.

This is a vision we have to keep alive. We shouldn't be easily satisfied and say, "Oh well, give him a break." Obama deserves respect. But you don't respect somebody when you give them a blank check. You respect somebody when you treat them as an equal to you, and as somebody you can talk to and somebody who will listen to you.

So what I'm saying is that Obama has a lot of wonderful qualities and seems to be a decent man, but he's a politician. And worse, he's surrounded by politicians. And some of them he picked himself. He picked Hillary Clinton, he picked Lawrence Summers, he picked people who show no sign of breaking from the past.

We are citizens. We must not put ourselves in the position of looking at the world from their eyes and say, "Well, we have to compromise, we have to do this for political reasons." We have to speak our minds.

This is the position that the abolitionists were in before the Civil War, and people said, "Well, you have to look at it from Lincoln's point of view." Lincoln didn't believe that his first priority was abolishing slavery. But the antislavery movement did, and the abolitionists said, "We're not going to put ourselves in Lincoln's position. We are going to express our own position, and we are going to express it so powerfully that Lincoln will have to listen to us."

And the antislavery movement grew large enough and powerful enough that Lincoln had to listen. That's how we got the Emancipation Proclamation and the Thirteenth and Fourteenth and Fifteenth Amendments.

That's been the story of this country. Where progress has been made, wherever any kind of injustice has been overturned, it's been because people acted as citizens and not as politicians. They didn't just moan. They worked, they acted, they organized, they rioted if necessary.

They did all sorts of things to bring their situation to the attention of people in power. And that's what we have to do today.

19

Talk on Democracy and Citizenship in Greece

French Institute, Athens, Greece, May 25, 2009

Zinn's play Marx in Soho *has been translated into many languages and performed in a number of countries, including Cuba, France, and Greece. He gave this address a day before attending a performance of the play in Athens.*

Today I want to talk about the relationship between democracy and citizenship. Of course "democracy" is a Greek word, right? We have a lot of Greek words in the English language, and "democracy" is one of the most important: "rule by the people." In the United States democracy is often defined in the words of Abraham Lincoln. Lincoln said democracy is government of the people, by the people, for the people. In my talk today I want to use the United States as an illustration of this problem, of the tension between democracy and real citizenship. I know American history better than I know Greek history, and I know the situation in the United States better than I know the situation in Greece, so I will do something unusual; I will talk about something I know something about! And I will leave it to you to extrapolate from that, to take what I say about the United States and apply it to your country.

There is no country in the world where the word "democracy" has more often been implied, and more often connected with, than the

United States of America. From the time we go to first grade, the time we start school, we learn that the United States is a democracy. There's no question about that. Nobody ever questioned that the United States is a democracy. Not only are we a democracy, we are the most democratic nation in the world. We are so democratic that we want to spread our democracy everywhere in the world. I suppose anything that has gone unquestioned should be questioned; so it's time for Americans to question whether in fact the United States is a democracy and whether in fact we are really spreading democracy in the world by our actions.

You probably know better than people in the United States about the Truman Doctrine of 1947. It was that time very shortly after World War II when President Truman made a speech in which he said that the United States was going to give military aid to Greece and to Turkey in order to support democracy in these countries. He said, "We are sending this military aid in order to support the democratic government." Well, you know better than most people in the United States whether the money that was used for military aid, which was given to Greece at that time, really furthered the cause of democracy in Greece. That same principle, that same idea, same claim, has been used in all of the interventions that the United States has made in the world since the end of World War II. The justification for these military interventions has been that the United States is going to bring democracy to these places.

When the United States invaded Korea and started the Korean War in 1950, the justification was that we were going to defend democracy in South Korea, although South Korea was a dictatorship. But a little fact like that does not have to be paid attention to. Once the press says, once the government says, once it is heard on television, again and again, that we are in Korea to support democracy, then it doesn't matter what the reality is, a new reality has been created. And the new reality is, we are defending democracy in Korea. And at the end of three years of war in Korea, in which two to three million Koreans died, a war, by the way, not really studied in the United States, where it is just barely known, a forgotten war in which several million people died, how does it end? Does it end with democracy in Korea? It ends as it began: a dictatorship in North Korea, a dictatorship in South Korea. The only difference is that two to three million people have died. And the use of military power to spread democracy continues. Many people remember the war in Vietnam, and there too, the United States sent an army, sent an air force and the navy, to support democracy in Vietnam—although democracy was being run by a dictatorship in Saigon. And the use of armed force to presumably establish democracy in other places has gone on in Southeast Asia and, in fact, all over the world.

I want to say something about Athens. I know I shouldn't talk about Athens; what do I know about Athens? In the United States we know very little about Greece. Greece is off the map. Don't feel bad. It is not only Greece that is off the map. Many places are off the map, because we are a very egocentric country and we decide who's on the map and who's off the map. And Greece, I am sorry to say, happens to be off the map. So we don't learn much about Greece. We do learn something about ancient Greece, because in American education it is accepted that Athens is the cradle of democracy. I went on a bus tour today, the first bus tour I ever took in my life. But I thought, well, yes . . . The bus tour always has a guide who points out the buildings you're passing: the Parthenon, the library, and the museums and so on. The guide not only does that, but also takes advantage of those moments when you are not passing the Parthenon to deliver a little lecture on Greek democracy and to remind you that Athens was the cradle of democracy. We learn this in American education, about Athens being the cradle of democracy. We are not told actually that the word "democracy" as applied to ancient Athens is not exactly true. That in fact, in ancient Athens there was no democracy for the slave population. There was democracy for the citizens, but the citizens were actually a minority of the population. Still, there was representative government and people elected councils, and there were juries, and people were tried by large juries. The fact that there were slaves, the fact that the citizens were a minority, this isn't really taught. Typical of education: you learn certain things, which are ingrained again and again, but there are little footnotes that are left out. For instance there is a scholar named J. D. Kitto who writes about Greece, and I remember him writing about ancient Athens. He says how wonderful Athens was as a democracy; however, there was a little blot on that democracy, which was slavery. And he talked about how in the mines there were ten thousand slaves and how they were worked to death under horrible conditions, and that, he says, was a little blot on Greek democracy. It is interesting because in the United States we often have the same attitude: The United States is a great democracy; we always have been a great democracy. Well, we did have a little blot on our democracy. We did have slavery. We did have four million Black people who were slaves, and this was a little blot on our democracy. Nothing serious. Nothing to get excited about. Nothing to prevent us from continuing to say, "Ah, yes, we are a democracy." And the idea is that if you have certain institutions, if you have representative government, a legislative body, if you have certain procedures in the judicial system, something that in the Anglo-Saxon world is called "due process of law," that is one of the signs of a democratic country.

I guess it was similar in ancient Athens. I know I keep talking about Athens as if I am an expert on Athens; I will leave it to you if I have said anything that is wrong about Athens. I can depend on you to correct me, where else is somebody going to correct me except here? But ancient Athens also had due process of law; they had procedures, which proved that Athens was a democracy. And Socrates was put to death by democratic procedure. He was tried by jury, and the jury decides that he must die. So he must die, it's okay. It will be a democratic death, because he has been found guilty by a jury. This is underlined and studied by American students when they do get beyond the first little introduction of ancient Athens, especially in courses in political philosophy, courses in political science. They will read Plato, and they will read the dialogues of Plato and they will read the *Crito*. They will learn that Socrates refused the offer of escape from prison. And why did he refuse the offer of escape from prison? Because he believed he had an obligation to the state. And he must not violate this obligation and therefore he must go to his death, even though his sentencing was based on something considered a crime, things that he had said. That's interesting, because freedom of speech is presumably one of the prerequisites of democracy, and Socrates, after all, was not an activist; he was not a terrorist, as far as I know, he was not a bomb thrower, he only talked a lot. But he didn't say the right things, so he was sentenced to death, and it's okay because it was due process. And now he is not going to escape, he is not going to violate his due process, because he believes that, as he put it, the state is like a father and mother and you must obey it, whatever it does. If it sends you to war, if it sends you to death, you must obey the state.

Well, that's interesting. In my education in the United States, when I was learning about Plato and Socrates and the dialogue *Crito*, nobody ever questioned this proposition, because Plato was a god in the history of philosophy in the United States and Socrates is a god too. So if Plato says this or Socrates says this (I am not sure that Socrates really said it—we don't have a tape recording of Socrates, we only have Plato's claim that this is what Socrates said, but we'll accept it), there is no questioning of this proposition, that you must obey the state. And what is the result? The result is that certainly in the United States—and I suspect in other countries, too—it goes uncriticized, and it is therefore part of the education of Americans to accept what is a totalitarian principle, not a democratic principle. It's a totalitarian principle that the individual must obey the decisions of the state. It has been done by due process, it has gone through the procedures, and in the United States we are familiar with this. In the United States the most terrible injustices can take place in the courts and innocent people can be sent to prison. Justice can operate differently for rich people and for poor people, Black people and white people, men and women, radicals and conservatives. Justice operates differently for all of these groups, but there are courts, there's a judge, there are juries, there are laws, there is due process. And the result of these procedures is looked upon as democratic. So if you are sentenced to death unjustly you shouldn't complain, because it has been done in a democratic way.

Some of you may remember the trial of Sacco and Vanzetti—not personally, even I don't remember this personally. As old as I am, there are actually things that have happened in history that I don't remember personally. I don't know to what extent you learn about this in Greece. I mean it happened in the United States but even there we don't really teach about the trial of Sacco and Vanzetti. I can tell you very briefly that Sacco and Vanzetti were put on trial in the United States after World War I. They were two Italian immigrants and anarchists, and they were put on trial presumably for a robbery and a murder that took place in Massachusetts and were sentenced to death. It was a ridiculous trial, presided over by a judge with a jury of people who didn't like foreigners, by a judge who didn't like foreigners, a judge who would refer to the defendants as "anarchist bastards," and so they were sentenced to death.

There is a great American journalist, Heywood Broun, who wrote about this. He pointed to the fact that not only did they have due process, not only did they go through all the courts, and all the courts affirmed their death sentence and the Supreme Court wouldn't even consider their case, but when there were complaints, protests, demonstrations all over the United States and all over the world against the impending execution of Sacco and Vanzetti, the governor of Massachusetts, in order to quiet these protests, appointed a special commission of very important citizens to go over all the evidence and make a decision. He appointed the president of Harvard, the president of MIT, and a judge—in other words, typical Americans! They use a phrase sometimes, "a jury of your peers," a jury of people who are in your class. . . . So the president of Harvard, the president of MIT, and a retired judge go over the evidence and come to the conclusion that in the case of Sacco and Vanzetti, yes, justice has been done. And this journalist writing about this case says that well, Sacco and Vanzetti, this poor shoemaker and this fish peddler—that was their work—can take unction to their souls that they are put to death by men in academic gowns and suits. . . . And this has happened again and again since the case of Sacco and Vanzetti and before the case of Sacco and Vanzetti; we have had—in what can only be called political trials—people sentenced to death or given long sentences in prison not really on the basis of what they did but on the basis of who they are. But so long as it is due process, then it is all right.

I quoted Lincoln before, defining democracy as government of the people, by the people, for the people, but Lincoln himself violated this principle, because he did not consider black slaves "people." This is a hard thing to accept, because Lincoln was a compassionate man. He really didn't like slavery. He didn't believe in slavery. But he believed in due process. He believed in the formal arrangements of government, and he believed that you must obey those arrangements; and the formal arrangement in the United States was the Constitution, and according to the Constitution, the United States government, the national government, could not interfere with slavery, even though it was a horror for four million human beings. No, the Constitution did not permit Lincoln to do anything about slavery. As a result, he did not feel that he could act against slavery, because he believed in due process. And this is a notion that is ingrained not only in the United States but also in much of the world, especially much of the world that seems to emulate the United States in what is called a democracy. The idea is that if you just go through the proper procedures, then everything is all right.

And so there is a grand deception that takes place in the United States about democracy, and the deception starts very early. It starts with the American Revolution, with the war for independence against England. It starts with the Declaration of Independence and the Constitution. In fact the Declaration of Independence, which is adopted at the start of the American Revolution, at the start of the war for independence against England, is a remarkable manifesto for democracy, because it says that government is not supreme, government is not to be deified. Government is established by the people for certain ends, and those ends are for everyone to have an equal right to life, liberty, and the pursuit of happiness. And when governments fail to fulfill this obligation, then "it is the right of the people," and these are the words of the Declaration of Independence, "it is the right of the people to alter or to abolish the government."

Well, that's democracy! That's a very good statement of democracy, but that's at the beginning of the Revolution. At the end of the Revolution, when the United States has been victorious in the struggle for independence against England, it adopts a constitution. Fifty-five men gather in Philadelphia. I might say, rich white men gather in Philadelphia. I'm sorry to say that; I'd like to say that a representative group of Americans gathered in Philadelphia, that there were whites and Blacks, men and women, rich people and working people, and Indians, and they established a constitution. But it didn't happen that way. Fifty-five rich white men. And in the Constitution they take that phrase that was in the Declaration of Independence, "life, liberty, and the pursuit of happiness," and they change it a little and now it is "life, liberty, and property." That's the signal about what has happened to democracy, what has happened to the principles of democracy as they were set forth in the Declaration of Independence. The democracy has now been turned over to men of property.

And we see this, as the government is established by the Constitution. It is a government that is set up to protect the interests of—what a surprise—rich white people! As governments set out to protect the interests of property owners, of bond holders, of those who want to expand into the western lands, that's the kind of government that is set up. It is a government that is set up to be a strong government. In American education what you learn is that before the Constitution we had weak governments: that thirteen states had separated themselves from England, but we had a weak national government, and now the Constitution established a strong national government, so we are all supposed to feel very good and proud. But the reason the Constitution has established a strong national government—a government that can raise an army and levy taxes—is because now this government can control rebellion; it can control the rebellions of slaves, the rebellions of farmers. Now the government can protect the Americans who want to move into Indian territory to take the land that the Indians live on. This is what the strong central government was set up for.

In fact you see an immediate reason for this strong central government to be set up: in the year 1786, the year before the Constitution was created, there were rebellions in western Massachusetts and in other states, rebellions of small farmers, many of them veterans of the Revolutionary War. They fought in the Revolutionary War, but of course they are going to suffer the fate of all war veterans. They fight in a war for liberty, for freedom, for democracy, and then they come home after the war and discover that liberty and democracy is not for them. In the year before the Constitution was adopted, small farmers in Massachusetts and other places rebel—thousands and thousands of them. They talk about citizen action. They surround the courthouses where their farms are being taken away from them because they can't pay their taxes—high taxes that are levied on them by the rich who control the state legislatures; they surround the courthouses and they do not allow their homes to be taken away from them.

These rebellions are finally put down by armies that are sent into the rebellious areas by the government, the national government, and by the state governments. But the rebellions put a scare into what we call the founding fathers. We call these fifty-five men who gathered in Philadelphia to frame the Constitution "the founding fathers," which is a very nice phrase. It is like we are all their children and we must, you know, obey our fathers. Well, the founding fathers are frightened by these rebellions, and after the rebellions they write letters back and forth, and I've read some of these letters, secretly of course, and the letters are about these rebellions. One of these letters is addressed to George Washington by one of his officers, and the letter says: "We mustn't allow this to happen, this is wrong; these people think that because they fought in the Revolution, they deserve an equal share of the wealth of this country." So the founding fathers are worried about these rebellions, and they set up a government that is strong enough to deal with and to suppress these rebellions. And you see the result. The government is set up by the Constitution, and it has all the procedures, it has, well, many of the procedures. It has voting, it has representative government, it has a legislative body, it has a president who, well, is not exactly elected by the people, but soon he will be, and we'll have the institutions of democracy and we will have the procedures;

we will have due process, we will add a Bill of Rights to the Constitution, which will talk about free speech and free press and the right to a trial by jury and the right to a lawyer, so that's democracy.

But, of course, that's not the reality of the United States after the Revolution, not the reality of the United States between the years of the Revolution and the present day. Because in that whole history between the years of the Revolution and the signing of the Constitution, that history is not a history of government by and for all the people, as Lincoln said. A woman who was a leader of the farmers' movement in the late nineteenth century in the United States, a leader of what was called the populist movement, said: "What we have now in the United States is a government by Wall Street, for Wall Street, of Wall Street." And, in fact, that has been the case of the legislation we have seen come out of Congress from the time of Alexander Hamilton, secretary of the treasury under Washington, from the very first laws passed by Congress, to the present day. They are laws that favor the wealthy. The tax laws, the subsidies to the corporations, that has been the history of legislation of the government by, for and, yes, of Wall Street.

Even when amendments were added to the Constitution, presumably to grant democracy, they were turned in a different way. In what we call the Bill of Rights, the First Amendment guaranteeing freedom of speech says that Congress shall make no law abridging the freedom of speech; Congress shall make no law interfering with the freedom of speech. A few years after the amendment was passed, Congress makes a law interfering with the freedom of speech, and people are sent to jail for speaking out against the government. Later, after the Civil War, the Constitution is amended, presumably to end slavery. The Thirteenth, Fourteenth, and Fifteenth Amendments are supposed to now give equal rights to Black people. What happened? Did it become reality? No, slaves are freed in a technical sense; they are free but not really free, because they are not given the resources to be free people. So from being slaves they now become tenant farmers and serfs, you might say. Have they been given by the Fourteenth and Fifteenth Amendments the promised equal rights? No, the Fourteenth Amendment is soon interpreted by the Supreme Court—and talk about a government by rich men: the Supreme Court is dominated by wealth and by people who represent wealth. The Supreme Court decides that the Fourteenth Amendment really does not apply to Black people, it applies to corporations and it must be used to defend the rights of corporations. So, yes, the government becomes an instrument of the wealthy, and the laws that are passed, the tax laws that are passed, the tariff laws that are passed, those are laws that favor corporate wealth. That is the history of American legislation!

There are two moments in American history when there is a departure from this history of legislation for the privileged. The reason there are departures in those two moments is that in those times citizens act, citizens rise up, citizens protest. In the 1930s, early 1930s, Franklin D. Roosevelt becomes president of the United States, and when he comes into office he does not plan to make any important changes. But he comes into office in the midst of an economic crisis; he comes in a time when the nation is in turmoil. Just before he comes into office, war veterans of World War I march on Washington; it is called the Bonus Army because they were promised a bonus, they were promised money as a result of serving in World War I. Thousands and thousands of them come to Washington. So Roosevelt is faced, as he comes into office, with strikes all over the country. A general strike in San Francisco ties up the whole city; a general strike in Minneapolis, Minnesota, ties up the whole city; hundreds of thousands of strikers, textile workers in the South go on strike; tenants organize and break the law—they are being evicted from their little tenements, and they gather and move the furniture that has been put out on the street back into the apartment, and they defy the police and the forces of law and order. Unemployed people get organized, and yes, the country is in turmoil. In this situation, Roosevelt and the Congress decide they need to quiet things down. They pass legislation and, for the first time really in the history of legislation in the United States, they pass legislation to benefit the lower classes. They pass unemployment insurance and social security and subsidized housing and a minimum-wage law. That is one of the moments in which citizen action overrides the historic function of government to serve the interests of the rich.

The other moment comes in the 1960s. What happens is citizens' action against racial segregation in the South. At the time I was teaching in the South, I was teaching at a Black women's college in Atlanta, Georgia, and I could watch this movement grow. It started in a very tightly segregated racist society, as Black people began to break the law, sitting in places where they weren't supposed to sit and refusing to move, demonstrating in the streets by the thousands, then by the tens of thousands, going to jail, creating agitation all over the South, which soon reached into the North and started rebellions in the ghettos of the North.

In this atmosphere, the government, finally, after failing to enforce the Fourteenth and Fifteenth Amendments as I pointed out, it now begins to enforce these amendments. When they're faced with this agitation in the country where citizens take action, they then pass laws to give Black people in the South the right to vote and to do away with the segregation laws. And then the energy of this Black movement moves into the movement against the war in Vietnam. There too we have a government that is determined to carry on this war, as I said, to bring democracy to Vietnam; and of course it is not really democracy, it's killing people by the millions. But an antiwar movement grows. It grows and it grows, to the point where the government cannot ignore it: where active civil disobedience takes place, where priests and nuns invade draft boards and destroy government records, and where soldiers refuse to fight and flyers refuse to fly. Toward the end of the Vietnam War young men refuse to serve in the armed forces, and the great antiwar movement develops and there is anarchy. At that point, the United States government decides we cannot carry on this war, and war comes to an end. And the energy of these movements, the Black movement and the movement against the war in Vietnam, becomes part of other movements, the women's movement for women's liberation, for sexual equality, for the gays and lesbians to be treated as human beings, and movements of disabled people, whose rights have not been recognized, as they have now become a force to campaign for legislation to protect them.

So in the '60s we see a breakthrough, a departure from the historic role of government in serving the interests of the privileged and the rich. Of course that period comes to an end; certain victories are won and wars ended, racial segregation and so on, certain consciousness has been raised, but then we're back to the usual thing that we call democracy. And since then—we know that because we're getting closer now to the era in which we live—we go back to the same situation, and not just with Bush, not just with the Republican Party, but also with the Democratic Party. Well, yes, we have due process, we have two parties, and this proves we have democracy, though two parties is only one more than one party! And we know what that situation gives us: it gives us war after war, and it gives us the wealth of the country being funneled more and more into the top richest 1 percent of the population. Yet we still call ourselves a democracy, even though forty-five million people are without health insurance, even though one out of every five children in the United States is born into poverty.

The economic dimension of democracy is something that is omitted from definitions of democracy, and certainly in American education, democracy is sort of a political thing. It's a procedural thing, it has nothing to do with wealth and corporations and poverty. But, of course, behind all of the procedures, behind the Constitution and laws and due process, behind all that, is the class system. As Marx said, "The history of mankind is the history of class struggle." In the United States the word "class" is not really part of our education, but yes, we are a class society, and this factor of wealth and economics lies behind the procedures of all the political institutions that we claim represent a democracy.

I guess the question is, what do we do, and how do we overcome this? We who believe in real democracy, we who believe that wealth should be distributed in a fair and equal way, we who believe in a peaceful world, how are we going to achieve peace, how are we going to achieve justice? We're not going to achieve it by due process, by the procedures, by voting in a new leader, by utilizing all the forms of representative government. We know that. We have the experience of the United States, the leading democracy of the world. We are not going to achieve democracy by using these procedures, certainly not a democracy that applies to people in other parts of the world. Right? Democracy, if it really is to be democracy, shouldn't be circumscribed; it shouldn't be limited by national boundaries. If we want one government of the people, by the people, for the people, it should be for people everywhere, it should be for people outside national boundaries.

These procedures obviously have not led to democracy in the United States and they have not led to democracy abroad, no matter how many armies and navies the United States has sent abroad. Then what is the answer? Is it violence, is it violent revolution, is it armed uprising, is it armed struggle? I would suggest that the history of the use of violence to achieve just *ends* is not really a comfortable history, because violence by its nature is corrupting. Violence, by its nature, poisons the soul of people who engage in it. And then, even if it seems to achieve a certain end, that end becomes in some way twisted. After all the violence that has taken place, presumably you've brought about change, but suddenly those changes disappear and something else happens.

Hannah Arendt, the political philosopher who studied revolutions and violence and studied the Nazis, said there's a cost to be paid when you use violence to achieve your ends. And it is not just the cost that you administer to the victims of your violence, people you bomb, it is not just that cost; the cost is to you, you who engage in that violence. So when you think about it in terms of political philosophy, which talks about *means* and *ends*, and the relationship between *means* and *ends*, then you see where violence fits in. You have to admit, even if you think the *end* is good, even if you think you are doing it for good *ends*, the *means* are horrible. Even generals and war makers say, "Oh, war is terrible, war is hell." The generals say this, they all say this, everybody agrees that war is hell, but it's "for a good cause." So the *means* are unquestionably bad, but the *end*, even if the *end* is proclaimed as a good cause, even if it might actually be a good cause, it is never certain. The *means* are certain—and they are certainly horrible. The *ends*, however good they seem to be, are never certain; they are unpredictable. The result of violence, whether in war or revolution, is unpredictable. This means that we must find ways that are between these two poles. Too often we have been brought up to believe it is just one or the other, either you follow the procedures or you engage in violence, though there's a whole spectrum of possibilities, an infinite number of possibilities, between due process and procedures on the one hand and violence on the other.

When I look at the history of the United States, what I see is that whenever anything good has been accomplished, whenever any injustice has been remedied, it does not come about through the processes of government, it does not come about through voting, through elections, through due process. It has come about only when citizens became aroused. That's how slavery was abolished. Slavery was not abolished because Abraham Lincoln issued the Emancipation Proclamation. Slavery was abolished because the slaves, the ex-slaves, the escaped slaves, and some white abolitionists got together and formed a great movement against slavery. That movement grew from a small group of people into a national movement that committed acts of civil disobedience and violated the law, violated the Fugitive Slave Act, which required the government to return escaped slaves to their masters. People broke into courthouses, broke into police stations; they rescued slaves, and all kinds of acts of civil disobedience took place. Only then did Lincoln act, only then did Congress act, to abolish slavery, to pass constitutional amendments. And we see this all through American history.

The working people of the United States had no protection in due process, no protection in the Constitution. There is nothing in the Constitution that says you cannot work sixteen hours a day, there is nothing in the Constitution that guarantees health care. The Constitution talks about life and liberty. The Constitution doesn't guarantee any of the things that give you life and liberty. There are no economic rights in the Constitution. And so it happens, working people decide they must do it themselves, the procedures won't do it. So in the late nineteenth century they organize, they go on strike all over the country for the eight-hour day. They face the police, and they're beaten and they are killed by the police, and the army is sent out against them, but they continue, they go on strike, and after a series of strikes in the United States the eight-hour day is won. That's how working people have gained whatever justice they have achieved. This has been the history of citizen action in the United States, and this is the only thing that has resulted in the rectification of injustice.

Today we are not seeing the kind of movements that we had in the past, the labor movement of the late nineteenth century, the great agitation of the 1930s, the nationwide movements of protest of the 1960s; we're not seeing this today in the United States. We are seeing signs of such a movement, we are seeing maybe the beginnings of such a movement, but we are still intoxicated with voting and elections and now with the idea that we have a new president and we have gotten rid of this warmonger, this idiot. We now have an intelligent and compassionate and articulate man that we've elected. Well, we'd better look at our history: it is not enough to elect a president, it is not enough to go through the procedures, it is not enough to elect Obama. No, in fact we already see the signs that Obama is not departing in a fundamental way from the history of the United States, which is the privilege of the wealthy, pouring hundreds of billions of dollars into the financial institutions hoping that some of it will trickle down into the hands of poor people. Obama, following the tradition of militarism in the Democratic Party, of intervention, almost as soon as he comes into office he sends missiles over Pakistan, which kill innocent people. Oh yes, maybe they killed a few, as they say, suspected terrorists. They are always suspected, it's not sure they're terrorists. How do you identify a terrorist? How do you find them? They are always *suspected* terrorists, and so if you suspect that there's a terrorist in this house you bomb the house, no matter who's in it.

That thinking, that terrible, primitive, violent militaristic thinking, is still there in Washington, DC, even with Obama as president. So it's obvious that we need citizen action in the United States; we need the euphoria that accompanied the election of Obama, the excitement, the exhilaration. Yes, I felt good after the election of Obama—ah, what a relief to get that murderous gang out of the White House. But well, one moment after he was elected I was watching him very carefully, ready to criticize, and knowing some of the history of the country, I know now that it will take citizen action in the United States to change policies very fundamentally and to give us real democracy. And there is hope, because as I said before, there are the beginnings, there are people protesting, there are high school students who walk out of classes to protest the war, there are antiwar vigils, gatherings in towns all over the United States. There are longshoremen, workers on the West Coast on the docks, who called a one-day strike, closed down the docks in protest against the war. We had doctors and nurses going to the halls of Congress, refusing to leave and getting arrested because they were demanding free national health care for everybody. We have some veterans of the Iraq War now speaking out against the war; still not a large number of them, still not the way it was during the Vietnam War, when so many veterans came back and formed an organization, but we have desertions from the army, more desertions than ever before, and it is hard for the army to recruit people into its ranks. There are signs of the possibility of a citizens' uprising.

It's very important to understand that in the United States and everywhere, wherever we are confronted with these twin evils of violence on the one hand and something called democracy on the other, we want something different and we wonder: Can we do it? Are we capable of changing things? Are we capable of creating a new world? It is important to understand something about power—the power of the people who hold power, the military, the wealthy, the corporate elite: whether the country is called a dictatorship or whether it is called a democracy, those are the people who hold the power. But their power is fragile; their power depends on the obedience of the people. When people stop obeying, their power disappears. We saw this in the United States. General Motors, you cannot make GM recognize the union. Ford Motor Company? No! But when their workers went out on strike, GM was helpless; Ford Corporation was helpless. When workers go out on strike, the corporations cannot do anything with their power, which has suddenly disappeared.

Same when consumers boycott a product; in the United States it happened in the 1960s when the farmworkers of California organized a boycott of grapes and all over the country people stopped eating grapes—very hard to do, grapes are delicious, but people stopped eating grapes. It was a successful boycott, and the farmworkers won some victories as a result, because the power of the farm corporations depended on the obedience of the consumers to buy their products. And when soldiers refuse to fight, armies cannot continue a war, governments cannot continue a war.

That was a crucial element in the decision of the United States government to withdraw from Vietnam; they could not count on the military anymore. It is very important to understand the power of people who do not seem to have power. But yes, people organized, withdrawing their obedience; suddenly they have power and then you see things happening, then you see governments topple, tyrannical governments disappear; then you see dictators rushing to get on their helicopters with a million people gathered in the streets. And in our times we have seen changes, we have seen surprises: we have seen governments in Eastern Europe fall, we have seen governments in Latin America change, we have seen governments, tyrannies, suddenly collapse in Indonesia and the Philippines, because that power was so fragile. And what we learn from history is that even the smallest of acts that people engage in matter. It is important to know this, because otherwise people think they have to do something heroic to change things. There are people who do things heroic, but most people do not do things heroic. Social movements come about not through a few heroic acts. Social movements, great social movements that achieve something, come about because millions of people do small things and, at certain points in history, all these small things come together and then something good happens, then change takes place.

And one more thing: if you engage in a movement, even in the smallest of ways, participate in the struggle for real democracy, whether you win or lose in the immediate sense, whether you see a victory or not, tomorrow or next week or next month, just by engaging in the struggle, your life will be better, your life will be fulfilling, your life will be more interesting.

20

Three Holy Wars

Boston University, Boston, Massachusetts, November 11, 2009

This was Zinn's last major speech. He saw it as the quintessential expression of his view that there is no such thing as a just war and of his desire to see an end to all war.

Three holy wars. When I tell people the title, very often they're a little puzzled, because they think I'm going to talk about religious wars. No. I'm speaking about three wars in American history that are sacrosanct, three wars that are untouchable, three wars that are uncriticizable.

I think you will probably agree with me that nobody criticizes the Revolutionary War, right? Especially here in Boston. No, not at all. The Revolutionary War is a holy war against England. Here in Boston, Paul Revere and Lexington and Concord and Sam Adams and all the Adamses, all of that. No, the Revolutionary War was a great war of independence from England. Heroic battles, Bunker Hill. It brings tears to my eyes. Not only in Boston but elsewhere. The Revolutionary War, you don't criticize that. If you did, you would be a Tory. They would deport you to Canada, which might be good.

Then there is the Civil War. You notice the quiet. You don't criticize the Civil War. And it's understandable. Why would you criticize the Civil War? Slavery? Freedom? The Civil War. The slaves are freed. It's Abraham Lincoln. You can't criticize the Civil War. It's a good war, a just war. Emancipation.

And then there is World War II. Again, the good war—except if you read Studs Terkel's oral history called *"The Good War,"* in which he interviews all sorts of people who participated in World War II, military, civilians. When he adopted the title of this oral history, his wife suggested, after reading the manuscript, he put quotation marks around *"The Good War,"* suggesting that, well, maybe there's a little doubt about how good that war is. But very few people have doubt about the good war. You turn on the History Channel, what is it all about? The good war, World War II, heroism, Iwo Jima, D-Day, the Greatest Generation. World War II is the best, the best of wars. I was in it.

And now I'm going to subject all three of those good wars to a kind of examination, which is intended—I'll tell you frankly what my intention is: to make us reexamine the idea of a good war, to make us reexamine the idea that there is any such thing as a good war, even the Revolutionary War, the Civil War, World War II. No. It's not easy to do, because, as I said, these three wars are holy. And all three wars accomplished something. No one would doubt that. That's why they're considered holy: they all accomplished something. Independence from England, freedom for the slaves, the end of fascism in Europe. So to criticize them is to undertake a heroic task. I only undertake heroic tasks.

The reason I think it's important to subject them to criticism is that this idea of good wars helps justify other wars which are obviously awful, obviously evil. And though they're obviously awful—I'm talking about Vietnam, I'm talking about Iraq, I'm talking about Afghanistan, I'm talking about Panama, I'm talking about Grenada, one of our most heroic of wars—the fact that you have the historic experience of good wars creates a basis for believing, well, you know, there is such a thing as a good war, and maybe you can find parallels between the good wars and this war, even though you don't understand this war. But oh, yes, the parallels. Saddam Hussein is Hitler. That makes it clear. We have to fight against him. To not fight in a war means surrender, like Munich. There are all the analogies.

Let's start with the Revolutionary War. Let's do it in chronological order, because, after all, I'm a historian. We do everything in chronological order. I eat in chronological order. All Bran, we'll start with All Bran. We'll end with Wheatina. The Revolutionary War. Balance sheets. I don't want to make it too mathematical. I'll be falling in line with all these mathematical social scientists. Everything has become mathematical: political science and anthropology, even social work is mathematical. No, I don't want to get that strict. But a rough moral balance sheet, let's say. What's good about the Revolutionary War? Oh, there is another side? Yes, there is another side to the balance sheet. What's dubious about the Revolutionary War? Let's look at both sides, because if you only look at "oh, we won independence from England," it's not enough to do that. You have to look at other things.

Let's first look at the cost of the war on one side of the balance sheet—the cost of the war, in lives, I mean. Twenty-five thousand. Hey, that's nothing. Twenty-five thousand? We lost fifty-eight thousand in Vietnam. Did you even know how many lives were lost in the Revolutionary War? It's hardly worth talking about. In proportion to the Revolutionary War population of the colonies, twenty-five thousand would be equivalent today to two and a half million. Two and a half million. Let's fight a war. We're being oppressed by England. Let's fight for independence. Two and a half million people will die, but we'll have independence. Would you have second thoughts? You might. In other words, I want to make that twenty-five thousand, which seems like an insignificant figure, palpable and real, not to be minimized as a cost of the Revolutionary War, and to keep that in mind in the balance sheet as we look at whatever other factors there are. So yes, we win independence against England. Great, and it only cost two and a half million.

Who did the Revolutionary War benefit? Who benefited from independence? It's interesting that we just assume that everybody benefited from independence. No, not everybody in the colonies benefited from independence. There were people right from the outset who knew they wouldn't benefit from independence. There were people from the outset who thought, "I'm just a working stiff, I'm just a farmer. Am I going to benefit? What difference will it make to me if I'm oppressed by the English or oppressed by my local landlord?" Maybe one-third of the colonists—nobody knows because they didn't take Gallup Polls in those days; there are various estimates—maybe one-third of the colonists were opposed to the Revolutionary War, and maybe even about one-third supported the Revolutionary War against England, and maybe one-third were neutral. I'm going by an estimate that John Adams once made, just very rough. But there obviously were lots of people who were not for the revolution.

That's why they had a tough time recruiting people for the revolution. It wasn't people rushing around, "Wow, it's a great crusade, independence from England. Let's join." No, they had a tough time getting people. In the South, they couldn't find people to join the army. George Washington had to send a general and his troops down south to threaten people in order to get them into the military, into the war. And in fact, in the war itself, the poor people, the working people, the farmers, the artisans who were in the army, maybe some of them were there for patriotic reasons, independence from England, even if they weren't sure what it meant for them, but some of them were there for that reason. Some of them had actually listened to the Declaration of Independence read from the town hall. And it was inspiring—liberty, equality. We will all have an equal right to life, liberty, and the pursuit of happiness. Some people were inspired and they joined. Other people joined because they were promised land. They were promised, you might say, a little GI Bill of Rights, just as today recruiting officers make promises to young guys that they want in the army. They give them bonuses and they promise them, maybe, a free education afterward. People don't naturally rush to war. You have to seduce them, you have to bribe them or coerce them. Some people think it's natural for people to go to war. Not at all, no. Nations have to work hard to mobilize citizens to go to war. And they had to work in the Revolutionary War.

Especially when they found out that although there was a draft, there was a conscription, the rich could get out of the conscription by paying a certain amount of money. But the farmers who went into the revolutionary army and who fought and who died and who were wounded in the war found that they, the privates, the ordinary soldiers in the war, weren't treated as well as the officers, who came from the upper classes. The officers were given splendid uniforms and good food and were paid well, and the privates very often did not have shoes and clothes and were not paid. And when their time was supposed to be up, they were told, no, they had to stay. There was a class difference in the Revolutionary War. In this country we're not accustomed to the idea of class differences. We're all supposed to be one big happy family, one nation indivisible. We're very divisible. No, we're not one nation. There are working people and there are rich people, and in between, yes, there are nervous people.

So yes, the conditions of the ordinary farmer who went into the Revolution, the privations were such that they mutinied against George Washington and the other officers. When I say mutinied, I mean thousands of them. Did you ever hear about this in your classrooms when you learn about the Revolutionary War? When you learn about Bunker Hill and Concord and the first shot heard 'round the world, do you ever hear about the mutinies? I doubt it. I never heard about it. I didn't learn about it in elementary school or high school or college or graduate school. You find very often that what you learn in graduate school is what you learned in elementary school, only with footnotes. No, I never learned about the mutinies. But there were mutinies.

Thousands of soldiers mutinied, so many of them that George Washington was worried. He couldn't put it down. He had to make concessions to what was called the Pennsylvania line, thousands of mutineers. However, shortly after he made those concessions and quieted down the mutiny by promising them things and promising them he would get them out of the army soon and give them pay and so on, soon after that there was another mutiny in the New Jersey line, which was smaller. And Washington put his foot down. He couldn't handle the thousands in the Pennsylvania line, but he could handle the hundreds in the New Jersey line. He said, "Find the leaders and execute them." Did you hear about this in your classrooms about the Revolutionary

War? Did you hear about the executions of mutineers? I doubt it. So they executed a number of the mutineers. Their fellow soldiers were ordered to execute the mutineers.

So not everybody was treated the same way in the Revolution. In fact, when the revolution was won, independence was won, and the soldiers came back to their homes, some of them did get bits of land that were promised to them, so many of them became small farmers again. And then they found that they were being taxed heavily by the rich, who controlled the legislatures. They couldn't pay their taxes, and so their farms, their homes, were being taken away from them, auctioned off. Foreclosures, they call them today. It's an old phenomenon.

So there were rebellions. I think everybody learns about Shays' Rebellion. They don't learn much about Shays' Rebellion, but they learn it enough to recognize it on a multiple-choice test. In Shays' Rebellion, in western Massachusetts, thousands of farmers gathered around courthouses in Springfield and Northampton and Amherst and Great Barrington, and they stopped the auctions from going on, they prevented foreclosures. It's a real rebellion that has to be put down by an army paid for by the merchants of Boston. It's put down. But it puts a scare into the founding fathers.

There is as interesting chronology there. Shays' Rebellion takes place in 1786. The founding fathers get together in 1787 for the Constitutional Convention. Is there a connection between the two? I don't remember ever learning that there was a connection between Shays' Rebellion and the Constitution. What I learned is, oh, they got together for the Constitution because the Articles of Confederation created a weak central government. That we needed a strong central government, and everybody likes the idea of a strong central government, so it was great thing to have a constitutional convention and draft the Constitution. What you were not told, I don't think—I wasn't told—was that the founding fathers, on the eve of the Constitutional Convention, were writing one another and saying, hey, this rebellion in western Massachusetts, we'd better do something about that. We'd better create a government strong enough to deal with rebellions like this. That's why we need a strong central government.

There was a general, General Henry Knox of Massachusetts, who had been in the army with George Washington, and he wrote to Washington at one point. I don't have his letter with me; I do have it somewhere. I'll paraphrase it; it won't be as eloquent as he was. You know, they were eloquent in those days. Take a look at the language used by the political leaders of that day and the language of the political leaders of our day. So Knox writes to Washington and says something like this. He says, "You know, these people who fought in the Revolution, these people who are rebelling, who have rebelled in western Massachusetts, and other states, too, not just in Massachusetts." Knox says to Washington, "These people who have rebelled, they think that because they fought in the war against England, that they deserve an equal share of the wealth of this country. No." Those are the kind of letters that went back and forth. "We've got to set up a government that will be strong enough to put down the rebellions of the poor, the slave revolts, the Indians, who may resent our going into their territory." That's what a strong central government is for, not just because, oh, it's nice to have a strong central government. There are reasons for that. The Constitution was a class document, written to protect the interests of bondholders and slaveowners and land expansionists. So the outcome of the Revolution was not exactly good for everybody and created all sorts of problems.

What about Black people? Slaves, did they benefit from the winning of the Revolution? Not at all. There was slavery before the Revolution, there was slavery after the Revolution. In fact, Washington would not enlist Black people into his army. The South, southern slaveowners, they were the first, doing it for the British. The British enlisted Blacks before Washington did. Blacks didn't benefit.

And what about Indians? Should we even count the Indians? Should we even consider the Indians? Who are they? Well, they lived here. They owned all this land. We moved them out of here. They should be considered. What was the outcome for them when we won the Revolution? It was bad. Because the British had set a line called the Proclamation of 1763. They had set a line at the Appalachians where they said, "No, the colonists should not go beyond this line into Indian territory." They didn't do it because they loved the Indians. They just didn't want trouble. They set a line. The British are now gone, and the line is gone. And now you can move westward into Indian territory, and you can move across the continent and you can create massacres and you can take that enormous land in the West away from the Indians who live there.

These are some of the consequences of the Revolution. But we did win independence from England. All I'm trying to suggest is that to simply leave it that way, that we won independence from England, doesn't do justice to the complexity of this victory.

Was it good to be independent of England? Yes, it's always good to be independent. But at what cost? And how real is the independence? And is it possible that we would have won independence without a war? How about Canada? Canada is independent of England. They don't have a bad society, Canada. There are some very attractive things about Canada. They are independent of England. They did not fight a bloody war. It took longer. Sometimes it takes longer if you don't want to kill. Violence is fast, war is fast. And that's attractive, right? You want to do something fast. And if you don't want killing, you may have to take more time in order to achieve your objective. And actually, when you achieve your objective, it might be achieved in a better way and with better results and with a Canadian health system instead of an American health system.

I won't say anything more about the Revolutionary War. I just want to throw a few doubts in about it, that's all. I don't want to say anything revolutionary or radical. I don't want to make trouble. I just want to think about these things. That's all I'm trying to do—have us think again about things that we took for granted: oh, yes, the Revolutionary War, great! No, let's think about it.

The Civil War. It's even tougher to critically examine the Civil War. Slavery. Nothing worse. And at the end of the Civil War there is no slavery. You can't deny that. So yes, you have to put that on one side of the ledger, the end of slavery. On the other side you have to put the human cost of the Civil War in lives. Six hundred thousand. I don't know how many people know or learned or remember how many lives were lost in the Civil War, which was the bloodiest, most brutal, ugliest war in our history from the point of view of dead and wounded and mutilated and blinded and crippled—600,000 dead in a country of thirty million. Think about that in relation to today's population. It's as if we fought a civil war today and five or six million people died in that civil war. You might say, "Well, maybe that's worth it to end slavery." Maybe. I won't argue that. Maybe. But at least you know what the cost is.

The slaves were freed, and what happened after that? Were they really freed? They were, actually. There was no more slavery. But the slaves, who had been given promises, forty acres and a mule—they were promised a little land and some wherewithal so they could be independent so they needn't be slaves anymore—well, they weren't given anything. They were left without resources. And the result was they were still in the thrall, still under the control of the plantation owner. They were free but they were not free. There have been a number of studies made of that in the last decade. Free but not free. They were not slaves now, they were serfs. They were like serfs on a feudal estate. They were tenant farmers, they were sharecroppers. They couldn't go anywhere, they didn't have control of their lives, and they were in the thrall of the white plantation owners. The same white plantation owners who had been their masters when they were slaves were now their masters when they were serfs.

I don't want to minimize the fact that it's still not slavery in the old sense. No, it's not. It's better. It's a better situation. So I want to be cautious about what I say about that, and I want to be clear. But I want to say it's more complicated than simply, oh, the slaves were freed. They were freed and they were betrayed. Promises made to them were betrayed, as promises made during wartime are always betrayed. The veterans are betrayed, the civilians are betrayed. The people who expected war to produce great results in freedom and liberty are betrayed after every war. So I just want us to consider that. And to ask the question, which is a very difficult question to answer, but it's worth asking, is it possible that slavery might have ended without 600,000 dead, without a nation of amputees and blinded people? Is it possible? Because, after all, we do want to end slavery. It's not that we're saying that we shouldn't have a bloody war, just let people remain slaves. No, we want to end slavery. But is it possible to end slavery without a bloody civil war?

After all, when the war started, it wasn't Lincoln's intention to free the slaves. You know that. That was not his purpose in fighting the war. His purpose in fighting the war was to keep southern territory within the grasp of the central government. You could almost say it was an imperial aim, which is a terrible thing to say, I know. But that's what the war was fought for. It's put in a nice way: We fought for the Union. We don't want anybody to secede. Why not? What if they want to secede? We're not going to let them secede. No, we want all that territory. Lincoln's objective was not to free the slaves.

The Emancipation Proclamation came—and, by the way, it didn't free slaves where they were enslaved; it freed the slaves that the national government was not able to free. It declared free the slaves who were in the Confederate states who were still fighting against the Union; in other words, it declared free the slaves that we couldn't free. And it left as slaves the slaves that were in the states that were fighting with the Union. In other words, if you were a state that was a slave state and you were fighting on the side of the Union, we'll let you keep your slaves. That was the Emancipation Proclamation. I never learned that. I learned, oh, the Emancipation Proclamation, great!

Yes, Congress passed the Thirteenth, Fourteenth, Fifteenth Amendments. The Thirteenth Amendment ends slavery; the Fourteenth Amendment declares equal rights, you can't deny people equal protection of the law; the Fifteenth Amendment, you can't prevent people from voting because of their color, their race. However, these promises of equality in the Fourteenth and Fifteenth Amendments, the promise of the right to vote, they were honored for a few years, when there were federal troops in the South to enforce them, and then they were set aside. Black people in the South were left at the mercy of the white plantation owners. So there was a great betrayal that took place, a betrayal that lasted one hundred years—

those hundred years of segregation and of lynching and of the national government looking the other way as the Constitution was violated a thousand times by the white power structure in the South.

Congress passed those amendments why? Not because Lincoln or the Congress itself initiated it. They passed those amendments because a great movement against slavery had grown up in the country from the 1830s to the 1860s, a powerful antislavery movement which pushed Congress into the Thirteenth, Fourteenth, and Fifteenth Amendments. A very important thing to keep in mind, that when justice comes and when injustices are remedied, they're not remedied by the initiative of the national government or the politicians. They only respond to the power of social movements. That's what happened in the relationship of the anti-slavery movement and the passage of those amendments.

Of course, then those amendments, the Fourteenth and Fifteenth Amendments, had no meaning for the next hundred years. The Blacks were not allowed to vote in the South. Blacks did not get equal protection of the laws. Every president of the United States for one hundred years, Democrat or Republican, liberal or conservative, every president violated his oath of office. The oath of office says you will see to it that the laws are faithfully executed. Every president did not enforce the Fourteenth and Fifteenth Amendments, collaborated with southern racism and segregation and lynching and all that happened. So the Civil War had this aftermath. It has to be looked at in a longer perspective.

Yes, the question needs to be asked also, is it possible that slavery could have been ended without 600,000 dead? We don't know for sure. When I mention these possibilities, it's very hard to imagine how it might have ended, except that we do know that slavery was ended in every other country in the Western Hemisphere. Slavery was ended in all these other places in the Western Hemisphere without a bloody civil war. That doesn't prove that it could have been ended—every situation is different—but it makes you think. If you begin to think the only way it could have been done is with a bloody civil war, maybe not. Maybe it would have taken longer. Maybe there could have been slave rebellions which hammered away at the southern slave structure, hammered away at them, a war of attrition, not a big, bloody mass war but a war of attrition, guerrilla warfare, and John Brown–type raids.

You remember John Brown, who wanted to organize raids and the slave rebellion? Little guerrilla actions. Not totally peaceful, no, but not massive slaughter. John Brown was executed by the state of Virginia and the national government. He was executed in 1859 for wanting to lead slave revolts. The next year the government goes to war, a war that cost 600,000 lives, presumably, as people came to believe, to end slavery. It was kind of a tragic irony in that juxtaposition of facts.

So it's worth thinking about the Civil War and not to simply say, "The Civil War ended slavery; therefore, whatever the human cost was, it was worth it." It's worth rethinking.

Now we come to World War II. The good war, the best. Fascism. That's why I enlisted in the air force, the fight against fascism. It's a good war, it's a just war. What could be more obvious? They are evil, we are good. So I became a bombardier in the air force. I dropped bombs on Germany, on Hungary, on Czechoslovakia, even on a little town in France. Three weeks before the war was to end, when everybody knew the war was to end and we didn't need to drop any more bombs, but we dropped bombs on a little town in France. We were trying out napalm. The first use of napalm in the European theater. I think by now you all know what napalm is—one of the ugliest little weapons. We were trying it out. And adding medals. Who knows what reason, what complex of reasons, led us to bomb a little town in France when everybody knew the war was ending? And yes, there were really German soldiers there hanging around. They weren't doing anything, they weren't bothering anybody, but they were there. And it gives us a good excuse to bomb. We'll kill the Germans. We'll kill some Frenchmen, too. What does it matter? It's a good war. We're the good guys.

I didn't think about any of this while I was bombing. I didn't examine, "Oh, who are we bombing and why are we bombing and what's going on here, and who is dying?" I didn't know who was dying, because when you bomb from thirty thousand feet, this is modern warfare, you do things at a distance, it's very impersonal. You just press a button and somebody dies. You don't see them. I dropped bombs from thirty thousand feet. I didn't see any human beings. I didn't see what was happening below. I didn't see children screaming, I didn't see arms about ripped off people. No. You just drop bombs. You see little flashes of light down below as the bombs hit. That's it. And you don't think. It's hard to think when you're in military. It's hard to sit back and examine, ask what you're doing. No, you've been trained to do a job and you do your job.

I didn't think about any of this until after the war. And I began to think about that raid on France. And then I began to think about the raid on Dresden, where 100,000 people were killed in one night and day of bombing. Read Kurt Vonnegut's book *Slaughterhouse-Five*. He was a prisoner of war in Dresden in the basement in a kind of meat locker, a slaughterhouse. Then I became aware of the other bombings that had taken place. But when you're in a war, you don't see the picture. I didn't know until afterward, 600,000 German civilians were killed by our bombing. They weren't Nazis. Yes, you might say they were passive supporters in that they didn't rebel. A few rebelled. How many Americans rebel against American wars? Are we all complicit for what we did in Vietnam, killing several million people? Maybe we are. But there was a kind of stupid, ignorant innocence about us. And the same thing is true of the Germans. We killed 600,000. If some great power, while we were dropping bombs in Vietnam, had come over here and dropped bombs on American cities in retaliation, and they say, "Well, these are imperialists, we'll kill them all," no, the American people were not themselves imperialists, but they were passive bystanders until they woke up. So I began to think about this.

Think about Hiroshima and Nagasaki. I had welcomed the bombing of Hiroshima when it took place. I didn't know what it really meant. We had finished our bombing missions in Europe, we had won the war in Europe, and my crew and I, we flew our plane, the same plane we had flown missions on, back across the Atlantic and we were given a thirty-day furlough. And then the idea was we were going to go on to the Pacific, because the war against Japan was still going on. During this thirty-day furlough in early August, my wife and I decided—we had been married just before I went overseas—we would take a little vacation in the country. We took a bus to go into the country, and at the bus stop there was a newsstand and there was a newspaper and the big headline "Atomic Bomb Dropped on Hiroshima." Oh, great. I didn't really know what an atomic bomb was, but it was sort of obvious from the headline that it was a big bomb. Well, I had dropped bombs. This was just a bigger bomb.

I had no idea what it meant until I read John Hersey's book *Hiroshima.* John Hersey had gone into Hiroshima after the bombing and he had talked to survivors. Survivors? You can imagine what those survivors looked like. They were kids and old people and women and all sorts of Japanese people. They were without arms or legs or they were blinded or their skin could not be looked at. John Hersey interviewed them and got some idea and reported—he was a great journalist—on what the bombing of Hiroshima was like to the people who were there. When I read his account, for the first time I understood, this is what bombing does to human beings, this is what my bombs had done to people. I began to rethink the idea of a good war, of our war against fascism. Oh, well, it's okay because we did defeat Hitler. Just like we did get independence from England, we did end slavery. But wait a while. It's not that simple. And World War II is not that simple: Oh, we defeated Hitler, therefore everything is okay. We were the good guys, they were the bad guys.

What I realized then is that once you decided—and this is what we decided at the beginning of the war, what I decided—they were the bad guys, we were the good guys, what I didn't realize was that in the course of the war the good guys become the bad guys. War poisons everybody. War corrupts everybody. So the so-called good guys begin behaving like the bad guys.

The Nazis dropped bombs and killed civilians in Coventry, in London, in Rotterdam. And we dropped bombs and killed civilians and we committed atrocities. And we go over Tokyo several months before Hiroshima, and I'll bet you 90 percent of the American people do not know about the raid of Tokyo. Everybody has heard about Hiroshima. I'll bet 90 percent of the American people don't know that several months before Hiroshima we sent planes over Tokyo to set Tokyo afire with firebombs, and 100,000 people died in one night of bombing in Tokyo. Altogether we killed over half a million people in Japan, civilians. Some people said, "Well, they bombed Pearl Harbor. That's really something." *These* people did not bomb Pearl Harbor. Those children did not bomb Pearl Harbor. This notion of violent revenge and retaliation is something we've got to get rid of.

So I began reconsidering all of that, rethinking all of that. I investigated the bombing of Hiroshima, investigated the excuse that was made: "If we don't bomb Hiroshima, we will have to invade Japan and a million people will die." I investigated all of that and found it was all nonsense. We didn't have to invade Japan in order for Japan to surrender. Our own official investigative team, the Strategic Bombing Survey, which went into Japan right after the war, interviewed all the high Japanese military and civilian officials. Their conclusion was Japan was ready to end the war. Maybe not the next week. Maybe in two months, maybe in three months. We can't wait. We don't want to wait. We've got these bombs and we've got to see what they look like.

Do you know how many people die because of experimentation with weapons? We were experimenting. We were experimenting on the children of Hiroshima. "Let's see what this does. And also, let's show the Russians we have this bomb." A British scientist who was an adviser to Churchill called the dropping of the bomb on Hiroshima "the first step of the Cold War." The Soviet Union was in the minds of the people around Harry Truman, James Byrnes and James Forrestal and others. So yes, I began thinking about the good war and how it corrupts and poisons.

Then I looked at the world after the war. What are the results? I said bad things about the war, I'm sorry, all those casualties. But it stopped fascism. Wait a while. Let's look closely at that. It got rid of Hitler, got rid of Mussolini. Did it get rid of fascism in the world? Did it get rid of racism in the world? Did it get rid of militarism in the world? No. You had two superpowers now arming themselves with nuclear weapons—

enough nuclear weapons that if they were used, it would make Hitler's Holocaust look puny. And there were times, in fact, in the decades that followed when we came very, very close to using those nuclear weapons.

So the world after World War II—and this is so important—you just don't look at "Oh, we won." What happens after that? What happens five years after that? What happens ten years after that? What happens to the GIs who came back alive five or ten years later? Maybe one of them will go berserk at Fort Hood. Think about that. Think about all the superficial comments made of "Let's examine this guy psychologically, his religion." Let's not go deeper into that and say these are war casualties. Those people he killed were war casualties, he was a war casualty. That's what war does: war poisons people's minds. So we got rid of Hitler. But what was the world like?

When I was discharged from the air force, I got a letter from General Marshall. He was the general of generals. He was sending a letter—not a personal letter to me, "Dear Howie," no—a letter that was sent to sixteen million men who had served in the armed forces, some women, too. The letter was something like this: "We've won the war. Congratulations for your service. It will be a new world." It wasn't a new world. And we know it hasn't been a new world since World War II. War after war after war after war. And fifty million people were dead in that war to end all wars, to end fascism and dictatorship and militarism.

Yes, I came to the conclusion that war cannot be tolerated, no matter what we're told. And if we think that there are good wars and that therefore maybe this is a good war, I wanted to examine the so-called good wars, the holy wars, take a good look at them and think again about the phenomenon of war and come to the conclusion that war cannot can tolerated. No matter what we're told, no matter what tyrant exists, what border has been crossed, what aggression has taken place, it's not that we're going to be passive in the face of tyranny or aggression, no, but we will find ways other than war to deal with whatever problems we have. War is inevitably—inevitably—the indiscriminate, massive killing of huge numbers of people. And children are a good part of those people. Every war is a war against children. So it's not just getting rid of Saddam Hussein. Think about it. Oh, we got rid of Saddam Hussein. In the course of it, we killed huge numbers of people who had been victims of Saddam Hussein. When you fight a war against a tyrant, who do you kill? You kill the victims of the tyrant.

Anyway, all this is simply to make us think again about war. We're at war now—in Iraq, in Afghanistan, and sort of in Pakistan, since we're sending rockets over there and killing innocent people in Pakistan. We should not accept that. We should look for a peace movement to join. Look for some peace organization to join. It will look small at first and pitiful and helpless, but that's how movements start. That's how the movement against the Vietnam War started. It started with handfuls of people who thought they were helpless, thought they were powerless.

But remember, the power of the people on top depends on the obedience of the people below. When people stop obeying, they have no power. When workers go on strike, huge corporations lose their power. When consumers boycott, huge business establishments have to give in. When soldiers refuse to fight, as so many soldiers did in Vietnam—so many deserters, so many fraggings, acts of violence by enlisted men against officers in Vietnam, B-52 pilots refusing to fly bombing missions anymore—war can't go on. When enough soldiers refuse, the government has to decide, "We can't continue." So yes, people have the power. If they begin to organize. If they protest. If they create a strong enough movement, they can change things.

That's all I wanted to say. Thank you.

Acknowledgments

This project would not have been possible without the support, encouragement, and editorial input of Myla Kabat-Zinn. I also want to thank Jeff Zinn, John T. "Ike" Williams, Kathryn Beaumont, and Hope Denekamp for their support of my work with Howard over many years. Rick Balkin has been a great champion for this book and for Howard's work generally. My colleagues at Haymarket Books, especially Ahmed Shawki, Julie Fain, Sarah Macaraeg, Rachel Cohen, John McDonald, Rory Fanning, and Jim Plank, were inspiring, as always, in their dedication for this project. Abby Weintraub very generously took time out of her busy schedule to design the beautiful cover to this edition.

David Barsamian has been a longtime friend and a true comrade. Without his important work on *Alternative Radio*, many of the recordings I drew on for these materials would not have been available. I encourage people to check out his website (www.alternativeradio.org) to find recordings of these and other talks. For help with additional recordings and transcripts, I am indebted to Rossella Miccio, coordinator, Humanitarian Office, Emergency; Alan Maass of the *Socialist Worker* newspaper; David Whitehouse of the *International Socialist Review*; the Campaign to End the Death Penalty; and Alex Green of Back Pages Books. Samantha Fingerhut helped me immensely with archival research and transcriptions. Most of all, I want to thank Brenda Coughlin, who has done so much to sustain Zinn's legacy through her vital work with *The People Speak* and *Voices of a People's History of the United States*. She has also shared many of my most memorable moments with Howard and constantly reminds me of what it is we are fighting for.

Index